Roberto Alomar

Roberto Alomar

The Complicated Life and Legacy of a Baseball Hall of Famer

DAVID OSTROWSKY

ROWMAN & LITTLEFIELD
Lanham • Boulder • New York • London

Published by Rowman & Littlefield

An imprint of The Rowman & Littlefield Publishing Group, Inc.

4501 Forbes Boulevard, Suite 200, Lanham, Maryland 20706

www.rowman.com

86-90 Paul Street, London EC2A 4NE, United Kingdom

British Library Cataloguing in Publication Information Available

Library of Congress Cataloging-in-Publication Data Available

ISBN 978-1-5381-5802-9 (cloth) | ISBN 978-1-5381-5803-6 (ebook)

In memory of Seth Roberts,
whose brilliant legacy continues to inspire us.

Contents

Acknowledgments

Ted Williams used to say that the first rule of hitting was to get a good ball to hit. It seems fair to say that the first rule of writing a book is to get a good story to tell. And, boy, does Roberto Alomar's life make for an intriguing story.

And you are about to read this intriguing story because the folks at Rowman & Littlefield believed in this project and were devoted to bringing it to life. A heartfelt thank you to Senior Vice President and Publisher Julie E. Kirsch, Senior Acquisitions Editor Christen Karniski, Associate Acquisitions Editors Samantha Delwarte and Erinn Slanina, and all of their passionate and talented colleagues.

Writing a book during a once-in-a-century pandemic presents unique challenges (namely no in-person contact), and I never could have reached the finish line without the help of the following people who arranged interviews and provided invaluable sources of information: Earl Luckett, Dan Griffin, Jon Chapper, Charlie Dowd, Randy Grossman, Eli Egger, Joe Penno, Patrick O'Connell, Madison Hannum, Daniel Clifford, Saul Wisnia, Rebecca Rienzi, Kristen Porzio, Chuck Pool, and Shane Philipps.

It should be noted that Roberto Alomar, himself, was invited to participate in this book project on two separate occasions. Both times, he declined the offer.

Of course, there is no book without browsing through dozens, if not hundreds, of newspaper and magazine files. And for that, as always, Cassidy

Lent, manager of Reference Services at the National Baseball Hall of Fame and Museum, gets well-deserved credit. I would also like to thank longtime baseball writer and author Danny Gallagher for providing valuable material along the way as well.

If you enjoy the photographs on the following pages (and you certainly will), credit goes to Carly Goteiner, Shelby Cravens, Zachary Weber, Craig Vanderkam, and Ron Vesely.

I would like to thank Aaron Fischman for providing some very helpful edits in the beginning that helped steer me in the right direction. I want to send another special shout-out to Bob Segal, who has provided me with such brilliant literary insight that has surely enhanced this project.

Closer to home, my in-laws, Jim and Judi, doubled as my office mates during summer 2020. Thank you for all the Donelan's lobster rolls and mini bottles of Diet Coke (not to mention the quiet workspace) during what was a very chaotic time, to say the least.

Thank you to my sister-in-law Jill for finding a guy in Adam who is also a sports nut. His genuine interest in this project (as well as yours, Jill) was always meaningful.

While the pandemic has prevented me from seeing Jonathan and Sharon as much as we would all like, their support and encouragement, even from afar, has been greatly appreciated.

A full one-second wink to my dad for providing such keen editorial interference in the early stages of manuscript preparation. On a different note, while I'll never be confused for a Hall of Fame ballplayer like Robbie Alomar, I believe I'm inching closer to being a Hall of Fame "athletic supporter" and that's a credit to you.

It was too bad that when my mom took me to Game 4 of the 1999 ALDS between the Red Sox and Indians at Fenway Park, she didn't have her camera with her. With all due respect to the photographers whose images grace this book, hers would have been the best photo of Roberto I could ever hope to obtain.

As I'm wrapping up this section, *Curious George* is blasting in the background. As friends and family are aware, it means Colby is present. While it is hard to articulate how Colby helped me write this book, her courageous journey remains a source of great inspiration. I am so proud of you and love you more than words can describe.

From 1996 to 1998, Roberto Alomar called Camden Yards home. Baltimore's splendid ballpark holds special meaning to our family as our young son Camden was (partially) named after it. In fact, in February 2022, as I was grinding through the final stages of this biography, Camden made us a family of four.

My wife, Lauren, probably deserves more than a paragraph for having spent nearly four years listening to stories of Roberto Alomar . . . while reading (more like getting through) my prior book, *Pro Sports in 1993*. Alomar played for eight teams, the Boston Red Sox not being one of them, so to say that his career interested Lauren would be a stretch. But, as always, she was a good sport and there for me every step of the way.

So, here's the second paragraph: this section begins by quoting Ted Williams and will end by quoting another Hall of Famer, Lou Gehrig, who famously referred to himself as being the luckiest man on the face of the earth. And that's exactly how I feel about being your husband, Lauren.

Introduction

Roberto Alomar knew he had messed up. Big time.

On the evening of September 27, 1996, as umpire John Hirschbeck was forced to wipe saliva from his brow and squinted to remove the spittle from his eyes under the beaming SkyDome's lights, Alomar, the greatest second baseman of his generation, who was on the cusp of leading the Baltimore Orioles to their first postseason berth since 1983, instinctively knew that spitting on the veteran ump would be his undoing.

In ninety seconds, Alomar went from being a revered major-league ballplayer to one of the most reviled public figures in America.

On a full-count pitch in the first inning, Alomar, a switch-hitter batting lefthanded, calmly watched as a heater from Toronto's Paul Quantrill sailed several inches off the plate. To Alomar's amazement, however, Hirschbeck inexplicably called strike three.

In disbelief, Alomar snapped back his head like the girl in *The Exorcist*.

"What?"

"You better swing at that pitch," Hirschbeck blurted.

"I'll swing if it's a strike," Alomar fired back.

"Another word, and you're gone."

As Alomar returned to the dugout, he snapped, "Just pay attention to the game!"

No ejection.

Alomar was barely back in the visiting dugout when a teammate barked a profane comment toward home plate.

Assuming Alomar was the offender, Hirschbeck screamed, "You're gone!"[1]

A livid Alomar, along with his fifty-three-year-old manager Davey Johnson, bolted toward Hirschbeck. Once a cussing Alomar got within spitting distance of the umpire, Johnson wrapped his left arm around Alomar's chest. It made no difference. With his face still exposed, Alomar leaned in and spat a wad of saliva all over Hirschbeck's face. More words were exchanged before Alomar was shoved off the field by his mortified manager.

Meanwhile, back at home plate, John Hirschbeck was cleaning himself off. The highly respected umpire had stayed in baseball, despite losing his eight-year-old son John to a rare brain condition, adrenoleukodystrophy (ADL), three years earlier. The umpire's other son, nine-year-old Michael, was also afflicted by the malady.

And there, trudging down the tunnel to the clubhouse was Roberto Alomar, who could hear the jeers from his erstwhile fans, well aware this episode would be the new hot topic in sports.

For Alomar, everything else would be an afterthought to this ghastly moment: the defensive gems that left the entire ballpark breathless; the dramatic home run off Dennis Eckersley in the 1992 ALCS; the Doritos commercials; the Reebok endorsements; the flocks of teenage girls who would await in hotel lobbies, begging security to divulge his suite number; the mothers who would present their daughters for Alomar to marry at autograph signings; the legacy.

Damn—*the legacy.*

For the previous five years in this very building, Alomar, the son of fifteen-year veteran infielder Sandy Alomar and brother of all-star catcher Sandy Alomar Jr., had emerged as perhaps the most gifted second baseman since World War II, while helping the Toronto Blue Jays win consecutive World Series titles. For the first half of the decade, Alomar was deservedly the most popular athlete in hockey-crazed Toronto and, as a first-year Baltimore Oriole, was in the discussion as being the best player in the game (if not of his generation). Could he at times be self-centered and immature like other multimillionaire superstars? Sure. But he never drew comparisons to, say, the violent slugger Albert Belle. Until now.

Would the public perception of Alomar change if people knew that Hirschbeck had supposedly called him a derogatory homosexual term? (There had been rumors at the time that Alomar was gay.) Or uttered a vile remark about his mother? Doubtful. Meanwhile, the Orioles were a win away from the postseason, and Alomar would soon be roasted outside of the Chesapeake Bay region. A likely first-round matchup against the Cleveland Indians meant facing the music when at bat at Jacobs Field—with his brother Sandy crouched behind the plate. If the O's advanced to play the New York Yankees in the ALCS, one hell of a Bronx Cheer surely awaited Alomar at Yankee Stadium.

Less than three hours later, after the game (the Orioles lost 3–2, which meant no postseason clinching celebration to divert attention from the incident), Alomar politely answered reporters' questions, while admitting that he had indeed spat at Hirschbeck.

When a reporter felt inclined to mention Hirschbeck's family tragedy, Alomar said of Hirschbeck: "I used to respect him a lot. He had a problem with his family when his son died—I know that's something real tough in life—but after that he just changed, personality-wise. He just got real bitter."[2]

The reporters swarming around Alomar's locker in the cramped Baltimore clubhouse were stunned. *He just got real bitter?* How could Alomar not only hold himself unaccountable, but excuse his behavior by hiding behind the ghost of Hirschbeck's deceased son? Did he really think providing that justification would make him any less of a vilified public pariah?

The next morning, Hirschbeck didn't read Alomar's comments in the *Toronto Sun*, but did arrive at the SkyDome early, knowing that reporters were interested in his take on the situation. Ninety minutes before the first pitch, in the umpires' dressing room, Hirschbeck met with a handful of scribes.

"Can we talk to you about what Alomar said last night?" one writer asked.

"What did he say?" Hirschbeck wondered.

"He said you'd become bitter after your son died," the writer responded.

Hirschbeck saw fire red.

"That son of a bitch is going to mention my son? . . ."[3]

Hirschbeck couldn't finish his thought before attempting to jump from his seat. Colleagues Jim McKean and Jim Joyce wrapped their arms around him while directing the reporters into the corridor outside the room. After shoving away McKean and Joyce, Hirschbeck bolted to Baltimore's clubhouse (the visiting clubhouse and umpires' dressing room were only about ten feet apart), stormed through the doors, and barked, "You talk about my kid, I'll fucking kill you!"[4]

The enraged ump never made it to Alomar's locker (supposedly, he was not even in the clubhouse at the time). This time Joyce was more assertive in restraining his friend. Knowing that Hirschbeck already had enough on his plate with a son at home suffering from the severe neurological effects of ALD and that he didn't need to be charged with aggravated assault, Joyce twisted his arms around Hirschbeck's neck and pushed him out of the clubhouse.

Ironically, Alomar, having been counseled by Baltimore's PR staff, had been preparing to read a carefully crafted statement of apology to reporters before the start of the game, but was advised to hold off in light of Hirschbeck's outburst. For Alomar, there would be no semblance of closure, at least for now. The fact that Hirschbeck had threatened his life made Alomar realize how he had compounded his heinous act with insensitive remarks. Alomar *knew* Hirschbeck had provoked him at home plate. (A quarter-century later, Baltimore teammate Rick Krivda reflected: "I just remember hearing that something personal was said about him [Alomar]. That's where I thought, 'Hey, if somebody said something about my mother in the heat of battle, I might have swung a fist, which could be even worse.'")[5] But the postgame reference to Hirschbeck's late son was utterly inexcusable.

The longer Alomar sat at his stall early that Saturday afternoon, the less he cared about baseball. Baltimore was in the throes of a thrilling wildcard race, but it wasn't so exhilarating for Alomar. He wanted to disappear from Toronto, the city where, from 1991 to 1995, he had batted a combined .307 and won a handful of Gold Gloves to go along with the two World Series rings. He wanted to return to his hometown of Salinas, a quiet little fishing village on Puerto Rico's south coast, and embrace his mother, Maria, who, as the wife of a journeyman infielder, knew baseball was a game of failure and constantly prayed for Robbie to succeed on the diamond.

Thankfully, for Alomar, he wouldn't have time to sit around and dwell on the matter. American League president Gene Budig gave Alomar a veritable love tap of a suspension (five games), which was supposed to have covered the final two regular games this season and first three contests in 1997, with no postseason ramifications; however Alomar appealed the suspension and was in the starting lineup, batting second and playing second. (Meanwhile, Hirschbeck, who couldn't stomach being in Alomar's presence, left the ballpark that morning and the next evening returned home to Poland, Ohio, where television crews were already lining his street. So, while Alomar would be manning second base, there would be no umpire hovering around second. As crew chief Jim McKean noted, "The wrong guy is sitting out.")[6]

The 36,316 fans at the SkyDome expressed great pleasure when Alomar went hitless in his first four at bats and were particularly giddy when an inside fastball from Toronto starter Erik Hanson forced Alomar to hit the dirt.

But Alomar, the most talented player on either team, upped his game when it mattered most. In the top of the tenth inning with the scored tied at 2, Alomar stepped in against reliever Paul Spoljaric and belted the southpaw's first offering over the right-center field wall to give the O's a 3–2 lead, leaving the ballclub three outs from returning to the postseason for the first time since winning the 1983 World Series. Indeed, Baltimore held on for the 3–2 win, eliminating the Chicago White Sox and Seattle Mariners from playoff contention.

Under normal circumstances, *the* storyline would have been Cal Ripken Jr.'s return to the playoffs. But these were not normal circumstances and while the Baltimore Orioles may have been Ripken's team, the 1996 playoffs would be all about Alomar's story. As the disgraced ballplayer trotted around the SkyDome base paths and later sprayed bubbly with his mates in the clubhouse, it was hard to shut out thoughts of what opposing fans—furious over the lenient suspension—might resort to. (In fact, there would be incidents of AA batteries and empty Bud Light bottles being flung at him in the days ahead. Not to mention, there would be a two-foot-wide strike zone against Alomar and the customary seventeen-inch one against everyone else . . . during high-octane October baseball. Perhaps it wouldn't even matter that Hirschbeck was unable to enact frontier justice on him.)

What could Robbie do now? A profuse apology and $50,000 donation (matched by the team) to ALD research at the Kennedy Krieger Institute at Johns Hopkins were in the works, but would that be enough to prevent the world from closing in on him? Would anyone outside of the Baltimore clubhouse walls care about his side of the story? As the postseason dawned, that now mattered little to the masses of angry fans hellbent on justice.

1

Béisbol 24/7

In the travel industry, Puerto Rico is often referred to as the shining star of the Caribbean. "Spain moved to a tropical island" is how travel agents frequently describe it. Travel brochures highlight the hundreds of miles of sparkling coastline and forest-clad mountain peaks. Tourists are reminded that the year-round temperature typically falls between 75 and 85 degrees and that Old San Juan has some of the finest Latin restaurants in the Caribbean.

The Puerto Rico of Sandy Alomar Sr.'s youth hardly resembled this fabled island oasis. Santos Alomar Conde grew up in Guayama, a small quiet town on the island's south coast in the 1940s—a half-century after Puerto Rico was ceded to America upon the conclusion of the Spanish-American War. The son of a sugar-mill machine operator who originally came from Ponce, the south coast's largest city, Alomar walked to school along unpaved, rocky roads flanked by sordid wooden shacks. Poverty was omnipresent. Refrigerators and telephones were scarce. Toilet facilities were located outside most homes—inconvenient during the best of times and life threatening when there was a tropical storm. When a tempest roared through the island, sustenance consisted of bread, water, and sugar. Possibly even for three or four days.

For Alomar's father, Demetrio Alomar Palmieri, and thousands of his contemporaries trying to raise families, devastating macroeconomic and political forces were at work. By the mid-twentieth century, cataclysmic hurricanes, lower prices from global competition, pitiful labor conditions in the fields, and a protectionist American Congress hellbent on setting quotas on exports and imposing higher taxes were spelling doom for the sugar industry, one that had been the financial mainstay for Puerto Rico ever since Columbus reached the island on his second voyage to the New World.[1] (In fact, the name Puerto Rico stems from the Spanish words for "rich port.") Consequently, most employment opportunities were not only part-time and seasonal but barely provided laborers with subsistence-level wages. While Puerto Rico had attained commonwealth status within the United States, Puerto Ricans were barred from voting in US elections, thus depriving them of a critical vehicle for wielding any political influence.

As one of eight children living in an overcrowded house, Sandy may not have had much, but he had baseball, or béisbol, as his fellow countrymen called it. The youngest of four Alomar boys, Sandy grew up in the game, as his three older brothers (Rafael, Tony, and Demetrio) all signed professional contracts with major-league clubs in America, although none reached the big leagues. By his early teenage years, when he wasn't dazzling for Luis Muñoz Rivera High School in his hometown and for the local American Legion team, Alomar was regularly making the eighty-mile round trip to play in the Pony League in San Juan, the bustling capital city whose vibrancy stood in stark contrast to the tranquil simplicity of Guayama. It was here that Milwaukee Braves scout Luis Olmo, the second Puerto Rican to play in the majors, saw a serious and brawny teen who had raw but undeniable talent, especially with his glove. Alomar was a very cerebral shortstop, a classic good-field no-hit guy who had decent speed. Prior to the 1960 season, the Braves inked the sixteen-year-old to a $12,000 contract, which meant he would be spending the following summers playing minor-league games in Wellsville, New York, and later Davenport, Iowa.

The pro contract was a mixed blessing. Getting paid to play baseball was nirvana, especially compared to toiling in the sweltering sugarcane fields as his friends back home were doing, but, as a shy Latino with limited English skills, Alomar often felt isolated in such white-bread rural outposts. (By mid-century, as Puerto Rico's economy was undergoing a drastic transformation toward becoming more industrialized, a mass exodus of rural, agrarian-based Puerto Ricans did immigrate to the mainland; however, the majority settled in prominent East Coast cities, e.g., New York City.) When he got promoted to play for the Braves' Double-A team in Austin, Texas, Alomar found the metropolitan environment even less hospitable, often being barred entrance to whites-only restaurants given his dark-skin complexion. The atmosphere on the field and in the clubhouse was hardly more welcoming. In the highly conservative—as well as explicitly and implicitly racist—baseball culture of the 1960s, Alomar, like all Hispanic players, was stereotyped as being lazy and soft. Alomar knew he was neither lazy nor soft, as the Braves organization soon found out. If a groundball took a tough hop and bloodied Alomar's face, he stayed in the field. If Alomar got plunked in the ribs by a four-seam fastball, he put his head down and jogged to first. Indeed, he proved to be a gamer who continued to be rock-steady in the middle infield.

By the end of the 1963 season, it was not a question of if, but when, Alomar would get called up to the big-league team. Feeling confident he could earn a steady paycheck playing baseball, Alomar returned home to Guayama and wed his hometown sweetheart, Maria Velasquez. Soon thereafter, the young couple (Sandy was twenty, Maria nineteen) settled into a house in a newly developed middle-class neighborhood named Monserrate in Salinas, a nearby sun-washed town whose economy largely hinged on fishermen trawling the Caribbean Sea for barracuda, tuna, and lobster. In the cookie-cutter Monserrate neighborhood, the Alomars' single-story white stucco house had a pastel-colored tile roof laced with white iron grillwork. A prominent statue of Jesus in the front yard was perhaps the only feature distinguishing the Alomars' house from the dozens of small rectangular flats lining the narrow street.

While the Alomars' house bore a strong resemblance to those of their close neighbors, their home life did not. Certainly, by Puerto Rican standards, theirs was an unconventional marriage, as by spring 1964, Maria grew accustomed to spending weeks (and soon months) away from her husband, who began that season with the Triple-A Denver Bears before getting called up to Milwaukee in September. After all, bringing a spouse on road trips—especially one from a remote island—was out of the question in the mid-twentieth century.

The more pressing matter, however, was that of financial security. In his first big-league stint in fall 1964, Alomar batted .245 with six RBIs in nineteen games. With no guarantee he would be a full-time big leaguer the following season, Sandy worried that the relatively small pittance of a minor-league salary (or prorated major-league one) wouldn't suffice. But he couldn't give up the dream of establishing himself in the big leagues, especially after his three older brothers had come tantalizingly close to realizing that very dream themselves, only to fall short. Mostly, though, the prospect of laboring in the sugarcane fields indefinitely was enough to motivate Alomar to wring every last ounce of talent out of his five-foot-nine, 150-pound frame. In fact, Alomar's situation was remarkably similar to Mickey Mantle's, as a couple decades earlier, the prodigious slugger viewed a career in baseball as a means for escaping the monotony and hazards of the zinc and lead mines in northeast Oklahoma.

During spring training in 1965, the baseball gods smiled on Alomar. The Braves suddenly found themselves in dire need of an everyday second baseman after their initial plan of shifting veteran shortstop Denis Menke over to second fell through. Eager to establish himself as a versatile utility player, Alomar raised his hand for the assignment, despite having played second base only a handful of times in his entire life. The twenty-one-year-old newbie second baseman played errorless defense that spring, while sporting a .300 batting average. Once the Braves realized that Alomar could make a seamless transition into becoming a more than serviceable second baseman, he cracked their 1965 opening-day roster.

"He has been absolutely amazing," manager Bobby Bragan raved to the *Sporting News* that April. "We take him away from a position he has played all his life and he looks like he had never been anywhere but second base. He makes the pivot. He makes the tough throw for a force-out after going to his left. He does it all."[2]

Undoubtedly, 1965 would be a good year for Alomar, as three months later his first child, daughter Sandia, was born. There was bittersweetness, however. While it is now acceptable for pro ballplayers to leave their teams for a few days to jet home and be present for their child's birth, this was not the case then. In fact, it was even more taboo than spouses traveling with the club. That Sandy would have to wait until October to return home was probably harder on Maria. Although the parental support provided by the Monserrate neighborhood certainly helped Maria, her husband still was two thousand miles away. While Maria would sometimes break into tears when Sandy first moved to the States, she eventually settled into the role of a baseball wife.[3] And once Sandy proved to be a sure-handed big-league middle infielder, the couple felt emotionally and financially stable enough to expand the family. On June 18, 1966, less than a year after Sandia's birth, the first son, Sandy Jr., was born.

Unfortunately, at this juncture, Alomar's career had taken a turn for the worse. While Sandy remained a pitcher's dream on defense—he made but one error all season—he was proving grossly inept at the plate. While shuttling back and forth between the majors and minors during the '65 season, Alomar had posted a respectable .241 average for Milwaukee. But the following season, the franchise could no longer justify offering him significant playing time; in thirty-one games, Alomar hit a putrid .091. Compounding matters was that the Milwaukee Braves had morphed into the Atlanta Braves, which meant more exposure to the racial hostility embedded in the Jim Crow South—at least when he was playing for the big-league team. (While MLB's emerging foothold in the Deep South was undoubtedly a boon to the league's coffers, the development was met with less fanfare from players of color, who had to start growing accustomed to eating meals on their team buses while teammates were dining in whites-only restaurants.) As summer 1966 dragged on, it became clear that Alomar was not long for Atlanta as the club viewed him as an offensive liability whose primary role would be that of a late-inning defensive replacement. In December 1966, the Braves sold Alomar to the Houston Astros, who, a few months later, jettisoned him to the New York Mets. When Alomar went hitless in his first twenty-two at-bats, the Mets demoted him to their minor-league affiliate in Jacksonville.

For pragmatic reasons, Alomar began to wonder if he could ever make a living as a pro ballplayer. The Mets were a last-place team and if they had no use for his services, then who would? The thought of supporting a wife and two kids on a minor-league salary for any length of time felt daunting. As Sandy was seriously contemplating quitting baseball in June 1967, a call from Maria crystallized his plans. There would soon be a fourth mouth to feed back home, she said. He would have to find a permanent home on some big-league club.

On August 15, the Mets sent Alomar to the Chicago White Sox—his fourth organization in six months. Feeling more like a disposable scrap heap item than a valuable commodity, Alomar grew resentful toward his former employers. In fact, a few years later, while an established veteran for the California Angels, Alomar would tell the *Los Angeles Times*, "They treat me like I was something they could throw away when they want to. . . . They brainwash me. They tell me I cannot hit, that I good glove man but that I not able to drive ball at all or get the run in from second base. They tell the press and public. And they say I am too little to not wear down. They make me believe these things myself . . . almost."[4] (Unfortunately, when Alomar was quoted in dailies, he received the same treatment afforded to his more famous countryman, Roberto Clemente. Rather than lightly editing the remarks, newspapermen transcribed the broken English verbatim, presenting the immigrant ballplayers as less sophisticated.)

Although Alomar scuffled down the stretch for the ChiSox in September, the club believed in Alomar and his considerable potential. To make himself a more versatile player, Sandy had become a switch-hitter. While gobbling up scorching groundballs was still his forte, the wiry utility player was steadily improving as a situational hitter, no longer perceived as an automatic out. Teammates liked Sandy, soon dubbing him the "Iron Pony" as nary an injury could shelve him.

As spring training 1968 dawned, the White Sox felt comfortable committing to Alomar as their starting second baseman. Finally, Alomar would be a full-time major leaguer with a well-deserved big-league salary.

Good timing. He was now a father of three.

Less than a week after North Vietnam launched the Tet Offensive against the United States and South Vietnam, Roberto Alomar came into the world. He was born on a Monday, February 5, 1968, the year of not only the Vietnam War escalation but also the Prague Spring, the assassinations of Martin Luther King Jr. and Robert F. Kennedy, the infamous Democratic National Convention in Chicago, and worldwide student protests.

Roberto, who soon became more commonly known as "Robbie," was a quiet and timid little boy with large brown eyes and long, curly hair. He seldom left his mother, his sole caretaker for eight months of the year. But as Roberto became a toddler, he started idolizing his ballplaying father. Nearly every story from Alomar's childhood begins with a small boy and a ball and mitt or a bat. There was neighbor Carmen Pabon, who recalls an eighteen-month-old Roberto, wearing only a diaper and sideways cap, trying (unsuccessfully) to cross the street with a glove on one hand, ball in the other, bat tucked under his armpit.[5] Older sister Sandia remembers how Alomar would carry his baseball equipment all across town, whether it was stopping by Uncle Dimitri's rundown bar or the downtown pharmacy owned by close family friend Nestor Pabon.[6] Even as a four-year-old, Roberto spent hours on end playing ball in the nearby vacant lot that doubled as a baseball diamond.

In contrast to Robbie, who had an all-encompassing passion for baseball, older brother Sandy did not have a singular focus on the sport. Once elementary school began, Sandy still played ball with the neighborhood kids but started gravitating toward more action-packed hobbies such as flying model airplanes, practicing karate, playing with remote-control cars, and riding go-karts. At times, Sandy simply tired of the glacial pace of baseball and entertained thoughts of dropping the sport. Whereas Robbie was enamored with his father's chosen profession, Sandy was not. During a time when young kids are starting to tell adults what they want to be when they grow up, Sandy's response was always "pilot." This was fine with his mother, who knew the challenges of being a big leaguer. Maria knew about the seemingly interminable minor-league bus rides and inevitable batting slumps, the latter of which could inflict significant emotional distress on the player and his family. She also knew that alternatives to a life of agrarian labor awaited her sons, considering the family could possibly afford private Catholic school and higher education thereafter.

It was a classic catch-22. Sandy's professional baseball career provided the family with a comfortable middle-class existence—something many of Sandy Jr.'s and Roberto's friends sorely lacked. But with the respectable salary came an inconvenient lifestyle in which every February, Maria and her kids would have to brace for Sandy's departure to the mainland, knowing they wouldn't see him until school ended in June. As Sandy became an established big leaguer (he was named to the AL All-Star team in 1970 as a member of yet another team, the California Angels) and Roberto grew old enough to start idolizing his father, Maria worried that this could become a vicious cycle. While Maria stressed academics over sports, especially to her two elementary school–aged children (the oldest child, Sandia, was never particularly interested in athletics, but instead developed strong artistic skills), she saw how much joy it gave Robbie to watch his dad play in Puerto Rican league games during mid-winter weeknights. Who was she to put a damper on his enthusiasm for a sport whose popularity was growing exponentially throughout the island, due in no small part to her own husband's success?

By the early 1970s, when the family started visiting Sandy in Anaheim every summer, it was strikingly apparent how Robbie, even at such a young age, looked like a natural on the diamond, running around the bases and playing catch with other players' kids during batting practice. The more Alomar hung out around the club, the more the players themselves started noticing how he seamlessly immersed himself in the game.

By summer 1972, one of Sandy's teammates, a young gunslinging pitcher named Nolan Ryan, took a particular interest in helping Alomar hone his throwing mechanics. In his first year with the Halos after coming over from the New York Mets, Ryan saw how seriously Robbie—who had only recently celebrated his fourth birthday—took instruction. When Robbie told Ryan that he, too, wanted to be a pitcher, the future Hall of Famer spent several mornings serving as a pitching coach to his teammate's son.

Even in his pre-K years, Robbie was perceived similarly to a musical prodigy—the supreme gracefulness and instincts were simply undeniable to anyone who watched him for more than twenty seconds. Maria had an inkling that it was only a matter of time before her husband, despite being a big leaguer himself, would eventually become known first and foremost as Roberto Alomar's father.

Robbie was now old enough to recognize that his dad, as a fleet-footed, switch-hitting middle infielder, was the spark behind California's offense. Sandy Alomar Sr. was a pitcher's best friend and a manager's dream. He had played in every single game during the 1970 and 1971 seasons—a true iron-man whom teammates fittingly called a man "of iron and steel."

But even Robbie knew his father was no Roberto Clemente.

Throughout the Caribbean and United States, Alomar Sr.'s reputation as one of the American League's top leadoff hitters was vastly overshadowed by that of Clemente, the Pittsburgh Pirates' right fielder whose legend had already grown to mythic proportions. While Alomar was a hero to the masses back home (his mural already adorned the wall of a famed Salinas ballfield), Clemente was a god, not only in Puerto Rico, but throughout Latin America. By 1972, within a year of leading the Pirates to a World Series title over the Baltimore Orioles, the perennial Gold Glove Award winner was nearing three thousand hits. Puerto Ricans—from the Bronx to his hometown of Carolina—

were anxiously awaiting Clemente's enshrinement into the Baseball Hall of Fame by the end of the decade.

But the back of his baseball card alone didn't justify the deification. It was Clemente's unwavering humanitarianism, most notably his passion for helping children and staunch advocacy for mentoring Latino and African American players, that so endeared him to the masses. In the spirit of his mentor Martin Luther King Jr., Clemente sought to give voice to the voiceless. Naturally, thousands of young boys born in Puerto Rico in the 1960s and 1970s were named Roberto, including, of course, Sandy and Maria's younger son. Even though Alomar Sr. hardly knew Clemente—they grew up in different regions of Puerto Rico and never played on the same team—selecting Clemente as his son's namesake was an easy decision.

While Roberto never had the chance to meet Clemente or watch him play, the man's omnipresent influence was strikingly discernible even for a young child such as Alomar. For when Clemente returned home every winter, residents and tourists came in droves to hover outside his long, pink stucco home in Rio Piedras, hoping to lay eyes on the man they commonly referred to as "El Magnifico." Many of the Alomar brothers' older friends, some of whom were starting to be exposed to the pervasiveness of cocaine in the Caribbean, attended the free baseball clinics that Clemente held in the offseason. It was impossible to walk more than a couple blocks anywhere on the island without seeing Clemente's black and gold "21" jersey. Clemente was constantly invited to speak at banquets and civic clubs in Puerto Rico—and rarely, if ever, declined. (In fact, the demands on his time and encroachment on his privacy proved so relentless that in late November 1971, Clemente would embark on a month-long tour of South America with his wife, Vera, so that he could have some personal time.)[7]

Thus, New Year's Eve 1972 would be an evening indelibly seared into Roberto Alomar's memory. For this night, according to generations of Puerto Ricans, was the "night that happiness died in Puerto Rico." As the islanders were preparing to celebrate the new year and upcoming election of Governor Rafael Hernandez Colon, the devastating news broke: moments after takeoff from San Juan International Airport, a four-engine DC-7 piston-powered plane had crashed into the shark-infested waters off Isla Verde. Roberto Clemente was one of the five lost souls on the doomed aircraft as he had spearheaded a relief mission to bring supplies to Nicaragua in the wake of an earthquake that had already claimed the lives of thousands. (Clemente had insisted on accompanying the cargo plane to Nicaragua as he had feared that food and clothing would fall into the hands of profiteers under the corrupt dictatorship of General Anastasio Somoza.)

For Alomar, the lasting image of the ghastly episode was one of neighbors streaming toward the beachfront the following morning, effectively forming a pilgrimage in search of their missing hero. The throngs of townsfolk huddled on the shoreline in disbelief, some literally waiting for Clemente to walk out of the sea. Boys carried portable radios, mothers brought their newborns; a scream or glimpse of an irregular shape elicited a crush of people wading out to the waves in unison.

Of course, no such supernatural phenomenon occurred. As the hours passed on New Year's Day and the searches on behalf of the Coast Guard and Navy proved futile, the cruel reality set in. In his final day in office, Governor Luis A. Ferré announced a three-day mourning period. Regarding Clemente's transformation from human to mythical legend, acclaimed Puerto Rican writer Elliott Castro later observed, "That night on which Roberto Clemente left us physically, his immortality began."[8]

Months later, via a special election that bypassed the mandatory five-year waiting period, Clemente would be inducted posthumously into the National Baseball Hall of Fame—the first Puerto Rican to receive the prestigious honor.

He would not be the last.

2

Livin' la Vida Loca

Growing up as Sandy's younger brother, Roberto was just trying not to get killed.

Although Sandy was never purposely trying to inflict bodily harm on Robbie (except that one time when Robbie needed eighteen stitches after his brother shoved him into the corner of a table), his passion for motorcycles and go-karts often led to death-defying escapades for him and his younger brother. Such as when Sandy was motorcycling on mountainous terrain, with Robbie sitting in the rear, and a decent-sized pit lay ahead. Rather than side-stepping the imposing depression, Sandy channeled his inner Evel Knievel by going full throttle, launching his bike to the other side. A petrified Robbie begged his brother to return home. Another time, Sandy was recklessly driving his go-kart off-road while Robbie, palms sweating and heart racing, was riding shotgun. The joyride ended with a collision into a tree, which fortunately only left the vehicle damaged.[1]

Robbie, once again, begged his brother to return home.

While Sandy had an insatiable desire to engage in such daredevil activities, Robbie had too much to lose by jeopardizing his health and safety.

Less than a month after his sixth birthday, Roberto Alomar, while visiting his father during spring training, was playing catch and fielding grounders when a St. Louis Cardinals scout asked Sandy if he could sign his son right then and there. A year later, during his second year in Little League in his

hometown of Salinas, Alomar made the all-star team. He was soon, however, ruled ineligible due to age restrictions—typically a disqualification that
precludes ballplayers who are too old. Not Roberto. He was barred from all-
star competition because he was too *young*. It was remarkable. Even playing
among adolescents, many of whom had started shaving and asking girls out
on dates, a prepubescent Alomar stood out.

While it quickly grew apparent that Robbie's budding baseball career had
unlimited potential, his father, now on the wrong side of thirty, was slowly
coming to the conclusion that his days on a professional diamond were
numbered. Once Dick Williams became manager of the California Angels in
1974, Sandy saw his playing time significantly reduced. Shedding the label of
"organization man," Sandy went to management and requested a trade. His
wish was granted as he was dealt to the New York Yankees, a career move
that represented his first legitimate chance to win a World Series. That dream
never materialized, as the closest Alomar got to a World Series trophy was in
1976 when his Yankees fell in four games to Cincinnati's Big Red Machine
in the Fall Classic. While Sandy never got to the plate in the '76 World Series
and was limited to one at-bat in the American League Championship Series
against the Kansas City Royals, he was standing in the on-deck circle when
Chris Chambliss slugged the pennant-winning homer in the bottom of the
ninth inning of Game 5—a seminal moment in baseball history that Roberto,
to this day, remembers watching on television.

Meanwhile, Sandy's wife, Maria, was less than thrilled with having to
spend summers in New York City during the mid-1970s. She and the kids
were living in Queens, roughly equidistant from LaGuardia Airport and John
F. Kennedy International Airport. While Maria grew accustomed to jets constantly soaring overhead, she couldn't stop worrying about her kids playing in
the streets as yellow cabs whizzed by at all hours. Even though New York City
had a sizable Puerto Rican population by then, Maria and her kids rarely left
their Queens apartment, except for watching Sandy's games initially at Shea
Stadium (the Yankees' 1974–1975 home when Yankee Stadium was undergoing renovations) and then at a newly refurbished Yankee Stadium during the
bicentennial summer. For Roberto, the 1975 summer was the most enjoyable
because one of his father's teammates, Bobby Bonds, had a ten-year-old son
named Barry with whom he developed a close friendship.

From Maria's perspective, the lifestyle was getting old. Every spring, she served as a single parent before having to relocate to a remote American city each summer. All the while, her English skills remained fairly limited. But there was no other choice. While some of his contemporaries were starting to make handsome six-figure salaries, Sandy, essentially reduced to a glorified utilityman, was not. Nor had he ever, for that matter. As long as there was an MLB franchise in need of his services, he couldn't afford to retire prematurely.

And there was. In February 1977, the Texas Rangers needed a veteran middle infielder, so they acquired Alomar in a trade from the Yankees. He played in a total of ninety-three games over the next two seasons before Texas released him. Rather than exploring his options as a free agent, Sandy acquiesced to his wife's request that he retire.

Upon hearing the news, a ten-year-old Roberto was in tears, begging his father not to leave baseball; as his primary profession, that is.[2] Sandy promised his son that he would be playing in the Puerto Rican Winter League, at least for a few more seasons, while explaining that it was time to settle into his new full-time career, that of a small business proprietor.

As is often the case for many a former pro ballplayer, the transition to a new line of work proved to be anything but seamless.

Sandy had taken some of his savings (he was, to his credit, always very thrifty when playing) and purchased a gas station in Salinas. It turned out to be a poor investment, as the return fell drastically short of expectations. While Sandy was losing significant funds with his failed business endeavor, he was also being hounded for loans by long-lost friends who knew he had made a solid living in the big leagues.

In his brief 1993 book, *Second to None: The Roberto Alomar Story*, Robbie recalled how the family's financial situation took a turn for the worse during this time:

> It was tough. Even though they didn't really tell us about it, I knew those were rough times. My Dad went through some bad times with investments. When you have money, everybody comes up to you and says, "Hey, can you lend me money for this?" and then they never pay you back. My father has a big heart. He's too soft. They took his money, and whenever he had problems, he didn't have anybody to help him.[3]

Of course, even when Sandy was playing in the majors, the Alomars were never exactly flush with cash. One summer when the family was living in Texas, Sandy was on a road trip when he learned that his mother had passed in Puerto Rico. According to Robbie in his autobiography, Sandy didn't have the funds to fly his wife and kids to Puerto Rico for the funeral.[4] But a career in baseball—as opposed to being an entrepreneur—yielded a steady, guaranteed salary to support a middle-class household. As Roberto recalled in his autobiography, Sandy started second-guessing his decision to turn down the Rangers' offer back in 1978 to serve as a traveling instructor in their minor-league system—even though that would have meant continuing to spend an exorbitant amount of time away from his family.

At least he could have fulfilled his role as provider.

Ever cognizant of how success in professional athletics could be fleeting, Maria increasingly stressed education to her children, and in particular, Roberto. While Sandy was fascinated with math and Sandia was a serious (and gifted) art student, studying was often an afterthought for Roberto.

During Roberto's adolescent years, he spent many winter weeknight evenings at his father's Puerto Rican Winter League games. If he had a test the following morning, he would bring his books with him and breeze through the text between innings. Many of these games would start in the late evening and finish in the early morning. Thus, it was not uncommon for Roberto to return home well past midnight, sometimes as late as 1:30 a.m., which made the early morning wake-up routine a tiresome ordeal for Maria and Sandia. Like a night owl college student home for winter break, Roberto constantly needed much prodding to get out of bed in the morning, not exactly bursting with ambition to study geography or chemistry. That Roberto was able to bring home report cards peppered with B's was a testament to his high level of intelligence because he rarely exerted much effort in the classroom.

Roberto needed to exert even less effort on the baseball field to succeed. He made an exasperatingly hard game look preposterously easy. Such as when, as a thirteen-year-old, he started playing alongside professional players on winter evenings in San Juan. An invitation to take infield with his father's winter ball team during pregame drills was not only an opportunity to play on a smooth infield surface—a stark contrast to the island's many ballfields in which rocks jutted out along the base paths—but also to demonstrate his uniquely precocious talent. In terms of raw ability, it was impossible to discern between Alomar and the current big-league players when it came to snagging a scorching liner or diving to make a backhanded stop up the middle. These weren't only washed-up ballplayers in their early forties making a last-gasp effort to extend their MLB careers. These were also current all-stars, occasional MVP candidates, and potential Hall of Famers. (In hindsight, it was a situation fairly reminiscent of a fourteen-year-old Bobby Orr excelling against twenty-year-old opponents in junior hockey back in the early 1960s.)

Fearing that his father's time playing in Puerto Rico was coming to a close, Robbie made it a point to attend every single game, or at least try to. There were many weekday afternoons when he would rush home from school to make sure he didn't miss his father leaving for the night game in San Juan or Ponce. On days when Maria put her foot down, demanding her son hit the books instead of fielding more grounders, Sandy Sr. would have to sneak out of their house in Monserrate. The sight of his baseball-obsessed son and protégé sobbing at the kitchen table was too much to bear. Robbie was so adamant about accompanying his father to games that one time, when he was supposed to stay home, he snuck behind the front seat of his dad's car while it was parked in the driveway and didn't pop out until his dad was twenty miles from home and couldn't turn back.[5]

Robbie may have idolized his old man, but was Sandy his favorite all-time ballplayer? Depends whom you ask. As longtime friend and former MLB outfielder Jose Cruz Jr., who also hails from Puerto Rico's southern region, recalls about the dynamic between his father, Jose Cruz, a two-time all-star for the Houston Astros, and young Alomar:

> My dad was Robbie's favorite player. Robbie was always an excited person when he was around my dad. I think his style, the way he did things, it was a little bit different from everyone else. And at the time when Robbie was growing up, it's like, "How many Latino stars were there out there?" and at the same time it's like, "How many Latino stars were from Puerto Rico?" At the time, I'd say it was my dad, not many others. And you're from the same part of the island, so it was just an easy thing for him to root for my dad. There aren't that many guys from that part of the island.[6]

As Robbie had designs on following in the footsteps of his big-league heroes, his older brother continued to pursue his daring adventures in the front seat of his motorcycle. With motorsports, Sandy could experience a constant thrill that baseball sorely lacked while not being in the shadow of his father or brother—especially his brother. The more Sandy saw Robbie play, the more Sandy realized he was not as agile or deft-handed. Never a standout on his Little League teams, Sandy started growing disillusioned with baseball and expressed no desire to follow the career path of his father. In fact, between the ages of twelve and fourteen, Sandy Jr. stopped playing baseball, and there were moments when he contemplated leaving the sport for good.

Eventually, however, Sandy started to grow disillusioned with motorcycling when one afternoon he was riding in shorts and burned his knee on his bike's exhaust pipe. A wake-up call indeed, as the mishap could have led to reconstructive surgery, or worse, amputation. His father, who for the life of him couldn't understand how his son got such a rush from revving up a bike's engine, used this as an opportunity to explain how riding motorcycles was an inherently dangerous hobby. Baseball, on the other hand, could be monotonous at times, but at least it wasn't a life-threatening activity, and it could potentially serve as a viable career.[7]

Shortly thereafter, Sandy was hanging out in his father's gas station when a customer, well aware of the Alomar baseball family, entered and invited Sandy to join his amateur-league team for an upcoming tournament. He needed a catcher, and while Sandy had hardly any experience crouching behind the plate, he was bored and agreed to play, but only for a couple of games. If Sandy was going to give baseball another shot, it might as well be as a catcher as he knew he didn't have the pillow-soft hands to be a smooth infielder or the speed and quickness to chase down line drives in the outfield. Plus, on the field, catching was, by far, the closest thing to motorcycle riding, what with its nonstop action and potential for endangerment.[8]

In the small sample size of a weekend tournament, Sandy caught the attention of American Legion scouts who were impressed by the kid's arm strength and nimbleness behind the plate and his ability to line frozen ropes all over the field. Still, Sandy was hesitant to commit to a full season, fearing that he simply couldn't live up to the standards set by his baby brother. To quit after several games would reflect poorly on his highly esteemed family, one already synonymous with baseball royalty throughout the island.

(In 1992, when both brothers were established big-league all-stars, Sandy told Milt Dunnell of the *Toronto Star*, "I always knew Robbie had more talent than me. I never was able to do the things he can do. That's why I'm a catcher—not second base like Robbie, like my dad. When we were kids, playing ball in Puerto Rico, Robbie at age seven or eight, he was better than kids eleven or twelve. He was just so superior. I didn't have his blazing speed.")[9]

It was actually Robbie, even more so than Sandy Sr., who was most responsible for encouraging Sandy Jr. to stick with baseball. As a young teenager, Robbie knew baseball was going to take him to the mainland in the not-so-distant future, and he didn't want to embark on the journey alone. Robbie understood how helpful it was for his dad to have had his older brother, Demetrio, playing alongside him on the same minor-league teams in Wellsville, New York, and Davenport, Iowa, back in the early 1960s. For added incentive to stay with baseball, Sandy needed to just flex in the mirror. By his mid-teen years, Sandy had sprouted well over six feet and started shedding baby fat, which meant that he was not just driving the ball into the gaps, but now over fences as well. Eventually, the more Sandy kept playing American Legion ball and found his niche as a solid defensive catcher with power hitting potential, he warmed to the idea of playing baseball professionally.

Of the many pro scouts starting to pay close attention to the Alomar brothers, none was more interested than Luis Rosa, a longtime family friend who had a prominent presence in Caribbean baseball. A Puerto Rican native, Rosa had traveled the globe as an army brat before settling in New York City when he was fifteen. Several years later, the Montreal Expos hired him to do some part-time scouting in New York, before transferring him to Puerto Rico in 1976. By the mid-1980s, as Sandy and Robbie were coming of age, Rosa was employed by the San Diego Padres as their chief scout in Latin America. That Robbie was major-league material wasn't a hard sell. San Diego's general manager at the time was Jack McKeon. As skipper of the Santurce Cangrejeros in the Puerto Rican Winter League in 1976, he had managed Sandy Sr. and seen firsthand his youngest child's natural instincts and exceptionally quick reflexes. Now, as a seventeen-year-old, an age when most kids are getting their driver's licenses and perhaps starting to think about college, Roberto had the makeup of a big-league ballplayer.

If only San Diego didn't have to compete with the Toronto Blue Jays, an up-and-coming club in the American League East, for acquiring the rights to Roberto's services. The small-market Padres organization couldn't offer Robbie the high signing bonus that Toronto was dangling in front of him, but they could offer him a chance to play with his brother . . . and, as luck would have it, be coached by his father. After scouting Sandy Jr. for over a year, McKeon and the Padres front office signed him in 1984—a year after he had turned seventeen and was eligible to sign a major-league contract—and outrighted him to Spokane to play short-season Single-A ball in the Northwest League. By January 1985, Sandy Jr. was slated to begin the upcoming season for the Charleston Rainbows of the Class-A South Atlantic League. If Robbie agreed to terms with the Padres, he, too, would be sent to Charleston in a matter of weeks.

But Robbie hesitated on the Padres' offer. With the strong backing of executive vice president Pat Gillick, the Blue Jays were offering significantly more money as well as an opportunity to join a roster stacked with Latino stars such as Alfredo Griffin, George Bell, and Damaso Garcia.

The Padres weren't done wooing Roberto.

Rosa knew that Sandy Sr. was miserable in the gas station business and wanted a chance to return to baseball, especially now that his sons were leaving home to play professionally. But this was the mid-1980s, and Major League Baseball was not a progressive institution. Hispanic ex-ballplayers such as Alomar were frequently passed over for coaching and managerial openings because conservative front offices thought the language barrier might impede effective communication. The Padres, however, were at the vanguard of a movement emphasizing stronger recruitment and cultivation of Latin American ballplayers. With a steady influx of young Latin talent streaming through the Padres organization, a Spanish-speaking minor-league instructor such as Alomar would be a tremendous asset. It also didn't hurt that Sandy Sr., in addition to having played for McKeon in Puerto Rico, had also played for current San Diego manager Dick Williams a decade earlier in Anaheim. Serving as the infield instructor for the Charleston Rainbows was not exactly what Sandy Sr. had envisioned for his reentry to baseball, but accepting the offer was a no-brainer.

Rosa, whose golden reputation in the Latino baseball community would be tarnished a decade later when, as head of the San Francisco Giants' Latin American training program in the Dominican Republic, he was charged with sexually harassing over a dozen young Dominican players, was still not convinced that Robbie was committed to San Diego.

So, he cheated.

On February 2—three days before Robbie turned seventeen and would be legally allowed to sign a professional contract—Rosa nudged him into signing on the dotted line, post-dating the contract to February 5.[10]

The next week, it was officially announced: Robbie would be joining his brother and father as members of the San Diego Padres organization.

North of the border, Gillick was devastated, knowing that this once-in-a-generation phenom had gotten away.

Down in the Caribbean, Maria was ecstatic, planning on moving to Charleston with her family for the summer.

No way could her teenage sons return home hungry after games, pining for their mom's rice and beans.

3

Leaving Las Vegas

Roberto Alomar simply couldn't take it any longer.

As a seventeen-year-old middle infielder for the Charleston Rainbows of the Single-A South Atlantic League, he minded his own business, rarely engaging in prolonged conversation with anyone aside from his brother and father. His .293 season batting average spoke for itself. Meanwhile, many of Alomar's teammates, particularly those in their early to mid-twenties, perceived him as a thin-skinned, immature kid whom they could haze at will. Perhaps it was because they were jealous that Alomar would surely be in the majors by the time he was their age. Or because he was the young hotshot rookie and, well, that's just what you do to the young hotshot rookie—especially one whose daddy is on the coaching staff. Whatever the reason, Alomar was constantly being ridiculed by his older teammates, clearly not so mature themselves.

"Roberto was picked on and it bothered him a lot," says a former Charleston teammate. "I could see a lot of it going on, on the road, in the hotels. There were people doing pranks on Roberto. It was easy to pick on him."[1]

During a midseason road trip through the searing heat of the Carolinas, one of Alomar's biggest tormentors went into overdrive. After one game in which the Charleston club couldn't shower at the visitors' ballpark because of a plumbing malfunction (not an uncommon occurrence at minor-league facilities), the guys made a beeline back to the motel. A couple minutes into the well-deserved warm shower, a garbage can full of ice water was dumped onto the teenager's head. Before Alomar could jump out and towel himself off, his amused teammate bolted out of the room. Alomar was not particularly amused, his shrieks piercing through the halls of the dingy motel.

A couple of nights later, Robbie, upon getting under his covers, found himself smothered in shaving cream. He bellowed with rage, only to see the same ruthless teammate, now accompanied by roommates, descend upon his room, laughing hysterically.

No más.

The following morning during pregame stretching, Alomar spotted a taped fungo bat on the ground and snuck up behind his harasser. Aiming for the guy's upper back, Alomar, whose average was hovering around .300 at the time, unsurprisingly nailed him right between the shoulder blades.

Thump!

While his stunned teammate shriveled on the ground, Roberto broke into tears before running off to find his father. The incident left players on both teams breathless.[2]

Robbie had every right to stand up for himself after being humiliated for months. But perhaps not in this fashion. After all, he had experienced some (not-so-good-natured) hazing. This, however, was blatant assault. Truthfully, had the perpetrator been a mid-level prospect with even limited big-league potential, he probably would have been released—perhaps even brought to the attention of law enforcement.

Alomar was not released. In fact, he wasn't even reprimanded—at least not publicly. The Charleston organization knew the parent club had big plans for Alomar and the last thing they wanted to do was alienate a guy (no, a *kid*) who had been humiliated all season. If Robbie left the club of his own volition, the whole plan to recruit the Alomar family would have been all for naught—never mind the signing bonus they could never recoup.

When they had signed Alomar months earlier, San Diego's front office had an inkling that there could be some maturity issues. He was, after all, a seventeen-year-old boy among grown men. If Alomar had been raised in the United States, he would still have been playing high school baseball (likely as a *junior*). And, of course, because he hadn't been raised in the contiguous United States, English was not his native tongue, making it exponentially harder to articulate his anger in the predominantly English-speaking clubhouse. The Padres knew what they were doing when they signed both father and son.

"He [Sandy Alomar Sr.] was basically there to make sure that Roberto had someone to overlook him," says one teammate. "Because although he was very talented, he was very young. Sandy made sure that he did everything the way he should as an adult even though he was still a kid."[3]

Indeed, Robbie was a kid who was living with his family, whereas his teammates were living independently as adults. He wasn't missing out on anything. While some of the Charleston Rainbows would cram four or five into a two-bedroom apartment (nothing like sleeping on the floor after going 0–5), Robbie lived with his parents and older brother in a rented house. He not only had his own bed, but also dinners that didn't constantly alternate between Pizza Hut and McDonald's. The latter benefit was invaluable to a still-growing teen such as Alomar. With most guys at the Single-A level earning a mere pittance, junk food was the norm, both at home and certainly on the road with $11 daily allowances for meal money—a very unfortunate situation considering many players were easily shedding several pounds each day playing in the summertime in the Deep South.

But for at least half the season, Robbie, along with his brother, Sandy, could get proper nutrition from his mother's homemade Latin dishes. Even on road trips, when wholesome foods may have been at a premium (a handful of guys splitting an eighteen-inch pizza was a common scene), Robbie took care of what was in his control by leading a dull and inactive life away from the ballpark. Whether the ballclub was stopping in Macon, Georgia, or Florence, South Carolina, Roberto wasn't tempted by lurking opportunities for enjoying nightlife debauchery. Even during downtime at the motel, when guys would wander in and out of each other's rooms like freshmen in dorm halls, Roberto did not partake.

"You never saw him [Roberto] on the road," recalls one former Charleston Rainbows teammate. "He would stay in his room the whole time and just sleep and get appropriate amount of hydration. His dad was the key to all of that. He was like the infield coach/babysitter."[4]

Robbie knew that he wasn't going to have his father around much longer as his days in Low Single-A ball appeared numbered. Irrespective of his age, he simply had too much potential to stay in Charleston much longer. Amid the hazing and hazy summer days of his rookie minor-league season, some of which coincided with silly game day promotions like bikini contests and twenty-five-cent Busch can nights, Robbie was selected to play in the South Atlantic League All-Star Game. Soon thereafter, he was voted by *Baseball America* as the best young second base prospect in the game—despite having fairly pedestrian stats, at least in some categories. At this young age, he hardly had any power—he didn't belt a single home run this season. While he made some brilliant plays in the middle of the diamond, his final defensive numbers were far from spectacular, finishing the year with thirty-six errors while primarily playing second base and occasionally some shortstop. But what stood out, even more so than the .293 average, was Alomar's uncanny knowledge of the game, his natural-born instincts that separated him from teammates and opponents, all of whom were far more seasoned.

"He just seemed to be able to slow the game down in his mind," says another former minor-league teammate. "He was always in the right place at the right time. He just knew how to play the game."[5]

This was strikingly obvious to teammates and opponents alike, including one Roberto Clemente Jr., the son of Alomar's idol and namesake, who was now a third baseman for the Gastonia Jets, also of the South Atlantic League.

"I knew his IQ was completely at a different level," says Clemente Jr. "There were some guys who were in a different league at their age, and he was one of those guys. We were professionals when we played against each other for the first time. I remembered him as a kid growing up and seeing him evolve into this genius player."[6] (As the Clementes and Alomars lived on opposite sides of Puerto Rico, the boys from each family never played against each other in Little League or amateur tournaments and, truthfully, rarely spent significant time together.)

Even though Alomar had, at best, warning-track power at this stage, he was a dual threat at the plate. It seemed like every time Alomar came up, according to Clemente Jr., he would either drop down a perfect bunt or smoke a line drive into the right-center field gap.

"We would be having a conversation while he was at bat, because I was playing third and I was so close to him," says Clemente Jr., who repeatedly tried to discourage Alomar from bunting by inching closer and closer onto the infield grass. "I stood there talking to him during his at-bat."[7]

Unfortunately, for Roberto, playing against Clemente Jr.—just like playing for Sandy Sr.—was short-lived. By season's end, several months short of his eighteenth birthday, Alomar had amassed thirty-six steals and fifty-four RBIs to go along with the near-.300 average., a stat line that warranted a promotion to the Reno Padres of the California League (High Single-A) for the 1986 season.

This meant he'd be living without his family for the first time.

For the Padres, it wasn't ideal having a minor-league affiliate located in Reno, Nevada, especially when the home ballpark was around the corner from one of the city's premier gambling establishments, the Peppermill Resort Spa Casino. The Padres made a conscious effort to educate the young men in their organization about the transitory nature of their chosen profession and to stress that financial security, even when attained in the big leagues, could very well be fleeting. But there was only so much mentoring they could do when a glitzy temptation such as the Peppermill flashed 24/7. Indeed, the blackjack tables and high-end slot machines proved irresistible to the cash-strapped ballplayers, some of whom literally would spend their bottom dollar on the risky wagers. Had there not been the traditional postgame leftover food in the clubhouse ripe for stealing, some guys literally would have starved.

As one of Alomar's erstwhile minor-league teammates, who was also promoted to Reno in 1986, remembers,

> You had a bunch of single guys. They would go right from the game to the Peppermill every night. We would get paid every two weeks and a lot of the guys would just go cash their checks at the casino and there would be some guys that would leave the casino and have no money. They'd lose their whole check. They would have to live for two weeks, and they would be bumming off people. It wasn't the best city for people that had an addiction to gambling or any type of addiction gene.[8]

"There's quite a few boys that would spend their whole paycheck [on gambling]," adds former Reno shortstop Jim Wasem.[9]

However, Robbie was not one of those boys. The Padres were able to rest assured knowing that their brightest prospect wasn't going to go hog-wild at casinos . . . or even step foot in them for that matter. The sad reality was that the summer of 1986 was a pretty lonely one for Alomar. His dad had joined the big-league club's coaching staff and his brother had gotten promoted to

Double-A in Beaumont, Texas. Roberto, according to Wasem, who was a roommate for a couple of months in Reno, spent most of his downtime in solitude, often watching TV sitcoms to improve his English skills. Despite being a top-tier prospect, Roberto was making less than $1,000 per month and had no interest in blowing his limited funds at the gaming tables.

By late spring, Alomar was living alone in a two-bedroom apartment (his roommate had gotten transferred) and so when Wasem was called up from Charleston, he was assigned to live with Alomar to serve as a good example for the teenage prodigy. Wasem's lasting memory of the experience: "He was a great young man. Quiet young man. He was eighteen and we were all twenty-one, most of us, and so of course we were at the Peppermill, and he stayed inside. I'd come home, and he'd be on the couch watching TV, eating, and that's what he did. He couldn't go out with us."[10]

In a sense, by being a perpetual homebody, Alomar displayed great maturity for an eighteen-year-old. He knew how to take care of his body. In the scorching hot (albeit very dry) Reno weather, he hydrated himself with bottles of Poland Spring while many of his teammates were pounding cans of Bud Light. Naturally, some fellow Reno Padres who were of the legal drinking age (and surely a few who weren't) came stumbling back to the apartment or motel long past midnight . . . while Alomar was dead to the world.

For Alomar, the only real off-field excitement in what was otherwise a nondescript summer in western Nevada occurred during an incident at the Meadowood Mall in lower Reno. For the first time in his life, according to one former Reno teammate who wished to remain anonymous, Robbie got in trouble with the law when he and a couple of teammates were arrested for shoplifting cassette tapes at a music store. Later that evening, embarrassed club officials went down to the Reno jail and bailed out the young transgressors. The matter was not adjudicated further, as the shoplifting charges were soon dropped, and a mere two-game suspension followed.[11]

The misdemeanor served as a stark reminder of the drawback to having such a ridiculously young phenom on the roster. Alomar wasn't the first eighteen-year-old to shoplift, nor was he the only Reno Padre to ever run afoul of the law. That Alomar and his teammates were living paycheck to paycheck also warranted some sympathy. It wasn't as though they had wads of cash in their pockets and were just looking to cause trouble. They were, after all, poor minor-league ballplayers who actually may not have been able to afford the new Van Halen or Bon Jovi album. Nevertheless, the law was broken, which reflected poorly on the organization.

But especially this year, Alomar's (relatively) minor lapse in judgment could be overlooked. *Easily.* The kid's on-field performance was nothing short of astounding. While American-born baseball prospects his age were dancing at proms and receiving diplomas, Alomar was tearing up the Single-A California League, finishing the season with a league-leading .346 average and .397 on-base percentage while only fanning thirty-eight times. His defense had also improved considerably, as he cut his error total from the prior season (thirty-six) in half while demonstrating exceptional poise and grace in the middle of the diamond. Although a series of nagging injuries, including a split lip and groin pull, limited Alomar to 90 games (the team played a 142-game schedule), the sample size was substantial enough to justify the promotion to the Wichita Pilots of the Double-A Texas League for the following season.

Less than two weeks after his nineteenth birthday, Roberto Alomar reported to camp and upon arrival, learned that his roommate for spring training would be Carlos Baerga. A nice belated birthday present. Similar to Alomar, Baerga was a slick-fielding, switch-hitting teenage infielder from Puerto Rico (he hailed from the Greater San Juan area) whom the Padres didn't envision languishing in the minors for very long. Most critically, sharing Spanish as their native tongue naturally bred a sense of comfort and security. Subsequently, when Alomar had downtime this spring, he had an alternative to watching TV alone on the couch as the extroverted Baerga would nudge him into grabbing lunch at a local diner, hitting up a pool hall, or checking out a late-night flick at the movie theater.

Alas, the pairing was short-lived. Although Baerga had posted a respectable .270 average the prior summer for the Rainbows, the Padres didn't deem him ready to make the jump from Single-A Charleston to Double-A Wichita. Such was life in the minors with teammates (and roommates) constantly getting assigned to different affiliates across vast reaches of the country. The disparate geographic locations of Charleston, Reno, and Wichita served as a prime example of the cumbersome logistical situation.

There were quite a few reasons, actually, that the minor-league lifestyle was getting old. Now that Robbie was playing for Wichita in the Texas League, the travel was unbearably long and tedious, particularly during the fifteen-hour bus rides across the Great Plains to El Paso. Commutes to San Antonio and Shreveport, Louisiana, could approach ten hours. The closest destination from Wichita was Tulsa, still a nearly four-hour bus ride away. Often, it was virtually impossible to sleep on such long hauls with teammates' noises and smells wafting through the stuffy air of the Peter Pan bus as it coasted by one single-stoplight town after another. Rarely was a lunch or dinner not spent at a McDonald's or Pizza Hut in a rest area plaza. If you got motion sick from reading, listening to a Walkman could be your only form of entertainment.

On such road trips, the majority of games were played in the evenings given the scorching summertime conditions of the Deep South. This meant having all day to sit around and find ways to entertain oneself in a roadside motel nestled into a remote outpost of Texas or Oklahoma. Thus, most of the guys on Wichita's roster would lounge by the pool, perhaps catch up on sleep or breeze through a *Sports Illustrated*. But not Roberto and Sandy. This was the late 1980s and remote-control toy cars were in vogue for big kids such as themselves. Who needed a pool when you had such a hobby to indulge in?

"We were at the motel and for some reason those two got those battery-operated little cars," remembers Jim Wasem, who got called up to Wichita for a brief stint in 1987. "Most of us would just sit in the shade and watch Roberto and Sandy race these motor cars around the parking lots. That was our highlight of the day."[12]

When the road trips ended, Robbie would return home to an even more modest apartment than the one he was accustomed to in Reno. He was making more this year but could only afford a one-bedroom unit, given the steeper rental prices in Wichita. The silver lining to a truly pitiful living situation (you alternated nights between sleeping on the bed and kitchen sofa) was that his roommate this season was Sandy Jr. Sharing the apartment meant there was a little cash left over for purchasing a used car. However, the catch was that the brothers, being inexperienced drivers, subsequently had to purchase an insurance policy that proved costlier than the vehicle's $300 price tag.

Nevertheless, the bleak living conditions, once again, didn't hinder Robbie from having another spectacular season. While continuing to hit for a very high average (.319), Alomar, really for the first time in his professional career, demonstrated considerable power as he finished the year with twelve homers and sixty-eight RBIs. The parent organization was extremely pleased. When the Padres had signed Alomar a couple of years prior, they weren't expecting to get much pop from the skinny teenager. That Alomar didn't belt a single homer in that first summer in Charleston was of little concern, as he was still growing. But now, with three complete minor-league seasons under his belt, Alomar, filling out and sprouting to six feet, was emerging as more than just a contact hitter.

Everything was going to plan.

Well, almost everything.

In 1987, the organization instructed Wichita to move Alomar over to shortstop for the majority of the season (he would play only a dozen games at second this season). San Diego was concerned that Garry Templeton, their big-league starter, wasn't the long-term solution and wanted to try grooming Alomar into the role. The feeling was that because Alomar was such a gifted second baseman, he could make a fairly seamless transition. For whatever reason, this was far from the case. As evidenced by his thirty-four errors in 113 games, Alomar was simply not comfortable on the left side of the bag and was not shy about articulating his displeasure. However, even amid the error-ridden season, Alomar, being such a phenomenal athlete with tremendous instincts, still made some marvelous backhanded sliding plays deep in the hole of the Wichita Pilots' turf infield—plays not expected from a nineteen-year-old, regardless of his natural position. Nevertheless, by season's end, San Diego decided it was in everyone's best interest for the experiment to be considered over. (Ironically, when his father was in the minors, he had been asked to transition in the other direction, from short to second.)

Aside from a handful of games in the 1990 season when Alomar was already established in the big leagues, he was never penciled in to play short again. Considering his eventual supreme mastery of second base, it's hard to imagine that he couldn't have, at the very least, developed into a highly serviceable big-league shortstop had he stayed with it.

"He could have played short in the big leagues *easily*," remarks former Pilots teammate Jeff Yurtin. "I played with a lot of guys and there was nobody that I played with at second base, or even saw anybody, that could play near his level at second."[13]

Despite inching closer and closer to his big-league call-up (the offensive numbers vastly overshadowed the defensive hiccups at short), Alomar continued to keep to himself. His reclusive nature was even more pronounced with the naturally gregarious Sandy Jr. being his roommate and constant companion. Sandy was also young and not completely fluent in English, but he made a conscious effort to immerse himself in the fabric of the clubhouse while Roberto maintained his Lone Ranger persona. The juxtaposition between the two siblings, as former teammates recall, was striking.

"Sandy was more outgoing, more talkative," says Wasem. "Roberto was a little shyer and I wouldn't say he was scared, but it's just a different animal when you're nineteen years old and you have a bunch of twenty-one-year-olds, twenty-three-year-olds [around]."[14]

Of course, the American legal drinking age of twenty-one precluded Roberto from joining his teammates for late-night brews. Remembers Yurtin: "He didn't go out at all. He stayed in and just focused on his craft."[15]

Of which he was becoming a master.

When spring training began in Yuma, Arizona, in February 1988, San Diego manager Larry Bowa told Roberto Alomar that if he had a good spring, he would crack the Opening Day big-league roster.

It turned out to be a blatant lie.

Alomar did not have a good spring. He had a great one. In Arizona, he hit .360 and resumed his superlative play at second. Everyone in camp knew he was ready for the big leagues and that San Diego would be a superior club with him on its twenty-five-man opening-day roster. Yet the Padres broke camp without him, sending him to Triple-A Las Vegas in late March.

There were two official explanations issued by the club. One was that the current second baseman, Randy Ready, was, à la his surname, more prepared for the role. The front office also reasoned that, over the past two seasons, two second base prospects, Joey Cora and Bip Roberts, had been prematurely rushed up to the big leagues only to be demoted back to the minors.

Alomar knew this was a bunch of baloney. While Ready did hit .309 in 1987, he was essentially a glorified utility man whose average was due for an inevitable market correction. Meanwhile over the past month, Alomar had proved that, despite his lack of major-league experience, his defensive prowess was superior to that of the six-year veteran Ready. And Cora and Roberts? What correlation did their cumbersome transitions have with Alomar's nascent career trajectory? Not to mention, Alomar was a much higher-regarded prospect than either one.

Everyone—Alomar, teammates, coaches, reporters—knew the real reason was that San Diego's penny-pinching front office, one spearheaded by club president Chub Feeney, wanted to delay Alomar's eligibility for arbitration. According to the Basic Collective Bargaining Agreement at the time, a player would not be eligible for arbitration (and thus a higher salary) until he had three years of MLB service under his belt. If said player spent more than twenty days in the minors during a season, it would not count as a full year of MLB work. So, by delaying Alomar's ascension to the big-league club until later in the spring, the clock toward arbitration wouldn't start ticking until 1989.

Understandably, Alomar was left feeling not just devastated but also resentful over the procedural-induced demotion. His impressive three-year track record in the minors spoke for itself. But it wasn't just the numerical accomplishments. Aside from the aforementioned bouts of immaturity, Alomar actually had carried himself in a highly professional manner, particularly considering his teenage status. During that first summer in Charleston, when there were hardly any off days amid torrid weather, he didn't overexert himself in pregame warm-ups. He took his batting practice and fielded grounders but didn't push himself to participate in an excessive number of drills. It wasn't due to indolence, but rather prudence as he knew the limits of his not-yet-fully-developed body. Young Alomar's mindfulness of proper nutritional health and conditioning also manifested itself away from the diamond. After the final out, he would be drinking water before going to bed, while his teammates were pounding lager as they looked forward to cavorting at nightclubs and casinos. The Padres organization simply couldn't have asked for anything more from Alomar over the past three years.

After being called into Bowa's office and told he had to clean out his locker in Padres' camp and report to the Las Vegas Stars within seventy-two hours, Alomar went into the weight room, where he sobbed uncontrollably for nearly an hour. Not only were they depriving him of far superior big-league working conditions, but he was also being separated from his father, who was now a fixture of San Diego's coaching staff. After finally collecting himself, he met with reporters anxious to chronicle his reaction. While Alomar had not one day of big-league service, he felt inclined to express his sincere feelings on what he perceived as a gross injustice by delivering the following remarks in a public setting:

They told me they have to give the job to Randy Ready because of the year he had last year. But with the spring training I had, I think I made the club. And now they tell me I don't make it. I don't know what I have to do to make it.

This is one of the toughest days for me since I began playing baseball. [Being cut] hurt my heart. The last day [of cuts] they send me down. That hurt me. If the team wants to send me down, why didn't they do it before?

At second base, I know I can be with any team in the major leagues. It's going to be hard in the beginning. The first day will be tough, maybe by the third or fourth day, I will be okay.[16]

There almost wasn't a first day in Las Vegas. Before traversing northward through the Mojave Desert to Sin City, Alomar expressed some reluctance to report until the Padres bumped up his Triple-A salary, to which they soon agreed. Alomar was destined to make millions playing in the majors, so, in a sense, it seemed a little ridiculous that he was making a fuss over a few thousand dollars. But, on the other hand, at least from a teammate's perspective (certainly from that of star Tony Gwynn, who publicly expressed his frustration with the move), it was understandable given how skinflint management was so hell-bent on manipulating Alomar's MLB service time for its long-term interests. Perhaps the only ballplayer not empathizing with Alomar was Sandy Jr., who had no interest in placating his younger brother. The following year, when *Los Angeles Times* columnist Bill Plaschke wrote a feature on the Alomar family, Sandy Jr. rehashed how he had called out Roberto after the demotion.

"I ask him, 'Who do you think you are?' I tell him, 'You are given a better chance than most of us young guys. We had no chance to make the team.' I tell him, 'You are now a minor leaguer like us, so you should like being with us.'"[17]

While he may have been peeved over the organization's decision to exile him to Las Vegas, Alomar saved his sulking and pouting for his personal life. However, he continued to exemplify professionalism on the diamond and, as usual, produced. Through nine games, he drove in a league-leading fourteen runs, while playing near-flawless defense, committing but one error.

Nine games. San Diego, and in particular manager Larry Bowa, couldn't wait any longer—not with the way Randy Ready was scuffling and Alomar was excelling. Even though delaying the promotion just a matter of days could have saved money down the road, Feeney and the rest of the front office simply couldn't get around the fact that Alomar was already a bona fide Major League Baseball player.

When Alomar walked into the Las Vegas Stars' clubhouse on the afternoon of Tuesday, April 19, he soon noticed that he was not penciled into the starting lineup. Today was the day. Finally, no more interminable bus rides and nights in rundown motels. He was, at last, a big leaguer.

While Feeney was cautiously optimistic, Bowa was unabashedly ecstatic. So much so that he went out of his way not to put added pressure on Alomar, who was expected to start at second base immediately for the Padres during their midweek series in Los Angeles.

"In my opinion, if Roberto Alomar hits .200," Bowa told reporters, "He will be an asset to your team because of the way he plays defense."[18]

But Roberto knew better. He knew he could be an asset to the Padres not just with his glove. After all, he had never flirted with the Mendoza Line at any point in his life and he sure as hell wasn't going to start now.

4

Caught in the Middle

April 20, 1988.

It looked like the apocalypse had hit Southern California. The traditionally sun-splashed, arid region was experiencing its second massive storm system in less than a week, one that included gale-force winds, localized flooding, hail, and minor tornadoes. While not quite left at a standstill, the greater Los Angeles area was severely affected by this uncommon burst of inclement weather. Due to the slick roads, dozens of non-fatal traffic accidents, several involving school buses, exacerbated rush-hour traffic conditions on the notoriously congested freeways. By evening, flooding forced the closure of transition roads from the westbound Ventura Freeway to the Golden State Freeway.

Naturally, the bizarre weather pattern also disrupted the Los Angeles Dodgers' home schedule. Going into the 1988 season, Dodger Stadium had been around a quarter-century and only had experienced a dozen rainouts. By the end of this week, three of the four games the Dodgers and Padres were slated to play had been washed out. As a result, Roberto Alomar had to wait until the weekend for his much-anticipated debut.

Initially, it seemed like a relief. After the rainout on Wednesday, April 20, the two clubs planned to play a twi-night doubleheader the next day. Alomar was expected to be in the lineup for both ends of the twin bill and face LA's two All-Star pitchers, Orel Hershiser and Fernando Valenzuela—not exactly an ideal scenario for making one's MLB debut. So, once the games were postponed, Alomar thought he caught a break . . . until he looked ahead at the upcoming schedule.

By Friday, the typical postcard weather returned to Southern California, and the Padres returned home to Jack Murphy Stadium to open a three-game set with the Houston Astros. Batting second and playing second would be Roberto Alomar, whose welcome-to-the-big-leagues moment would come against not just an All-Star caliber pitcher, but a future Hall of Famer in flame-throwing Nolan Ryan.

Ryan was of Robbie's father's generation, having debuted for the New York Mets in 1966—two years after Sandy Sr. had broken in with the Milwaukee Braves, not to mention two years before Roberto was born. Some of Roberto's earliest memories of his father's career involved the pregame lessons Ryan so graciously provided on the lawn of Anaheim Stadium. Now, Ryan was trying to ruin the kid's big-league debut.

No such luck.

In the bottom of the first inning, following Tony Gwynn's leadoff single and 1,000th career hit, Ryan had Alomar down 0-2 in the count and tried to fan him with a curveball down and away. Alomar slapped at the slow breaking ball and tapped a grounder deep in the hole between short and third. Houston shortstop Rafael Ramirez, playing Alomar to pull, had to shuffle to his right to make a backhanded stop. The ball banged off Ramirez's glove and rolled around the infield dirt for a couple seconds before the veteran infielder scooped it up. There was no point in firing a throw to first baseman Glenn Davis: Alomar already had darted past the bag.

The hometown scoring decision ruled it a base hit—probably a questionable call, and one that may not have gone Alomar's way had the game been played in Houston's Astrodome. Nevertheless, the youngest player in the majors was now batting 1.000, courtesy of the infield hit against Ryan, who was nearing three hundred career wins.

Across the diamond, San Diego third base coach Sandy Sr. beamed with parental pride over the poise his son just demonstrated. He could relate. Twenty-four years earlier, Sandy was ungraciously welcomed into the big leagues by digging in against another legendary right-handed hurler, St. Louis Cardinals pitcher Bob Gibson, in the second game of a doubleheader. But Roberto being unfazed by his imposing opponent was more impressive given his youthfulness and heightened expectations.

"I've always admired him," Alomar said of Ryan after he batted 1–4 in the Padres' 3–1 victory over the Astros. "He used to teach me how to pitch. But I really never thought he'd still be pitching when I got here."[1]

When Ryan began his MLB career in 1966, Ronald Reagan was a B-list actor who happened to be launching a political career by running for governor of California in the upcoming election. Now, in spring 1988, Reagan was the president of the United States who happened to have been an actor in his earlier life. (Ryan would not retire until after the 1993 season. Ironically, on May 1, 1991, the "Ryan Express" capped off his major-league-record seventh no-hitter by fanning Alomar for the game's final out.)

While Robbie had a fairly nondescript MLB debut, holding his own against a living legend such as Ryan vindicated the Padres' decision to call him up as a twenty-year-old. Indeed, as the ensuing months would prove, Robbie would never have to worry about riding minor-league buses again. While the Padres had a mediocre year in 1988 (the club finished with an 83–78 mark), the mustachioed, slender rookie remained the club's starting second baseman throughout the season. Although he didn't exactly tear up the National League with his .266 batting average, Alomar proved to be a solid contact hitter who, at least for a rookie, rarely got overpowered by opposing pitchers.

"It was hard to strike him out," remembers veteran pitcher Doug Drabek who was holding down the Pittsburgh Pirates' rotation in the late 1980s. "A guy who knew how to put the bat on the ball, even if it was to extend an at-bat. He just had a good eye at the plate and knew what he wanted to do."[2]

"When this guy came up, he just had a different swag about himself," recalls Mike Jackson, who was pitching for the Seattle Mariners at the time, but had seen plenty of Alomar during spring training in Arizona. "This guy knew he was good, and he knew he was probably one of the best in the game."[3]

Alomar was never really in the running for National League Rookie of the Year in 1988 (he finished in fifth place), but considering that he was literally the youngest player in baseball, his vastly improved play over the second half of the season was rather encouraging. In the final fifty-five games, he hit safely in all but nine while posting a .316 average and only made three errors after July 21. Perhaps even more encouraging was Alomar's ability to remain unruffled amid the turmoil engulfing the Padres organization in 1988. The Padres' fairly decent record belied significant internal chaos. After a 16–30 start, the front office canned Bowa, whose old-school, no-nonsense managerial approach had alienated many players—but not Alomar, who didn't mind the intensity evinced by Bowa's steely demeanor. After all, Bowa had been the staunchest advocate for Alomar's rapid ascension to the big leagues and stuck with him throughout his early-season struggles. While most teammates celebrated Bowa's replacement with the more avuncular Jack McKeon (the Alomar family's old friend from the Puerto Rican Winter League), Roberto, as he noted in his autobiography, found it a little disconcerting to have to get acclimated to a new manager after his first month in the majors.

Even though the team went 67–48 with McKeon and remained in contention until early September, a bizarre event during the penultimate weekend of the season highlighted the team's clownish and dysfunctional leadership. On the evening of September 24, in the middle of the seventh inning of an eventual 3–0 win over Houston, a couple fans paraded two levels below club president Chub Feeney's private box with a banner that read "Scrub Chub." Feeney, who had angered many fans and players not only for his reluctance to promote Alomar back in April but also for his inactivity regarding free-agent signings and trades, apparently forgot, or didn't care, that it was Fan Appreciation Night as he shuffled to the front of his box and flipped off the banner holders. While this was long before Twitter, TikTok, and screenshots, the obscene gesture was caught on camera and soon broadcast into living rooms across Southern California.

The following day, Feeney resigned his post as San Diego president.

So, this soap opera of a season taught Alomar that there was more to playing for the Padres than enjoying the gorgeous weather and laid-back fans. Being a Padre meant having to block out an excessive number of distractions occurring on a seemingly regular basis.

"If the Padres were the Yankees, they would have been a national story every year for all their infighting, confusion, the way they treated players, what went on in the front office," recalls veteran baseball writer Barry Bloom, who covered the Padres for the *San Diego Union-Tribune* throughout the 1980s. "It was just complete chaos."[4]

While the lingering aftermath of the humiliating Feeney incident hovered over the team going into the 1989 season, it got off to a decent enough start, heading into June with a 29–25 record. For Alomar, personally, his sophomore season was a mixed bag. While he was a versatile threat at the top of the order by hitting .295 and swiping forty-two bags, he regressed quite considerably on defense, committing twenty-eight errors, nearly twice as many as his rookie season total.

Back in spring training, there had been talk that Alomar could challenge Ryne Sandberg of the Chicago Clubs for the National League Gold Glove Award at second base. Clearly, such hype was premature, as Alomar was not only making his fair share of physical miscues but also mental ones. There were times when the normally cerebral Alomar made a dazzling backhanded stop . . . before making an ill-advised desperation throw into the dugout. On one occasion, he uncharacteristically committed the cardinal sin of forgetting to cover first base on a bunt that pulled the first baseman off the bag.

San Diego wasn't overly concerned. The organization knew that in time, Alomar's defensive play would justify his billing as a can't-miss second base prospect. Furthermore, Alomar's late-season offensive contributions began overshadowing the defensive lapses. In the heat of the NL pennant race, Alomar was emerging as one of the game's most dynamic leadoff hitters. Some writers and scouts' prediction back in February that Alomar could soon give teammate Tony Gwynn a run for the National League batting title no longer seemed outlandish.

Truthfully, however, Alomar was not yet an elite hitter ready to dethrone Gwynn, widely considered the greatest hitter since Ted Williams, who was having another stellar season coming off back-to-back NL batting crowns. By Labor Day, Gwynn was locked in an air-tight race for the batting title with Will Clark of the San Francisco Giants, coincidentally the team the Padres were battling for first place in the NL West and slated to play in a mid-September weekend series at Candlestick Park. For the first time since their 1984 NL pennant-winning season, the Padres were playing meaningful late-season games, and just like Gwynn, Alomar was an instrumental contributor to the team's resurgence.

These were heady days for the twenty-one-year-old kid from Puerto Rico. Whereas many young ballplayers may have wilted from the grind of their first entire big-league season or been intimidated by high-stakes September baseball, Alomar proved unflappable, as evidenced by his maintaining a near-.300 average down the stretch. After posting multiple multi-hit games against divisional foes Atlanta and Houston earlier in the month, Alomar came through in the rubber game of the pivotal three-game set against the

Giants by going 2–5, including a solo homer to lead off the game and an RBI single in the eighth inning. A clutch performance, indeed. After the Padres dropped the first game of the single-admission doubleheader, their 6–1 win in the nightcap kept them five games back of the Giants for first place in the NL West heading into a series in Cincinnati.

Naturally, upbeat vibes seeped through San Diego's clubhouse after the win. Starting pitcher Bruce Hurst answered fluff questions from reporters about his complete game gem. Catcher Benito Santiago lightheartedly shot the breeze with fellow Puerto Rican Joey Cora, now a reserve infielder. The postgame spread consisted of Mexican food from one of the Bay Area's finest cantinas. A bucket of ice-cold Corona bottles flanked the platters of home-made guacamole and savory chicken tacos. There was no need to worry about schlepping personal luggage to the team's coach bus parked outside Candlestick and soon departing for San Francisco International Airport. That's what a big-league clubhouse staff was for.

Life was good.

Or, at least, it should have been for Alomar.

He was in no danger of returning to Las Vegas. The days of peanut butter and jelly sandwich lunches and interminable bus rides were a distant memory. The many perks (more like luxuries) of being a big leaguer were here to stay, as he was San Diego's starting second baseman for the foreseeable future. His dad was still around as third base coach and the presence of fellow countrymen Cora and Santiago naturally provided extra comfort. Oh, and he was making a six-figure salary for the first time in his life. Yet at this particular moment in time, Alomar came across as uncomfortable and aloof, appearing rather out of his element.

One of Alomar's former minor-league teammates who had recently returned from playing professional ball in Italy was at the doubleheader and swung by the Padres' clubhouse to see some of his buddies following the twin bill. His lasting impression of the evening:

> I looked over at Roberto and it was unbelievable. He was just sitting there all by himself. I looked at him and I just thought, "Man, that's sad." I just felt so bad for him. He didn't really seem like he had even enjoyed himself. He didn't come over. He didn't say anything to me really. It had nothing to do with him and me. That was just his personality.[5]

As the next season would prove, however, Roberto's personality was not the troublesome one in the San Diego clubhouse.

After the Padres gave the Giants a run in 1989 (with an 89–73 record, they finished three games behind in the NL West standings), expectations were high heading into the 1990 season. Coming off an impressive sophomore season, Roberto was poised to crack the NL All-Star roster. Gwynn, the eventual 1989 NL batting king, appeared destined for Cooperstown. After a solid first year in San Diego, veteran slugger Jack Clark had proven he was not finished. But the biggest reason for the considerable buzz was that back in December the Padres had acquired outfielder Joe Carter from the Cleveland Indians. Carter had averaged thirty-one home runs and 108 RBIs the past four seasons in Cleveland and was not yet thirty years old. Thus, the asking price seemed reasonable as San Diego only had to part with spare outfielder Chris James, minor leaguer Carlos Baerga, and catcher Sandy Alomar Jr.

The organization was most reluctant to deal Roberto's brother and probably wouldn't have had Benito Santiago not blossomed into an All-Star in 1989. While the twenty-three-year-old Sandy had only eight days of big-league service, he had won the *Sporting News'* Minor League Player of the Year award the past two seasons and was clearly ready to be a full-time big leaguer.

Any frustration Roberto may have felt over the organization deeming his older brother dispensable did not adversely affect his on-field performance. While the club played below-.500 ball in April, Roberto was not the least bit responsible for the underwhelming start. Even when his bat went silent (his average dipped slightly this season), he could still impact a game by tearing up the base paths and making exceptional plays up the middle. Alomar was still making some airheaded decisions—like stealing bases on the wrong counts and trying to backhand too many groundballs—but such blunders were usually forgiven by Jack McKeon, who, according to former San Diego first baseman Phil Stephenson, "didn't get too excited about much of anything."[6]

Unfortunately, however, Roberto's strong first half was merely a sidebar to the Padres' underachievement—and subsequent drama engulfing their clubhouse this season.

By early May, the Padres were playing below-.500 and fading fast in the NL West standings. The unexpected struggles led to bitter internal dissension, which soon morphed into a public imbroglio when, on May 15, the *New York Daily News* quoted veteran third baseman Mike Pagliarulo as saying in regard to one teammate that "if he gets his hits and we lose, that's fine with him."[7] Several days later, Tony Gwynn learned from a San Diego writer that the barb was directed toward him. Several days after that, Gwynn learned that Pagliarulo was far from his only detractor in the San Diego clubhouse. During a players-only meeting held before the Padres' game on May 24 at Shea Stadium, the airing of grievances ensued. Starting first baseman Jack Clark, with the strong backing of Pagliarulo, and shortstop Garry Templeton, chastised Gwynn for, among other things, opting to bunt runners over instead of trying to drive them in to safeguard his batting average (even the best hitters get retired two out of three times when swinging away) and being a kiss-up to the media, all while having a sour attitude toward being the seventh-highest-paid player on the team. Younger, more impressionable teammates piled on by taking their weak shots at Gwynn—some even had the nerve to complain he failed to provide housing and restaurant advice for newly acquired players.

Ironically, it was the notoriously manipulative Clark, of all people, who, in so harshly criticizing Gwynn, alienated the most popular and successful athlete in San Diego history from many within the confines of Jack Murphy Stadium.

"Clark did what he did with every major player he ever played with," recalls baseball scribe Barry Bloom. "Whether it was Ozzie Smith, Rickey Henderson, Tony [Gwynn], he would take the guy who was the star when he'd get to a team, and he would get into a huge fight with him."[8]

Phil Stephenson has his own memories of playing with Clark that summer:

> The one thing about Jack was he was kind of his own dude. There were times he would come up to me the last day of a road trip or when we had an off day the next day and he would tell me, "Make sure you're ready." And he would get himself thrown out of the game in the first or second inning. He would leave the clubhouse and take off to wherever he wanted to go to spend his day off.[9]

Yet despite Clark's track record of shenanigans, at this hour, few members of the San Diego clubhouse were in Gwynn's corner, despite Gwynn's pedigree as a four-time NL batting champion and league-wide reputation for being exceptionally diligent and good-natured. Robbie was not one of those few.

"Robbie sided with him [Clark] against Tony," says Bloom. "Robbie was in Jack's corner."[10]

Even though Gwynn had long been a great admirer of Alomar's talents and advocated for his rapid promotion to the big leagues a couple of years earlier, many Padres, including perhaps Alomar, could be put off by Gwynn's apparent me-first attitude. While Gwynn was beloved by fans (and even many reporters), his exuded affability may have belied how some teammates genuinely perceived him.

"One of the things about Tony was that he was a self-centered player," acknowledges Bloom. "All he really ever cared about from the moment he came up to the major leagues was, 'How am I going to get to three thousand hits?' That was his goal."[11]

By 1990, Gwynn was easily on pace to join the three-thousand-hit club. But the pursuit came at the expense of sacrificing power, potentially an asset more conducive to winning. Everyone in San Diego knew that Gwynn was capable of hitting more than his traditional half-dozen homers per season. When the team held pregame home run derbies at cavernous Jack Murphy Stadium, the hefty Gwynn was often the victor. Yet Gwynn refused to turn on fastballs in games, instead opting to spray low line drives from foul pole to foul pole, and it wasn't until the mid-1990s when Ted Williams shamed him into hitting for power that Gwynn finally had consecutive seasons with double-digit home run totals. (Diagonally across the country, Boston Red Sox third baseman Wade Boggs was also carved up for prioritizing average over power.) Thanks to Clark and friends, it was open season on Gwynn, and while there were the perfunctory apologies following the outburst at Shea, frosty relations lingered.

As the following months unfolded, there was no happy resolution to this story. In September, a mutilated Tony Gwynn figurine with severed arms and legs was hung from its neck by a chain noose in the San Diego dugout. Clark would adamantly deny being the perpetrator of the racially tinged "prank" and eventually a groundskeeper admitted to hanging the doll; however, Gwynn thought the admission was the club's way of trying to cover for some of his own teammates. A week later, when Gwynn's season prematurely ended with a broken finger, he cleaned out his locker and returned home. When a reporter asked Gwynn if he would return to the team before the final game, Gwynn responded, "Hell no. Why would I want to hang around with those [expletive]?"[12] A half-year later, Clark, then part of the Boston Red Sox, was very forthright in articulating his resentment toward Gwynn when he told *Sports Illustrated*'s Tim Kurkjian: "He has a losing attitude about baseball. He protects Number One: himself. He does his own thing because everyone in San Diego kisses his ass. He's, like, Mr. Padre. But you don't know Tony until you play with him."[13]

As the season progressed, the Padres' disappointing June record (11–15) and even worse start to July (2–6) unmistakably reflected a dysfunctional clubhouse. By the All-Star break McKeon felt inclined to step down as manager (he stayed on as vice president of baseball operations) and was replaced by coach Greg Riddoch.

For Roberto, the managerial change wasn't necessarily at the forefront of his mind at this moment because he was participating in the MLB All-Star Game at iconic Wrigley Field. Being named a reserve second baseman was a well-deserved nod. After recuperating from a hand injury suffered the prior September that truncated his second MLB season, Roberto posted a sparkling .311 batting average to go along with thirty-seven RBIs in the first half of the 1990 season. The evening in Chicago was extra special, as Sandy Jr., now in his first year with the Cleveland Indians, was the American League starting catcher, making him the first-ever rookie backstop selected by the fans to start the Midsummer Classic. Sandy Jr., who had endeared himself to fans earlier in the season when he gunned down Oakland speedster Rickey Henderson from his knees, was, admittedly, humbled by the honor. The day before the game, he told the *Chicago Tribune*: "I was shocked. It's my first year. In Cleveland, people have only started to come to the games the last few weeks. They probably voted for me in San Diego and New York and in other places. . . . How could I have ever dreamed I would be an All-Star? I didn't think I'd ever be a major-league baseball player."[14] Meanwhile, Roberto, who had talked of becoming an All-Star since the day he put on a big-league uniform, wasn't exactly in awe of rubbing shoulders with Ozzie Smith, Andre Dawson, Ryne Sandberg, and other National League stars, but he did acknowledge that he and Sandy Jr. being only the third set of brothers to play for opposing All-Star teams—on their mother's birthday no less—was quite meaningful.

In hindsight, it meant even more, given the turmoil awaiting Roberto upon his return to San Diego.

Once the season's unofficial second half got underway, it took Roberto less than a week to realize that, in the newly hired Greg Riddoch, he had a manager he didn't care for. Really, for the first time in his life.

The relationship was irrevocably damaged during a mid-July series in Chicago. In the middle game of the series, Riddoch felt Alomar was dogging it on his way to first following a groundball. After the 7–2 loss to the Cubs, the newbie skipper called Roberto into his office. Following the thirty-five-minute, closed-door meeting, Riddoch told his All-Star second baseman he hoped their discussion would stay private. After Riddoch benched Roberto during the series finale the following afternoon, the new boss revealed to the press how he was miffed at Roberto for his lackadaisical approach ("I haven't liked what I've seen—not at all"). Less than twenty-four hours later, Roberto was, himself, miffed when he read Riddoch's comments in the paper, but to his credit, kept his emotions in check and simply walked over to his manager, showed him the paper, and walked away.[15]

As the Padres continued floundering (they started the second half 1–11 before finally winning a series against the Reds, which included Roseanne Barr's infamous national anthem rendition), Riddoch couldn't stop publicly calling out the young phenom. Alomar's average was nosediving, and his defense was wildly inconsistent, but at times Riddoch's criticism crossed the line. A couple of years later, when reflecting on the dynamic between player and manager for Roberto's autobiography *Second to None*, Sandy Sr. acknowledged: "Riddoch was saying some things about him [Robbie] in the press, making it look like he had personal problems. Then he was saying to the press that Robbie's head wasn't in the game."[16]

Robbie wasn't the only Padre who felt Riddoch could be disloyal and two-faced. Perhaps even worse, there was the fairly widespread sentiment that Riddoch lacked the baseball acumen to be a competent manager.

"He just couldn't find lineups that could win consistently," recalls Phil Stephenson. "I think the stress kind of wore on him a little bit. There were some guys that didn't like him, and I'm not sure why they didn't like him. I wasn't one of them. In '90, I think we were just underachieving more than anything else."[17]

After a disastrous July, the team played uninspired ball over the final two months to finish with a 75–87 record. Yet in a somewhat surprising move, the new ownership group headed by Hollywood producer Tom Werner (the

Kroc family had been replaced in mid-June) removed the "interim" label from Riddoch's job title before the season concluded. Less than a week after the season finale against the Dodgers, Riddoch, before leaving for a fishing trip in Idaho, relieved Sandy Sr. of his duties.

While Sandy Sr. was disappointed, he was not stunned. He knew Riddoch had it out for him and that the manager's recent promotion meant his days on the coaching staff were numbered. (On more than one occasion the previous summer Riddoch had organized outings with other coaches while going out of his way to exclude Sandy Sr.)

The press was eager to hear from Roberto, who once again demonstrated considerable maturity, by remarking: "I have no hard feelings, but I'm real disappointed because I thought that Dad was doing a real great job as a coach. . . . I don't know the reason he was let go. I don't know all that went on between Greg and my dad. I don't get into their lives, but I don't think it was a good decision."[18]

Irrespective of Riddoch's personal gripes, the dismissal of Sandy Sr. certainly was a questionable decision, as it not only irked Roberto, one of the franchise's cornerstone players, but it also stripped the clubhouse of one of its most revered figures.

Catcher Tom Lampkin, whom the Padres acquired in a mid-season trade in 1990, remembers,

> They [Roberto and his dad] were close. You could tell that they had a good relationship. He [Sandy Alomar Sr.] had a job to do and he took it seriously and he did his job. His dad was not hard in a bad way, but he was a demanding coach. He demanded guys treat the game the way the game was supposed to be played. He didn't take it easy on Robbie just because Robbie was his son. He still demanded the same perfection.[19]

The following season Roberto opened up about how he really felt toward the Padres for letting his dad go when he was quoted in the *Los Angeles Times* as saying: "The way they let him go, it wasn't a manly decision. It wasn't professional, either."[20]

As if Roberto needed further incentive to start entertaining thoughts of playing elsewhere, the Padres were still toying with the idea of having him play shortstop. In late June, Alomar, who loathed playing shortstop for

Wichita in 1987, was nudged into the position when veteran Garry Templeton was temporarily benched. After making two errors in a five-game span at the position, Roberto wasn't shy about voicing his displeasure and McKeon obliged by moving him back to second. But once the dust had settled on the 1990 season the San Diego brain trust resumed talks of Alomar permanently taking over for the aging and declining Templeton and slotting Joey Cora and/or Bip Roberts in at second.

This didn't go over too well.

"He [Alomar] pouted and insisted on playing at second base," says Barry Bloom. "I think he was ready to get the hell out of San Diego. I don't think he thought that he had any future there."[21]

Although Alomar may not have been miserable in San Diego (he had recently purchased an oceanside house in Del Mar, a picturesque suburb twenty miles north of San Diego, and appreciated having a couple fellow Puerto Ricans as teammates with whom he often socialized), he simply couldn't stomach the idea of playing shortstop for Riddoch. Fortunately, any uncertainty was short-lived, as on December 5, in the midst of the winter meetings held outside Chicago, San Diego's newly hired general manager Joe McIlvaine traded Alomar and Joe Carter to the Toronto Blue Jays for shortstop Tony Fernandez and first baseman Fred McGriff.

While 1990 had been a dumpster fire of a season, Alomar was the last person to blame for the club's misfortunes, as he went about his business of blossoming into an All-Star with boundless potential. Certainly, it was hard to imagine that the Padres would be a better team in 1991 with Alomar playing elsewhere.

Phil Stephenson remembers,

He was a really good guy, a tremendous player. Robbie was just one of those happy guys, nothing seemed to bother him. I was really saddened to see him get traded to Toronto. It wasn't so much a surprise that Joe [Carter] got traded because at that time the National League, I think, there was better pitching. I think Joe was a lot more comfortable as an American League hitter.

I was really surprised they traded Robbie. I thought he was a really good fit in San Diego. The fans loved him. He was good with the media. Just one of those guys that you liked to have on your team. He always had a lot of positivity around him. Tony [Fernandez] was a really good shortstop, but he didn't have the charisma that Robbie had. Tony wasn't very good in the clubhouse. Robbie was a great guy to have in the clubhouse.[22]

Tom Lampkin shares similar memories by noting,

Robbie was an exceptional athlete. He turned the double play as well as anybody I played with. He was one of those guys that didn't look like he was trying. It came so easy to him. Never had any problems with him. I never heard anybody that did. He was a great kid. He was fairly quiet and shy. I never saw him get upset. I never saw him snap after an at-bat or after a bad game. Even at a young age, he was very professional, the way he carried himself and the way he played.[23]

Nevertheless, in talk swirling around the trade's potential impact, Alomar, while certainly not considered a throw-in, was vastly overshadowed by Joe Carter, given his exuberant personality and prolific offensive track record.

"Joe could say what he wanted, laugh when he wanted, do what he wanted, and nobody said anything," adds Lampkin. "I don't remember Robbie putting himself out there. I remember it more as a rookie-veteran relationship between those two guys than it was like that they were on a par on everything."[24]

The snap judgment following the trade was that San Diego came out on top. They needed a slugging first baseman with Jack Clark's looming departure and got one in McGriff, who had averaged thirty-five homers per year since 1988. With Garry Templeton's rapid decline (and Alomar's unwillingness to move) they needed a shortstop and got a top-flight one in Fernandez, who had won four Gold Glove Awards in the 1980s. On the flip side, in acquiring Carter, Toronto was getting a slugger of McGriff's caliber, but one who was four years older. And while Alomar had tremendous upside, he was not nearly as established a middle infielder as Fernandez.

Meanwhile, Toronto general manager Pat Gillick felt he got the best of this deal. Ever since he was the New York Yankees' scouting director back in the mid-1970s and had seen Sandy Sr. practice with his youngest son, Gillick had coveted Roberto. Now, he couldn't wait to share what he considered good news with his wife, Doris. Perhaps he could get to her before she turned on the television.

When he called from O'Hare Airport to tell her about the trade, his spouse, upon hearing the breaking news for the first time, responded, "You better get home as soon as possible before you screw up the team anymore."[25]

In effect, she was speaking for legions of Ontarians who felt that the Blue Jays were getting fleeced in this deal. Fernandez was a defensive wizard (although the public didn't know that he had made multiple threats to the Blue Jays about retiring to join the ministry, which certainly factored into Gillick's decision to include him in the trade), and McGriff was one of the game's premier power hitters.

The fans weren't the only ones upset. On the morning of December 5, after learning the news from his agent (and soon thereafter meeting with reporters who had descended upon his new home), Roberto broke down in tears—just like he had nearly three years earlier following the demotion to Las Vegas. His parents got on the phone and tried to console him, but it was to no avail. It wasn't that Roberto was particularly upset about bolting from the Padres. It was more that Toronto was a great unknown, which bred great insecurity. He had never been to the Canadian metropolis and was unaccustomed to northern climes. In terms of baseball, he had never seen the Blue Jays play in person and had only seen them on television once, during the 1985 American League Championship Series.

There may have been some reporters interested in Alomar's take, but at the winter meetings, he was not the main topic of conversation. Essentially, he was more an afterthought than anything, as throughout the day, reporters were either coining the blockbuster deal the "Joe Carter trade" or the "Fred McGriff trade."

Gillick knew better. Very late in the evening of December 5, he spotted reporter Tim Kurkjian in a hotel lobby, walked up to him, and whispered, "This will always be known as the Roberto Alomar trade."[26]

5

"Home Suite Home"

Joe Carter was jealous.

For the second time in two years, he had to get accustomed to a different city, which meant settling into another house, buying furniture, and learning strange traffic patterns for commuting to and from work.

Meanwhile, his young bachelor teammate Roberto Alomar, in only his first move as a big leaguer, had no such hassles. From the moment he landed in Toronto in December 1991, Alomar, with only himself to care for, was treated like royalty as a resident of the SkyDome Hotel, which was part of the same edifice (SkyDome, now known as the Rogers Centre) that housed the ballpark. Alomar had stayed at the hotel for a night earlier in December right after the trade went down and liked it so much that the hotel designed a massive, freshly painted suite for him equipped with sofas, pool table, and two high-end televisions. In what was essentially a tenancy-at-will arrangement, it was his to move into when the season started. And he didn't have to lift a finger for anything. Within this climate-controlled, immaculate, and exquisitely outfitted private pad, the kid from the Caribbean quickly grew accustomed to never using the same towel twice in a day and to waking up to gourmet room service breakfasts. Copies of *USA Today* would appear at his doorstep each morning, followed by chocolate mints on his pillows come nighttime. But before Alomar's head even hit one of those plush pillows, he could expect a waiter to wheel in a minibar stacked with $8 mini-bottles of cognac and $9.75 jars of cashews—just in case the hotel's high-profile guest desired a late-night snack. And as if Alomar needed any more reasons to put off looking for a house, the hotel staff created a personalized daily menu that included the two meals he craved the most: hamburger and chicken stir fry. They also programmed his flat screen TVs to include a diverse selection of hit early 1990s movie titles.[1]

As the 1991 season unfolded, the hotel life was a perfect match for Roberto's personality, as he could stay perfectly content inside his all-inclusive bubble. If he needed laundry done, the concierge service was a call away. When he got hungry, room service was at the ready. Shopping for furniture was never on the to-do list. Living in occasionally wintry weather conditions was an adjustment coming from the sun-splashed postcard weather of Puerto Rico and San Diego . . . but hardly an issue in Toronto when the solution was to merely lower the window shades.

However, Alomar's private lifestyle meant he was even more of an enigma to Blue Jays fans, who knew little of his backstory. The fans knew he had been a fine player in the National League, but, at least in the early going, his unassuming and sometimes reclusive nature (not to mention his less-than-imposing physique) did not generate much hype about his new presence on the team.

The same could be said about the reactions of some of his teammates.

Back in February, when the Jays had reported to spring training in Dunedin, Florida, there wasn't excessive buzz over the club's new second baseman.

"In [Joe] Carter, we knew exactly what we were getting, as we had played against him a lot when he was in Cleveland. Robbie, we didn't know as much about," says veteran infielder Rance Mulliniks.[2]

"Seeing Robbie for the first time, he was just a short little Latin looking guy. He wasn't super impressive by any means," recalls Mike Timlin, a rookie pitcher for Toronto in 1991.[3]

Alomar didn't remain nondescript for very long. In fact, during an early spring training game there was one particular play that made heads turn. On a hot shot up the middle, Roberto glided to his right, slid down to snag the one-hopper, and in one fluid motion, popped up before slinging the ball to first for the out.

"I remember all of us in the dugout, that immediately got everybody's attention," says Mulliniks. "Because we hadn't seen anybody make a play like that before. That's when I think we all realized we really had something special in Robbie Alomar."[4]

Perhaps even more awe-inspiring than Alomar's off-the-charts talent was the ease with which he was mastering a craft that had wildly frustrated its most highly skilled practitioners for over a century. Timlin remembers,

> What impressed me the most was that he really enjoyed playing the game of baseball. He was always having a good time. It was something that just came naturally. He didn't have to really, really work hard. He lifted and he ran, and he did all the stuff that he needed to do. But I think he could have gotten by with the natural talent that he possessed, just literally showing up and doing it. That's how good he was.[5]

Once the regular season began in earnest, the rest of the American League took notice. After a mediocre April, Alomar put up MVP-caliber numbers in May, a month in which he drove in nineteen runs while making just one error. Not exactly a burner on the basepaths, Alomar still quickly became one of the game's elite base stealers because of his innate ability to pick up cues from pitchers and catchers. Aside from Rickey Henderson, Ken Griffey Jr., and Barry Bonds, no one impacted a game in as many ways.

"I just remember him [Roberto] creating panic in the dugout when I was with the White Sox," recalls former American League catcher Matt Merullo. (His late grandfather, Lennie Merullo, had been the last surviving member of another Chicago baseball team: the 1945 NL pennant-winning Cubs.) "He could kill you either way, right-handed, left-handed, had power, take hits away on defense, steal bases. He always had a cool, calm demeanor. He just made it look so easy. It was like a sense of envy, like, 'How could this guy be so good?'"[6]

It was painfully apparent that the Padres had committed their own E4 in letting their star second baseman go. In essentially trading him for an older, less complete player in Tony Fernandez, the new ownership group had severely mismanaged the precious asset that was Roberto Alomar.

"I don't ever remember being as impressed by a baseball player," says longtime Cleveland Indians beat writer Jim Ingraham when recalling the first time he saw Alomar play during a late June series between Cleveland and Toronto.

"I remember thinking to myself, 'How did San Diego ever trade this guy? Why would San Diego ever give this guy up?'"[7]

"He [Alomar] wasn't the tallest or necessarily the fastest, [but] he just did it all," says Hall of Famer Dave Winfield, who was playing for the California Angels in 1991. "One of the most well-rounded, versatile, high baseball IQ players that I played against."[8]

While Roberto was coming into his own as a top-of-the-order switch-hitter (on May 10, he became the first Blue Jay to go deep from both sides of the plate in the same game), his defensive feats were particularly impressive considering he played half the time on the unforgiving SkyDome carpet. In the 1980s, when Toronto had played in Exhibition Stadium with its rock-hard infield, the franchise had shuffled through an assortment of second basemen, none of whom felt particularly inclined to lay out for grounders, line drives, or bloops that came within a few feet of their outstretched mitts. Alomar was different. In his first couple months at the SkyDome (the Blue Jays had moved in midway through the 1989 season), he repeatedly showed no hesitation to go airborne in pursuit of a putout—while bracing for a crash landing, risking carpet burns, fractured ribs, or worse, a separated shoulder. After playing on the lush grass and groomed dirt at Jack Murphy Stadium the past few years, Alomar adapted perfectly to his new home turf, never once suffering such a debilitating injury while maintaining his horizontal approach to fielding.

"The turf's kind of tough, but I'm getting used to it," Alomar told the *National Post* in late May. "It's proper to play that way. . . . When you dive for a ball, you kind of get stuck. You can't keep going. On the grass, you dive and you keep going. It's more better."[9]

That's right, even in the early 1990s a Canadian daily such as the *National Post* deemed it necessary to quote Alomar verbatim, thereby not extending him the courtesy of cleaning up his broken English. Perhaps it is not surprising, therefore, that his relationship with the Toronto sports media would later turn sour.

The inhospitable playing surface may have posed the only real challenge in coming north of the border. With his fearless all-out approach, Alomar quickly endeared himself to Toronto fans who were blissfully ignorant of his purported half-hearted efforts in San Diego the prior season. The warm feelings were mutual. Before coming to Toronto, Alomar was unsure just how much the hockey-mad city would support its local nine. But all it took was one homestand for that feeling of uncertainty to subside. Although he occasionally would hear excessive chatter about the Maple Leafs' upcoming season or a reference to how many "points" the Blue Jays were down in the late innings, Alomar was impressed with the knowledgeable and engaged fan base—particularly when they started coming in droves to the futuristic SkyDome every night to support a team that was now often atop the AL East standings.

(A couple of years later former San Diego teammate Tom Lampkin was playing for the Milwaukee Brewers and visited Alomar in his SkyDome suite when he and the Brew Crew were in town. Lampkin's recollection: "It seemed like a lot of the Latin players liked it up there [Toronto]. He came across as being very happy there. He was laughing and smiling and joking a lot more. That might have had to do with the fact that he was becoming more of a veteran player at that time.")[10]

Alomar and the Blue Jays were an easy group to root for. Unlike the petty infighting that tarnished the reputation of Alomar's last team (1990 Padres), the 1991 Blue Jays came across as classy. On multiple occasions, flight attendants would rave to manager Cito Gaston about how polite his guys were. It was also refreshing to see a new team vie for American League supremacy, seeking to break the stranglehold on the AL pennant that the Oakland A's, Boston Red Sox, and Minnesota Twins had maintained since the mid-1980s. And certainly, by mid-season, baseball fans across North America appreciated Alomar's contributions to his club's contending season—so much so that he was voted in as the AL starting second baseman for the All-Star Game, which would be played at the familiar and comfy SkyDome. In that game, Alomar would play alongside older brother Sandy Jr., who was once again the starting catcher for the American League. This meant that the Alomar brothers would become only the third set of siblings in all-star history to start for the same team, with the famed DiMaggio brothers being the last to do so.

However, heading into all-star week, the fans' selections sparked controversy. Roberto and Sandy Jr. may have been the most popular players at their respective positions, but arguably not the worthiest honorees. After enjoying a white-hot May, Roberto had tailed off considerably in June and went into the game with a .284 batting average and thirty-seven RBIs. When Texas Rangers second baseman Julio Franco, who had superior numbers, griped about being a reserve to reporters ("If you can prove I can't start the game,

I'll kiss my ass"),[11] Roberto responded the afternoon before the game, "He can be nasty if he wants to. It's not me."[12] The selection of Sandy Jr. was even more head-scratching. In the season's first half, the elder Alomar brother went homerless with four RBIs, while only appearing in thirty-nine games. Upon learning that he had been chosen over Chicago's Carlton Fisk, Sandy Jr. remarked, "I don't know why the people voted for me. I didn't stuff the ballot box for me."[13]

The American League won the game 4–2, but it was a lose-lose for the Alomars and Franco, as the brothers went a combined 0–6 while Franco, the veteran, never got off the pine.

When meaningful games resumed after the break, Roberto resumed playing like an all-star. He posted a .359 average for the month of July en route to finishing the season with a .295 mark and career-high sixty-nine RBIs. All while flashing his now-trademark spectacular glove work every single night to earn his first Gold Glove. Rance Mulliniks reflects,

> Robbie was a special player. Robbie was the most complete and best all-around player that I ever played with. Playing sixteen years in the major leagues, I played with some other Hall of Famers, but Robbie was the most complete all-around. Not only was he a tremendous player, but he played the game the correct way. He really understood how to play and probably a lot of that can be attributed to his background, in particular his father. Robbie approached every situation during the course of the game in the terms of not what I need to do to pad my stats, but what do I need to do in this situation that is going to get my team the best chance to win this game?[14]

In a rather pedestrian AL East, Alomar's Jays (91–71) coasted to a first-place finish and ALCS match-up with the Minnesota Twins—an opportunity to win their first AL flag and cast aside their reputation as the chronically underachieving "Blow Jays." The franchise had acquired the unflattering moniker after blowing a 3–1 lead to the Kansas City Royals in the 1985 ALCS, folding in the final week of the 1987 regular season, and then losing in five games to the Oakland A's in the 1989 ALCS. But this year's club seemed destined for better fortunes. The acquisition of Alomar and Carter proved to be a stroke of genius by general manager Pat Gillick—as was the other offseason trade that plucked center fielder Devon White from the California Angels. The starting rotation was solid, if not spectacular, with the likes of

Jimmy Key, Tom Candiotti, and Juan Guzman anchoring the staff. The Twins entered October with a slightly better record (95–67) but were by no means prohibitive favorites against the Blue Jays.

Once again, however, Toronto couldn't shake its postseason demons, as it bowed out in five games to the eventual world champs. Yet Alomar was not the least bit responsible for the disappointing showing. Indeed, Sandy Sr.'s little boy delivered a clutch performance, cranking out a .474 average and four RBIs while playing errorless defense in the first of what promised to be many postseason appearances.

The following spring, the Blue Jays, with the offseason addition of future Hall of Famer Dave Winfield, boasted one of the league's most productive lineups. It was a star-studded roster loaded with the likes of Joe Carter, Devon White, John Olerud, and now Winfield. But Roberto was the farthest thing from an afterthought. With the season but a few weeks old, he wasn't just considered the best all-around player on his team, but in all of Major League Baseball. In addition to his truly never-before-seen defensive wizardry (this is not a typo, he made just *five* errors during this 1992 season), he was flirting with .400 in mid-spring.

And after the season extended into its second month, *Sports Illustrated* naturally deemed Alomar worthy of a feature story. As was the esteemed publication's M.O., when the June 8 edition of *SI* hit airport gift shops and dentist office waiting rooms, the sports world was taken on a deep dive into Alomar's very private life with the cleverly titled "Home Suite Home" article.

It was not entirely flattering.

Multiple employees of the SkyDome Hotel were interviewed (anonymously) about Roberto's private home life. There was the room service waiter who commented that "He is not a great tipper, no, no, no, no. Fifteen percent or less, never more." (Alomar was making close to $3 million that season after having recently signed a four-year, $18.5 million contract with Toronto.) And there was the housekeeper, who, when asked if Alomar ever speaks to her, unhesitatingly responded, "Never. No, never, ever."[15]

If Roberto was waltzing around with a swelled head, it may have been, in part, due to his emergent matinee idol status in Toronto. A member of the hotel's security staff, John Kalimeris, was quoted in *Sports Illustrated* as saying, "We've had girls running up and down the halls, knocking on every door

trying to find his room. You wouldn't believe some of the things I've been offered by girls to take them to his room. When he comes back from the games,
we have a special route for him that bypasses the lobby so people can't follow
him back to his room."[16]

Regardless of the reason, Alomar was surely in his own orbit in the space-
age SkyDome, a multipurpose facility showcasing cutting-edge features such
as a retractable roof and luxury suites. Matt Merullo acknowledges,

> He was hard to make eye contact with. He seemed kind of aloof at times, not
> very much emotion in his eyes. There were other guys that would interact with
> me. I think Kirby Puckett was a classic example of that kind of a guy. I had
> a conversation with George Brett one day before early batting practice. Cal
> Ripken would come up and pat you on the butt with his glove after you hit a
> double, but Alomar was not that kind of guy.[17]

Although others around the game would concur with that description,
close friends such as Jose Cruz Jr. felt differently:

> He never really looked for the attention, especially off the field. A lot of times,
> he was very charitable. He was very forthcoming with a lot of information,
> forthcoming with wanting to help. He was very much that guy. He'd engage in
> what you were doing and talk about it in depth. A lot of people didn't get that.
> They kind of just saw him being a little more aloof than some of the other guys
> at the time. That's just my opinion of what I saw, what I experienced with him.[18]

Meanwhile, in the clubhouse, on charter flights, during team dinners, Alomar was, by multiple accounts, a fine teammate—just as he had been in San
Diego years earlier. Rance Mulliniks, who in 1992 was wrapping up a sixteen-
year MLB career, the majority of which he had spent in Toronto, says, "The
way I would define Robbie is he was actually pretty quiet and reserved. Didn't
have a lot to say in the clubhouse. When he did have something to say, it was
meaningful. He was very friendly. Very positive attitude. Always had a smile.
He was everything you would want in a teammate."[19]

In his one and only season in Toronto, Dave Winfield was nearing the end
of an even longer career (he broke into the big leagues in 1973). He, too, looks
back very fondly on his time spent with Alomar in 1992.

He was an enjoyable teammate. I really respected him a great deal. When you can come to the park and you know a person enjoys being there and doing what they do and performing at a high level, those are the things that I can say about him easily because that's the way he was. A smile on his face. A confident walk. A contribution to help you win every day.[20]

Particularly on the afternoon of October 11, 1992—Game 4 of the American League Championship Series.

Coming off a spectacular 96–66 regular season and desperately hoping to avoid losing their fourth consecutive ALCS, the Blue Jays were clinging to a 2–1 series lead over the Oakland A's. As late-afternoon shadows crept over the Oakland Coliseum, Toronto, trailing 6–4, was three outs away from coughing up the one-game advantage. For the second consecutive inning, the Jays were facing eventual AL MVP Dennis Eckersley, who had been far from his dominant self that day. Normally a one-inning closer, Eckersley had been summoned in the eighth inning by A's skipper Tony LaRussa with his team up 6–2. However, he promptly served up run-scoring singles to John Olerud and Candy Maldonado, before settling down to retire the next three batters to preserve the two-run advantage. But the high-octane closer didn't exactly help his cause when, following his strikeout of pinch-hitter Ed Sprague for the third out, he pumped his fist in exultation, stared into the Toronto dugout and barked a string of profanities.

Naturally, the Jays were indignant. (It was probably a good thing that cameras weren't in the visiting dugout to pick up a live feed, because otherwise impressionable young school children from the Bay Area to Ontario would have learned some new words.) But they were also nervous. With their fourth October demise in less than a decade looming, the Jays were now forced to exorcise their well-chronicled postseason demons—and stave off further humiliation—by again rallying against Eckersley, a six-time all-star who apparently had rediscovered his mojo. So, when Roberto dug in against the mustachioed, fireballing right-hander in the top of the ninth with a runner on third and no outs, he didn't just represent the tying run, but, indeed, the potential savior to a long-suffering franchise.

On a 2–2 pitch, Eckersley hung a slider over the middle of the plate that Alomar turned on. He immediately dropped his bat and thrust both arms triumphantly into the air. No need to bolt out of the box. The rocketed line drive soared over the head of Oakland right fielder Ruben Sierra before landing next to a policeman stationed on the stairwell just beyond the outfield fence. Alomar took his time circling the bases before emphatically pouncing on home plate to tie the game 6–6. The deliberately slow stroll was understandable. This was a snapshot in time worth savoring. Finally, a Toronto Blue Jay had delivered in the clutch amid the pressure cooker of October baseball. It was unquestionably the biggest hit in franchise history and, at least for the moment, made millions of Ontarians forget about their team's past postseason blunders. For good measure, it came at the expense of Eckersley, who stood on the mound stunned as the Toronto dugout erupted against him.

Never short of a colorful sound bite, Eck was an emotional wreck in the postgame clubhouse, telling reporters: "I was all over the fucking place today. . . . I've had my good times and I've had my bad times. And this is one of the worst feelings I've had in a long time."[21]

The normally indomitable reliever wasn't exaggerating. Years later, when speaking to baseball author Danny Gallagher, Eckersley acknowledged that Alomar's bomb stung more than the famed long ball he had served up to a limping Kirk Gibson in Game 1 of the 1988 World Series.

"Oh yeah, that home run hurt more because I felt more responsible for that playoff," said Eckersley. "I had such a great year that year and that burst my bubble. It took away from getting those awards because of the pain of the Alomar thing. Oh, I was in tears. I felt so responsible. That really hurt more than anything, that Alomar home run."[22]

In the visitors' clubhouse, Alomar, who always showed the utmost respect for opponents, even acknowledged that the best closer in baseball was off his game, when he said, "It was a slider over the inside part of the plate. His slider wasn't big and his fastball was flat."[23]

In hindsight, Alomar's two-run shot turned out to be one of the defining moments of his illustrious career and the Blue Jays' eventual world championship season. Winfield says,

> There was a high intensity, great pitcher on the mound. And Eckersley didn't give up too many leads. That was an extraordinary matchup. It was one of those exceptional, timely hits that you always remember. You don't always expect the home run from him. That's not the thing that he walks up there and tries to do.

You could imagine something in the gap, taking extra bases, extending a rally or starting a rally. That was big time.[24]

Though not a power hitter by trade at this point of his still-nascent career, Alomar knew that, even on a two-strike count, Eckersley was not going to play games with Joe Carter lurking on-deck. Mike Timlin remembers,

It was almost like he [Alomar] said it in his head, "If you're going to throw the next pitch over the plate, I'm going to take you deep." And he did. The ball left the bat and I remember him raising his hands, skipping down the line. The ball never flew out very well in Oakland during a day game. I love Eck to death. I mean he's a good friend of mine. At that point, he was one of the guys that was so good at the time. If you had any chance to beat him and you did, it was a huge feather in your cap. The way Eck carried himself—there's always that guy on the other team that you love to hate—it did fire some guys up, it really did.[25]

A fired-up Toronto team went on to win 7–6 in extra innings before closing out the series three nights later to capture its first AL pennant. With the franchise-trajectory-altering homer and .423 batting average for the series, Alomar was a no-brainer choice for ALCS MVP.

Perhaps even more impressive than the ever-clutch postseason performance itself was that the twenty-four-year-old Alomar was just barely approaching his prime. And now, as the Jays closed in on their first world championship, Alomar had established himself as a transcendent talent with unreal potential.

As Boston Globe sports columnist Bob Ryan wrote following Alomar's Game 4 heroics: "There is an attitude on the Toronto bench the Blue Jays have never had before. Is it the thrill and inspiration they all get from watching Alomar play and knowing that someday their proudest collective boast might be that they once played alongside him?"[26]

With the Toronto Blue Jays being the first-ever Canadian pennant winners, the 1992 edition of the Fall Classic between the Jays and Atlanta Braves was showcased as the first true World Series. Major League Baseball was (desperately) trying to use this "Canada's Team" vs. "America's Team" storyline to stir up enthusiasm for a World Series that included two not-so-iconic franchises whose host cities, Toronto and Atlanta, were, to put it nicely, not quite as enamored with baseball as they were with hockey and football, respectively. Worse, the games were not slated to begin until after 8:00 p.m. (and likely to finish close to midnight), making it difficult for many working adults, including those in Toronto and Atlanta in the Eastern Time Zone, to watch the most meaningful parts.

With the series getting underway in Atlanta, the Braves organization did its part in upholding the global rivalry theme. On the evening of Game 1, Pat Gillick was sniffing around his team's dugout and commented that "It smells like horses down here."[27] He wasn't kidding. After Game 7 of the NLCS, when Atlanta's Royal Incontinent Mounted Police (fitting counterpart to Toronto's Royal Canadian Mounted Police) patrolled the field, the overexcited ponies urinated near the Jays' dugout and on the Braves' bullpen mound. The Braves' grounds crew made sure to deodorize their team's bullpen prior to Game 1 but conveniently forgot to purify the stench swirling around the visiting Canadians' dugout. The following night during the national anthems before Game 2, a US Marine color guard from Atlanta displayed the Canadian flag with the tip of the red maple leaf upside down. A seemingly innocuous mistake immediately caused such an uproar from Nova Scotia to British Columbia that in the second inning, Major League Baseball issued a public apology before a Marine Corps spokesman declared the act unintentional. With legions of unconvinced Canadians still up in arms the next morning, President George H. W. Bush even delivered an apology.

(Sadly, the shenanigans overshadowed Toronto's Cito Gaston becoming the first Black manager in a World Series and Coretta Scott King throwing out the ceremonial first pitch prior to Game 2—two developments made even more remarkable by their occurring in Atlanta-Fulton County Stadium, the very same building where Hank Aaron's pursuit of Babe Ruth was met with stinging vitriol a couple decades earlier.)

Toronto soon got even on the field. After dropping Game 1, the Jays took a commanding 3–1 series lead, eking out one-run wins in Games 3 and 4, the first World Series contests played on foreign soil. Days later, forever shedding their reputation as choke artists, Canada's team finished off the Braves in an instant classic 4–3 extra-inning win in Game 6.

After a career-defining ALCS, Roberto had a quiet World Series (.208 BA, no ribbies) that served as a mere sidebar to the heroics of some of his less-heralded teammates. It was, indeed, utility man Ed Sprague who turned the tide of the series with his two-run, pinch-hit-homer in the ninth inning of Game 2 that catapulted Toronto to a 5–4 win. MVP honors went to starting catcher Pat Borders (.450 series average), who continued a time-honored tradition of relatively obscure players inexplicably delivering clutch World Series hits.

The iconic play of the 1992 Fall Classic came courtesy of Devon White, when, with runners on first and second in the top of the fourth inning of a scoreless Game 3, the inimitable center fielder raced back to the wall to snag David Justice's scorching line drive. The play, which turned into a twin-killing as the runner on first, Terry Pendleton, had passed the runner on second, Deion Sanders, immediately drew comparisons to Willie Mays's famed Polo Grounds catch a half-century earlier.

"One of the most spectacular catches in the history of the game when a game was on the line," remembers Dave Winfield. "He caught it up against the fence like Spider-Man."[28]

It was Winfield, the surefire Hall of Famer in pursuit of his first World Series ring, who socked the game-winning double in the eleventh inning of Toronto's scintillating Game 6 series-clinching win. Unquestionably, he was the man of the hour in the victors' postgame clubhouse, the not-quite-over-the-hill superstar whose steadying leadership proved invaluable that year.

For Roberto, the Blue Jays' first world championship meant that he was now the best player on the best team in the world. The child of the Caribbean was the most popular athlete in the largest city of the Great White North, and with that came heightened celebrity status. More endorsement opportunities (Doritos, Speed Stick) started trickling in. His newly published book, *Second to None*, hit the shelves. During book signings, mothers would rush up to his table and (perhaps tongue-in-cheek, or perhaps not) present their daughters for marriage. Dinners in private curtained-off areas of Toronto restaurants became the norm.

The hype for the Alomar-led Blue Jays was certainly justified as they embarked on their title-defending 1993 season with a lineup closely paralleling the prior season's prolific edition—the only major difference was that the team replaced Winfield at DH with another one-day Hall of Famer nearing the end in Paul Molitor. If anything, it was an even more potent lineup, in no small part due to Alomar's emergence as a five-tool player with his enhanced power numbers. After shaking off a World Series hangover, he had a sizzling June and went into the all-star break on pace to finish with twenty homers and perhaps his first 100-RBI season. During the Midsummer Classic at Baltimore's Camden Yards, Alomar's newfound power was on full display when he crushed a solo shot off former San Diego teammate Andy Benes. He capped his finest season yet (.326 BA, 17 HR, 93 RBIs) by driving in forty runs over the final two months to propel Toronto to its second consecutive AL East title.

Alomar was not merely a five-tool star. He was a five-tool star who happened to be a good-looking bachelor with a suave manner. As such, there was no escaping the prying Toronto tabloids and their "reports" about his ever-changing love life.

Back in the spring, Alomar felt *Toronto Life* crossed the line when the popular magazine ran a cover story that included an unfavorable reference to his sex life based on an interview with a former romantic partner. Peeved that he was never given the chance to respond to the girl's comments that portrayed him negatively, Roberto decided to boycott talking to the Canadian-based press entirely—even baseball beat writers interested in chronicling his multi-hit days . . . and not his multi-girl nights.

Unfailingly polite to the media throughout his entire professional career up to this point, Roberto now had the following uncomfortable exchange with reporters at the onset of a late May/early June series at Anaheim Stadium:

"Can I ask a couple of questions?" a Toronto reporter inquired.

"What about?" Roberto answered.

"Your play this year."

"No, I'm not talking to you guys."

"Why not?"

"I don't want to talk about it."[29]

The writers on hand knew about (and understood) Alomar's gripe with the media. One even tried to reassure him that baseball scribes have no desire to pass on scandalous information to the tabloids. It didn't matter. He would talk at length to US reporters but not give Canadian ones the time of day. ("I've been nice to you guys. No more.")[30] From Alomar's perspective, everyone in the Canadian media—newspapers, magazines, television, radio—had the collective goal of uncovering dirt on celebrities such as himself. Anything to make their charmed and privileged lives just a bit miserable for a few days.

(Alomar was not the only star ballplayer to ever have a standoffish approach toward the media. While his boycott of the Canadian scribes proved to be short-lived, there have been other Hall of Famers, most notably Steve Carlton, who would completely shun the media for years.)

If baseball writers from Ontario resented Alomar's hardheadedness, they could not use their keyboards to exact revenge and run the most important player on the team out of town. Without Alomar's once-in-a-generation defense complementing his MVP-worthy offensive production, the 1993 Blue Jays, whose pitching staff had been depleted by the departures of David Cone and Jimmy Key to the Kansas City Royals and New York Yankees, respectively, would be no threat to repeat.

As longtime veteran pitcher Dave Stewart, formerly of the Oakland A's, who had been signed as a free agent to replace said rotation stalwarts, remarks about Alomar: "In the '80s, I can't think of anybody that played at the level that he did at second base. In the '90s, in my opinion, that was the Robbie Alomar period of time. He's the best that I've ever seen play at that position."[31]

Stewart is no different from any former Toronto teammate in that he remembers Alomar being an exceptionally cerebral player who minded his own business in the clubhouse. He continues,

> He was a great teammate. Robbie didn't talk very much. He was actually really, really quiet in the clubhouse. He was a quiet kid, but really fit in well. One of the smartest players I have ever played with. He had a knack for picking up little things from the pitchers that gave him a little bit of an edge. Today, you've heard of what's happened in Houston and picking up signs and the way that they did, relaying them back to teammates. Well, Robbie was ahead of that trend and did it the right way. He picked up things. Whether the glove was setting too high on the chest out of the stretch or too low out of the stretch. He also served as a player-type manager because it wasn't uncommon for Robbie to put on a hit-and-run.[32]

Ironically, when Robbie came home to play in the Puerto Rican Winter League, a young and impressionable Alex Cora, who would become one of the eventual ringleaders of the Astros' sign-stealing operation during the 2017 season, diligently studied how Robbie did things by the book.

With Alomar, John Olerud, and Paul Molitor, the American League's three best hitters in 1993, comprising the heart of his order, Jays manager Cito Gaston was, once again, careful not to overmanage. The laissez-faire approach worked as the Jays, behind a relentless lineup more than compensating for a fairly suspect pitching staff, followed up a 95–67 regular season by dusting off the Chicago White Sox in the ALCS en route to a franchise-first second consecutive AL pennant.

This time, Roberto saved his better offensive performance for the second, more important round of the postseason. In a World Series that will forever be remembered for Joe Carter's walk-off home run in Game 6 against the Philadelphia Phillies to clinch Toronto's second straight title, Alomar quietly hit .480 and knocked in six runs. Yet his finest moment came on defense. In fact, had it not been for Carter's heroics, Alomar's catch in the fifth inning of Game 1 very well could have been the iconic moment of the series. It was that incredible.

With the score tied 3–3 in the top of the fifth, Philadelphia leadoff man Lenny Dykstra lofted a soft flare over first baseman John Olerud's head. A bloop single, the 52,011 fans in the SkyDome figured. Alomar had other ideas. The now perennial Gold Glove winner dashed to his left and, once again showing total disregard for his body, suspended himself in mid-air to glove the first out before gliding to a gentle stop *near the right field foul line*. As Tim McCarver, television play-by-play man for CBS Sports, noted to a continent of viewers, no second baseman in baseball makes that play, or even comes close. Yet Alomar made this miraculous play—snagging a soft line drive with precious little hang time—look so routine, effortless, natural. Two seconds later, Alomar got to his knees, flipped the ball to Olerud to throw around the horn, bounced up, and respectfully nodded to the roaring home crowd.

Following Toronto's 8–5 Game 1 win, Alomar acknowledged that, even by his own high standards, this was a pretty damn good play.

"It might be one of my best. I don't really know how I caught the ball."[33]

In this regard, Alomar may have been selling himself short. Clearly, the breathtaking feat didn't result merely from his sheer physicality.

"Robbie had an intuitive mind," says Timlin. "He had an idea of where the ball was going to be hit. He almost had a half step ahead of what was going on. I believe at that point, he knew what the pitch was, he knew what the location was, so he might have been a half step going toward that area."[34]

For nearly any other second baseman—heck, nearly any other *position* player—who ever played the game, this catch would have been a career-defining moment. But not for Alomar. With his seemingly endless highlight reel of acrobatic plays, even the exceptional ones in the postseason all start to blend in with the others.

"I don't recall that play," admits Dave Stewart, when asked to go over the Game 1 catch. "Robbie made plays like that look easy and so to point out one play is difficult to do. When I sit and I think about second basemen that I played with, I played with some good ones, he is hands down the best that I ever played with. So, to recall one spectacular play is difficult to do when he's made so many."[35]

Although the Blue Jays finished with virtually the same record in 1993 (95–67) as they posted in 1992 (96–66), their second title season had been more of a grind. While Roberto was just reaching his prime, most of the lineup, albeit an extraordinary one, was past theirs; a rather mediocre pitching staff had been exposed on occasion; the pressure to repeat proved grating at times.

"The '92 team, we were extremely dominant," remembers Mike Timlin. "Cito didn't do a lot. It was almost like he could just fill the lineup [card] out and it didn't really matter who he put where; we found a way to win. We had that type of confidence in '92. In '93, it seemed like we had to work a little bit harder as a team."[36]

But that team proved good enough to capture its second World Series. In 1994, the Jays, with several of their aging vets underperforming, had to work a lot harder to even stay in contention and by mid-summer had no chance of catching the younger, up-and-coming New York Yankees in the AL East. Ultimately, it mattered not, as the now-infamous players' strike truncated the season.

While the 55–60 Blue Jays regressed dramatically, it was business as usual for Roberto, who hit .306 while tacking on another All-Star Game nod and Gold Glove Award.

Before the season was called in early August, Roberto began a streak of 104 consecutive errorless games at second base. The prolonged stretch of flawless play, which set an AL record for the position, was even more improbable considering how many times Alomar had to dive for grounders and then make an off-balance throw to first or make the split-second decision to keep the ball in his mitt so as not to risk an errant throw.

The incredible run finally ended on Independence Day (America's, that is) when the Jays were visiting the California Angels and Alomar was pegged with an E4 in the bottom of the sixth inning.

Understandably, Roberto may have been a little distracted that afternoon.

Only two days earlier, during the final game of a home series against Baltimore, Tricia Miller, an armed and deranged thirty-one-year-old fan (more like fanatic) who had grown frustrated in her failed attempts to develop a romantic relationship with Roberto, entered the SkyDome with a loaded .22-caliber Smith and Wesson revolver intending to murder her idol. Fortunately, she was apprehended by police around 2 p.m. that afternoon after seeking medical assistance from security upon her arrival at the SkyDome Hotel/Roberto's home. (Reportedly, she was planning to turn the gun on herself after the assassination.) As a precaution, Roberto was removed from the game in the ninth inning because the police couldn't wait any longer to ask him questions. Following Toronto's 9–7 loss, in which they blew a 7–2 lead in the ninth inning, Alomar learned that he would be assigned a private security detail for the upcoming West Coast swing.

On July 3, the first day of the trip and the last of his errorless streak, Alomar, well aware of the still-recent knifing of tennis sensation Monica Seles, used his considerably influential platform to call for systemic changes to stadium security. His remarks to the press: "The league has to start taking more precautions. Right now people can walk into the stadiums and nobody knows what they've got. Maybe they should start having people go through the same things they do at airports [metal detectors]. There really isn't a lot of security in any sport and to be honest, I've been thinking about it ever since Monica Seles got stabbed."[37]

Evidently, Alomar was ahead of his time, as the major North American pro sports leagues wouldn't implement such technology for their security framework until early in the next century.

(That Alomar even felt comfortable asserting himself with the largely white English-speaking press was a testament to the significant progress he had made in learning the English language. As Mike Timlin shares, "In '91, he was more of a physical leader and he always exuded that. He became more of a vocal leader. He had changed in that manner where he became comfortable with himself, speaking to the media, speaking in some of the team meetings.")[38]

Alomar's insightful comments demonstrated his genuine concern for fellow professional athletes, but they also reflected a deeply personal fear, namely that of gun violence.

Back in November 1970, Sandy Sr.'s older brother, Tony, a former minor-league shortstop in his late thirties, was shot in the forehead while attending a Puerto Rican citizen group's dance. Tony Alomar was soon flown to the Batavia Veterans Hospital (just outside of his minor-league Rochester home) where, over the next fifteen-plus months, he never regained consciousness, while his formerly hulking 220-pound frame was whittled down to its 155-pound paralyzed state, before eventually giving out.

While his brother was valiantly fighting for his life for over a year, Sandy Sr. was off playing for the California Angels, making trips to Upstate New York fairly challenging to coordinate. With many relatives still in Puerto Rico and he himself nearly three thousand miles away, Sandy Sr. appreciated the many well-wishers who visited, one of whom was the Cuban-born MLB pitcher Luis Tiant, a longtime dear friend of the Alomar family. In recalling his visit, Tiant remarks:

> It was a sad day. He [Tony Alomar] was sitting in bed like a vegetable. He couldn't move. He couldn't do anything. He was shrinking, getting smaller and smaller. It was a hard time going over there, holding his hand. It made me cry. He couldn't talk. Every time he looked at me, he held my hand tight. We're all going to die someday, but not like that. For no reason they shot him in the head.[39]

A toddler at the time, Roberto may not have had vivid memories of his late uncle and his long, sad demise, but he grew up in a household that remained haunted by the tragedy for years. Understandably then, at this moment in time, the threat of gun violence from a crazed stalker hit home for Alomar. That there were people roaming the earth interested in ending his life because he was a celebrity athlete had to be unnerving—both on and off the diamond.

If the error on July 4 was excusable, Alomar's performance (or lack thereof) at the end of the month was far less so.

As the July 31 trade deadline approached, the bean counters in Toronto's front office were intent on shedding high-priced veterans. With the team in the cellar of the AL East, the club effectively gave up on the season when it dealt newly reacquired ace David Cone to the contending New York Yankees on July 28 for a few mid-level prospects. Roberto was not a happy camper. Clearly, the franchise was in a rebuilding mode, which meant that not only would the losses keep mounting, but it was also increasingly unlikely that a contract extension would be forthcoming from the notoriously frugal front office. With free agency looming in a couple of months, Roberto figured that if the club wasn't going to re-sign him, at the very least it could send him to a contender for the stretch run.

So, the day following Cone's departure, Alomar did what many late twentieth-century entitled superstar athletes did to express discontent with management: he refused to play under the guise of a mysterious injury. Unsurprisingly, Alomar, soon to be one of the most sought-after free agents in the game's history, didn't get much sympathy from the press. As Bob Elliott, one of Toronto's most prominent sportswriters, remarked in the *National Post*: "Alomar is 27, who plays like he's 37, when it comes to baseball instincts and acts like an immature 17-year-old. Alomar wasn't hurt Saturday—only his pride. David Cone was dealt to a team with a chance. Alomar wasn't."[40]

With the media portraying him in such a negative manner, Alomar felt he needed to defend himself publicly. He wanted the fans (who were still on his side) to know that he still loved them. If it weren't for that dastardly ownership group, he would stay a Jay for life.

As Alomar told the *Toronto Star*, "I just want the fans to understand that I went to them [management] twice and they said no. I want the fans to know that if I'm not here, it's not because I didn't want to be."[41]

But his behavior spoke even louder. By not taking the field with his teammates for the July 29 game against Oakland (this raised a few eyebrows in the clubhouse), Alomar was essentially sending a "show me the money or send me to greener pastures" ultimatum to first-year Toronto general manager Gord Ash. Ultimately, however, the Toronto brain trust refused to accommodate Alomar via a trade, effectively forcing him to play out the final two months of his contract.

As the club nosedived to a 56–88 finish, Alomar looked like he was ready to check out of his SkyDome Hotel suite. Over the final two months he hit only two home runs while posting a .272 average in September. Yet, he went into the final weekend of the season (but more importantly, free agency) clinging to a .300 average. Conveniently, Alomar suddenly developed a sore back and didn't step on the field once during the entire season-ending series against the Yankees, thereby keeping the most important number on the back of his baseball card unblemished.

Alomar prioritizing his personal welfare over that of the team in this instance all but sealed his fate with the organization.

Thus, when it was time for offseason negotiations to begin, the Blue Jays, as expected, let Alomar—the most popular and talented player in club history—walk in free agency.

On December 21, the divisional rival Baltimore Orioles, who under new general manager Pat Gillick (he left Toronto after the 1994 season) were giving out free-agent contracts like Halloween candy, inked Alomar to an $18 million, three-year contract.

By this time, nearly the entire roster from the 1993 World Series title team had been gutted. And unfortunately, the rebuilding process would be a long and slow one as the Jays would not return to the playoffs until 2015. Mike Timlin acknowledges,

> I was a little surprised at that point that we let such a superstar go. I understand that they had people behind him that they were developing in that role, second base. As well as he was playing and the numbers that he was putting up, I understand the business side obviously that he was going to make a whole lot more money. I don't think they [Blue Jays] wanted to go in that direction so that's why they made the business decision. I do believe that Toronto made a mistake by letting him go.[42]

6

A Star among Stars

Roberto Alomar was in a good mood.

It was in the early afternoon of December 21, 1995, and the most popular Puerto Rican ballplayer since Roberto Clemente was hours away from signing the aforementioned $18 million contract with Baltimore and several days away from celebrating Christmas with his family. Wearing running shoes, short pants, and a green polo shirt, Alomar was standing in the entrance of a Chili's restaurant in San Juan, having just finished lunch with a friend, when a female patron came over, handed him a white ticket, and asked, "Can you get my car, please?"[1]

Because he was in such high spirits, Alomar was not the least bit offended; if anything, he was slightly amused.

After politely explaining to the stranger that he was not the Chili's valet parking attendant, Alomar turned to his friend and softly said, "I could buy this place. I could take all these cars home."[2]

Once an actual parking attendant came by with Alomar's black Lexus, the multimillionaire ballplayer hopped in and drove toward Castillo San Felipe del Morro in Old San Juan. As he got out and walked mostly unrecognized around the sixteenth-century fortress that serves as one of the island's most iconic landmarks, Alomar acknowledged to his companion, "I bet Cal Ripken can't even get out of his car in Baltimore."[3]

As Alomar was well aware, playing for the Baltimore Orioles in 1996 would indeed mean playing in the shadow of his new double-play partner. The prior September, the city of Baltimore held a parade for the Baltimore Orioles—not because they had clinched a long-awaited postseason berth (they actually didn't qualify for the playoffs), but because Ripken had broken Lou Gehrig's consecutive games played streak. Not even the arrival of Alomar, the hottest free agent on the market, could possibly dim the 24/7 limelight surrounding Cal Ripken Jr.

During their first day together in spring training in Fort Lauderdale, Ripken and Alomar participated in a joint news conference. Naturally, the first six questions went to Ripken before Alomar was acknowledged.

"So, Robbie," a television reporter asked, "how does it feel to be playing next to Cal Ripken?"[4]

Perhaps, the more appropriate question would have been asking Ripken how it felt to be playing next to a two-time World Series champion who had a chance to become the greatest second baseman ever.

"Ripken cast a long shadow over that franchise at that point," says former *Baltimore Sun* sports columnist John Eisenberg. "For a number of years there, all they [the Orioles] had going for them was Cal Ripken and that streak. Ripken was sort of in his own category. This was post-streak, so he was walking around with armed guards practically. He wasn't always available. Robbie was pretty available."[5]

After literally walking around with armed guards the prior July following the SkyDome incident, Alomar was okay not being the hometown team's most high-profile celebrity. Indeed, the Orioles would always be Cal's team, even as the shortstop was nearing the finish line of his Hall of Fame career. But for the second time this decade, Roberto still tried very hard to endear himself to a new fan base. During spring training, it seemed like he was spending more time than usual signing autographs and chatting with fans. Following his unceremonious departure from Toronto, Roberto didn't want Baltimore fans to assume he was this selfish diva. It was also important to acknowledge that he still loved performing for the masses and that Tricia Miller was one maniac out of millions of rational, devoted, and knowledgeable fans.

As such, the day Alomar learned of Miller's sentence (nine months in prison followed by three years of probation), he made it a point to tell reporters, "Not everyone should pay for one person. You can't do anything about it.

I think the guys who protect us do a good job. You just have to go out there and try to please the people. They're the ones who pay to see you play."[6]

And boy did Alomar please Baltimoreans this spring, posting a .352 average with eleven homers and fifty-three RBIs in the first half. Subsequently, during the All-Star Game at Philadelphia's Veterans Stadium, he received the well-deserved honor of batting third in the American League starting lineup. This meant he was batting ahead of Albert Belle, reigning AL MVP Mo Vaughn, Ivan "Pudge" Rodriguez, and Ripken.

"In '96, he got off to an unbelievable start," says former Baltimore outfielder B. J. Surhoff. "Watching him play, you were pretty sure you acquired Babe Ruth. You were pretty sure you had the best player in the game right at the moment."[7]

Alomar's emergence as one of the game's most dangerous hitters was not a shocker to those who had been around during the early stages of his career. Back in late May, when Alomar was flirting with .400, his former San Diego teammate Tony Gwynn, whose .394 average in the truncated 1994 campaign represented the closest anyone had come to finishing the season hitting .400 since Ted Williams batted .406 in 1941, remarked to Buster Olney of the *Baltimore Sun*, "I told him [Alomar] when he was here [San Diego] he was going to win his share of batting titles, and it's probably that time. He has the ability to hit a home run, or work the count and hit a double down the opposite line and do whatever he wants to do. He's probably the best all-around player in the game."[8]

At this point in the mid-1990s, it was hard to argue that Roberto was not the best all-around player in the game. While one could make a compelling case that sluggers Ken Griffey Jr. and Barry Bonds were MLB's two kingpins by virtue of their prolific power numbers, as outfielders, they certainly did not impact the game nearly as much defensively as did Alomar, the middle infielder who was now well on his way to a sixth consecutive Gold Glove Award.

But this is where things got interesting in Baltimore. If Alomar was arguably the best player in baseball, it was rather peculiar that within his own clubhouse, he was merely the fourth or fifth most prominent star.

Aside from Ripken's larger-than-life influence pervading Camden Yards, the O's roster included three-time all-star Mike Mussina, the ace hurler who came up in the farm system, one of the game's premier sluggers in first baseman Rafael Palmeiro, and flossy outfielder Bobby Bonilla, who thrilled crowds with his moonshots. For good measure, in mid-July Baltimore would reacquire future Hall of Famer Eddie Murray, one of the most beloved players in franchise history. As great as Alomar was, he didn't have the boisterous personality, juicy power numbers, or, most importantly, the track record in Baltimore to become a true fan favorite. "He was not a big figure in the clubhouse," acknowledges Eisenberg.[9]

Former Baltimore pitcher Rick Krivda says,

> I believe he probably felt like he wanted to be Number One. Being with a bunch of other guys like Cal [Ripken Jr.] and [Mike] Mussina, he might have taken a second or third tier to those guys because he wasn't the Number One guy. I don't mean that in a bad way or anything. I just felt like he had to adjust to that. Robbie wasn't the Number One Oriole guy because he didn't come up through the system.[10]

While he was perhaps content staying at arm's length from the public (not just in Baltimore but also back home in Puerto Rico), not being The Man on his new club eventually started grating on Alomar. The game's premier second baseman wasn't accustomed to playing second fiddle to anyone— especially now after coming from Toronto where he ultimately attained rock star status. Consequently, as is often the case with many superstar athletes, Alomar started gravitating toward less heralded teammates who had no illusions of ever attaining alpha male status.

One such teammate was Krivda, the young, affable southpaw, who, to this day, remembers how Alomar went out of his way to help him before a game during the 1996 season. Krivda explains,

> I remember after batting practice I came in and I had a pair of Oakley sunglasses and I think the side piece broke. And I couldn't wear them. He was like, "What's the matter?" I was like, "My friggin' Oakleys broke." Alomar said, "Come here." I went over to his locker and he unzipped the mega Oakley case that had eight pairs in there. He opened up this case and there was this little picture of Pamela Anderson in there, and it said something like, "To Robbie, my man. XOXO Pamela."[11]

Naturally, Krivda was hungry for more information. Without hesitation, Alomar described his brief fling with the *Baywatch* star that happened back in the early days of his Blue Jays career. Krivda remembers Alomar explaining, "When I dated her a little bit when I was with Toronto, I would bring her to games. We would go out to eat and I was basically holding her purse the whole time. There were like a million people around her and they think I'm like her bellboy. They [the public] just wanted her. They didn't even know who I was."[12]

So, Krivda walked away with high-end Oakleys as well as deeper insight into his all-star teammate's psyche.

"After I heard that story, I kind of thought like, 'Yeah, maybe he [Alomar] is kind of that way with some of the guys.' I mean he was great to me. But I think because of his experience with Pamela, I think he felt maybe kind of that way around Cal [Ripken Jr.] or Mike [Mussina], because they were [Baltimore] lifers."[13]

Outside of Baltimore, Alomar remained not nearly as recognizable as Ripken, who, despite being well past his prime, still reigned supreme as the face of Major League Baseball. How popular was Ripken? Consider that three years earlier, during the midpoint of the 1993 season, his average was hovering around .200, yet the fans still elected him as the AL starting shortstop in the All-Star Game. These days when Baltimore traveled, Ripken stayed in an undisclosed hotel separate from the one in which his teammates were lodging. At some level, it was understandable. The "Iron Man" was exceptionally generous with his time signing autographs during batting practice, but the crush of fans awaiting his arrival at hotel lobbies from Boston to Seattle grew overwhelming and borderline unsafe. Roberto? He was just another member of the Orioles' traveling party, one that drew considerably less fanfare with Ripken's well-publicized absence.

It also seemed that Alomar was vastly overshadowed by stars on other teams. While at this point in his career Alomar had done virtually nothing that could have possibly driven away big-name sponsors, it seemed that corporate America found Ken Griffey Jr., Barry Bonds, and Mark McGwire (in other words, ballplayers born on the mainland who spoke fluent English) more marketable. While McGwire and Griffey Jr. were making a bundle from endorsement deals with Rawlings and Nintendo respectively, and Bonds had enjoyed a cameo in the 1993 flick *Rookie of the Year*, Alomar, in his first year in Baltimore, got hardly any opportunities for cashing in on his baseball talents. In fact, it seemed like residing in Canada had meant more endorsements. In August, Alomar opened up to the *Baltimore Sun* about how he felt slighted in this regard when he remarked, "I don't get that many requests. Being Latin and being in the States, sometimes they think you don't speak the language real well and they don't approach you."[14]

Meanwhile, the lack of requests hardly made a difference when it came to Alomar's finances. By signing the $18 million pact with Baltimore the prior offseason, he was still one of the richest players in the game, even without the flashy endorsements. And he went to bed every night (often after watching hours of TV shows and/or movies, just like he did in the minors) knowing that he was living up to his massive contract, no small accomplishment considering the parade of past big-ticket free agents who flopped in their new homes.

As Tony Gwynn had said to the *Baltimore Sun* earlier in the season, "None of the attention is on him right now because he's doing what he's supposed to do."[15]

7

An Ugly Spat

Less than a half-hour after the final out of Game 4 of the 1996 American League Division Series Roberto Alomar stood by his locker in the visiting clubhouse of Jacobs Field and sobbed uncontrollably. He may have been Baltimore's hero in the series-clinching 4–3 win against the heavily favored Cleveland Indians that afternoon, with a game-tying single in the top of the ninth and go-ahead solo shot leading off the twelfth, but he was still baseball's biggest villain following the prior weekend's incident with home plate umpire John Hirschbeck. His clutch performance was nothing more than a sidebar to the bigger and more compelling story that accounted for dozens of local and national writers jockeying for position around his locker stall. So, as Alomar braced for yet another round of questions regarding the sore subject, he simply broke down.

"I know there was a lot of flak given to him during the series [ALDS]," recalls former Baltimore teammate B. J. Surhoff.[1]

Had Alomar maintained a squeaky-clean reputation before the ugly spat with Hirschbeck? Hardly. Before this internationally newsworthy dust-up, Alomar had been ejected for arguing balls and strikes three times, the most notable of which occurred on May 17, 1995, when he was peeved over ball-and-strike calls and tossed his glove in the direction of home plate umpire Rich Garcia at the end of the game. He subsequently received a two-game suspension (eventually reduced to one). And, of course, there was last season's unceremonious ending in Toronto when many fans felt Alomar was acting in a highly self-centered and immature manner. Alomar's image took a hit at these moments, but the seemingly interminable public shaming he was now facing was on a whole different level.

"He was public enemy number one in sports at that moment," says John Eisenberg. "It was not an easy thing. He had performed well under pressure before. This was a different kind of pressure."[2]

Throughout the ALDS, Alomar was mobbed by reporters after every game even though, up until the ninth inning of Game 4, he had been having a fairly quiet series with three soft singles in fifteen at bats and no noteworthy defensive plays. The media, largely intent on portraying Alomar as if he were a heartless sinner, knew that the ballplayer's formal apology three days after the incident was entirely scripted by Baltimore's PR department. They repeatedly tried to coax Alomar into saying something colorful, but he wouldn't budge. ("You guys want to talk about the incident, but I don't want to. I already did what I have to do.")[3] It got to the point where Alomar would almost perk up in excitement when a reporter asked him what kind of pitch he was looking for in a specific at bat.

Meanwhile, the Cleveland fans didn't exactly behave like laid-back, friendly Midwesterners. After the first two games at Camden Yards, Alomar was ruthlessly jeered every time he came to bat at Jacobs Field. In the third inning of Game 3 after Alomar struck out, four fans ran down to seats behind the O's dugout where they directed nasty taunts toward him before high-fiving each other.[4]

In a sense, Major League Baseball, by handing down the lenient five-game suspension that wouldn't have to be served until the beginning of the 1997 season, made it harder for Alomar to salvage his reputation. Now, he was viewed as heartless *and* sheltered by the all-powerful players union. (With Alomar eligible to play, the umpires, whose union had significantly inferior legal representation, started making noise about boycotting the postseason before ultimately giving in.) Over the past week, op-ed pages, talk radio shows, and talking heads across the country endorsed the narrative that the spoiled ballplayer got away with murder. There was Joe Morgan, the one-time Cincinnati Reds great turned ESPN broadcaster, referring to Alomar's decision to spit on Hirschbeck as "the most despicable act by a ballplayer, ever."

Rush Limbaugh, Larry King, and David Letterman brought up the incident on their respective shows. The hardball imbroglio even entered the arena of politics that autumn when Jim Lehrer was moderating the vice-presidential debate and posed the question of whether the episode indicated there was "something terribly wrong with the American soul," to which Al Gore responded, "I think [Alomar] should have been severely disciplined."[5]

But what really devastated Alomar, what really made him shed tears at this moment, wasn't the public ridicule. It was the fear that he had tarnished his family's legacy. He knew that spitting on Hirschbeck and then bringing up the umpire's late son in the postgame comments would cause undue humiliation for his esteemed parents and siblings.

Alomar's former manager, Cito Gaston, speaking from his home in Florida, told the *New York Times*, "Unfortunately, this is going to be with Robbie for a long time and he knows he has to deal with it. He hurt a lot of people. He hurt his brother. He hurt his family. His family is strong. Very much so. But it hurt."[6]

Meanwhile, when Dave Winfield was interviewed by Claire Smith for this story in the *Times*, he didn't go into how the situation impacted Robbie's family. He focused his thoughts on Robbie himself. One talking head after another over the past week compared Alomar to violent baseball characters such as Ty Cobb and Albert Belle so it was about time that someone came to his defense.

"If somebody would say this kind of thing would happen and it did during the regular season," said Winfield, "Roberto Alomar would be so far down the list of people you would think could do this. It's just not him. It is just hard to imagine him being so antagonized that he would act that way."[7]

Winfield wasn't the only former teammate shocked to see Alomar being embroiled in such controversy. (Dave Stewart once told *Sports Illustrated* that Alomar is "a harmless guy who doesn't bother anyone,"[8] while decades later Phil Stephenson says, "That's something I just never would have seen him [Alomar] doing, or even being a part of. Very out of character for him.")[9] But Winfield was one of the precious few who publicly defended Alomar during his darkest hour. This was a highly sensitive matter and saying something partial toward Robbie could have been perceived as a direct affront to the grieving Hirschbeck.

And, naturally, the other reason Roberto was bawling his eyes out at this moment was that he knew the road ahead would only be more treacherous. Awaiting the Orioles in the next round were the New York Yankees and Robbie was well aware that thousands of fans at Yankee Stadium wanted to harm him. (They certainly didn't care whether the behavior was out of character or not.) The heightened security presence couldn't shield him from the batteries and glass bottles launched out of the stands. It would be open season on the most reviled man in baseball in the Bronx.

In October 1996, Roberto wanted nothing more than forgiveness, but he also wanted his side of the story to be listened to. Perhaps even acknowledged. Alomar believed that he had been provoked by Hirschbeck's vile and insensitive remarks. Thus, spitting on the umpire was his way of standing up for himself. Barry Bloom, one of the longest-tenured baseball writers in America, says,

> I think that Robbie was unfairly characterized in that whole incident. Basically, there were always kind of rumors around that Robbie was gay. Hirschbeck called him a "fag." You can't do that to him. Especially a Hispanic player in front of other people. That's why he spit in his face. Now, I'm not saying what Robbie did was the right reaction. It would have been bigger of him to let it slide and go on and maybe go to management and complain about it. He didn't have to do it the way he did it, but it was just an instant reaction.[10]

There are only three men on the planet—Alomar, Hirschbeck, and Baltimore manager Davey Johnson—who could say with absolute certainty what exactly transpired during the altercation. No one was mic'd up, and the closest bystanders to the incident—Toronto catcher Charlie O'Brien, Baltimore's Todd Zeile who was coming to bat, and the rest of the umpiring crew—were out of earshot. That being said, there were reports that Hirschbeck not only referred to Alomar by the derogatory homosexual name but also called him a "son-of-a-bitch." The latter remark Alomar also took quite personally, believing it was a direct affront to his beloved mother.

Surhoff remarks,

> Even to this day, I still don't know exactly what transpired at the time and how it came about and what was said. I just know it was really, really unfortunate

because we're talking about it today, twenty-six years later. That's not the type of stuff that you want to be remembered for. It really put a mark on his career that people have to bring up unfortunately. I never really talked to him about it. I didn't really want to bring that up to him.[11]

As the postseason dragged on, Alomar knew that had he simply delivered a thoughtful apology after the September game in Toronto, the feud may still have been the story du jour around baseball, but the entire continent of North America wouldn't have perceived him as this heartless sinner. But Alomar delivered no thoughtful apology after the game. In front of cameras and tape recorders, he went on the record in declaring: "He [Hirschbeck] had a problem with his family when his son died—I know that's something real tough in life—but after that he just changed, personality wise. He just got real bitter."[12]

While there was no recording of what Hirschbeck said in the actual argument, Alomar's bombshell comments were dutifully recorded and transcribed, soon visible for the masses. John Eisenberg was one of those writers in Toronto's clubhouse meticulously chronicling every syllable uttered by Alomar. (Interestingly, it wasn't immediately apparent to the press that Alomar had spat on Hirschbeck. In fact, it wasn't until the fourth inning that Eisenberg and the other writers saw from slow-motion replays on press box monitors that spittle was involved.)

Eisenberg's memory of the infamous evening was: "That didn't go great for him [Alomar]. I vividly remember that. He said some things that proved to be true, that Hirschbeck had called him a name. But he [Alomar] said he didn't feel that badly about it [spitting]. He brought up his [Hirschbeck's] son, which was a mistake."[13]

But Alomar felt that in the postgame clubhouse group interview, he had once again been provoked. He had no interest in talking about Hirschbeck's dead son John—in fact, during a 2013 article for *Sports Illustrated*'s "Where Are They Now?" issue, he claimed that he had been unaware of Hirschbeck's family tragedy until a writer brought it up that evening—and so he felt he had been led on by the media. Furthermore, because Alomar's native tongue was Spanish, it is possible things got lost in translation. Perhaps, had the interview questions been asked in Spanish, Alomar's responses would have differed. Eisenberg adds,

I don't think there was any misinterpretation in terms of the questions, no. I do think that language might have been a bit of an issue there in hindsight, looking back all these years later. His English was good. He was a well-spoken guy. But maybe he didn't have the nuances of English. He may not have had everything mastered, and I'm not sure that helped him there. I think language was in play.[14]

Following Baltimore's 9–4 loss in Game 3 of the ALDS, as reporters continued their nightly routine of grilling Alomar, the maligned ballplayer hinted at the potential language barrier issue: "I don't want to comment anymore about it. Every time I say something, it gets twisted."[15]

Even before this ordeal, Alomar had grown wary of speaking with print reporters. At least in front of television cameras, there was documented evidence of exactly what he was saying. But the scribes could take liberty in interpreting his comments, which is why, especially now, Alomar spoke in clichés, expressed little emotion, used complete, yet simple sentences—a demeanor in marked contrast to his penchant for hamming it up with fellow Latinos on the field, his articulated Spanish loaded with inflection and animation.

But what was the point of trying to rationalize his behavior? Fair or unfair, over the past week the media had helped create a narrative partial to Hirschbeck and subsequently the public had made up its collective mind: Alomar deserved to be vilified throughout the 1996 postseason, if not longer.

While Alomar and his Orioles were advancing deeper into October baseball, John Hirschbeck was home in Poland, Ohio, with his wife, Denise, and their three children.

For the first time in his life, John was in the public eye away from the diamond. There were the television crews lining his street when he arrived home on the evening of Sunday, September 29; one interview request after another (how many times could he say, "I've moved on"?); authors reaching out about collaborating on book projects; there was even talk that a movie could be in the works. As an admittedly private, low-key guy whose idea of fun was having a few neighbors over for a cookout, Hirschbeck had no use for any of the hoopla.

Especially now.

As the Alomar-Hirschbeck feud became one of the biggest pop culture stories in America in October 1996, the umpire's tragic story came to light.

The public learned that Alomar spat on a man who not only lost one son to the deadly neurological illness adrenoleukodystrophy (ALD), but whose other son, ten-year-old Michael, was also battling the very same insidious genetic disease.

While Hirschbeck's older son, John, was diagnosed with ALD too late to receive a bone marrow transplant that could have slowed the progression of the disease, Michael did undergo the experimental transplant, from which he was now several years removed. But every day following the procedure was a struggle. In his preadolescent years, Michael grew accustomed to taking over a dozen pills each morning. He grew tired easily, developed shingles, repeat-edly experienced brain seizures that sometimes hospitalized him for days and sapped him of his memory. While Michael struggled to retain information and learn how to read, he was missing so many hours of school for medical appointments that he was held back. He often became confused and disori-ented and went days without an appetite. These were merely some of the daily challenges John and Denise Hirschbeck faced while also raising two elemen-tary school-aged daughters . . . only a few years after burying their first son.[16]

Naturally, as such disturbing details of Hirschbeck's homelife emerged that fall, the umpire, who, on game days carried a pager in case his younger son got sick and on days off visited his older son's grave, became one of the most sympathetic figures in the sports world.

Which, in turn, meant Roberto Alomar would remain one of the most despised athletes alive.

On the eve of the American League Championship Series between the Orioles and Yankees, the Roberto Alomar saga was grabbing headlines in the Big Ap-ple. The front page of the October 8 edition of the *New York Post* featured an image of Alomar under the headline, "NY's Most Wanted!" It was unbeliev-able. The sensationalistic tabloid deemed the Alomar story more newsworthy than the New York City cop who had just been acquitted in the choking death of a man during a fight sparked by a touch football game.[17]

Inside the paper, *Post* sports columnist Steve Serby claimed that in New York, Alomar was even more loathed than sports villains such as Pat Riley (the former Knicks coach had recently departed for the Miami Heat), Reggie Miller, and Bobby Bonilla. When asked to predict the fans' reaction in Game 1 at Yankee Stadium, Chris Convery, a forty-five-year-old Yankee fan from

Long Island, was quoted as saying, "People will be throwing batteries at him. There won't be a flashlight working in the Bronx after the game."[18]

Maybe the only saving grace for Alomar was the weather. The ALCS was slated to begin on the evening of Tuesday, October 8, however a rainstorm postponed Game 1 to the following afternoon, which meant that both games in the Bronx would be played (mostly) in daylight with presumably less alcohol-fueled emotion from the stands. Still, with legions of New Yorkers threatening to throw more than insults at Alomar, Yankee Stadium wasn't taking any chances as it doubled the typical game-day police presence (from 150 to 300). After all, Alomar was not only viewed as the devil for his actions toward Hirschbeck, but he was the best player on the team standing in the way of the Yankees as they marched toward their first World Series in fifteen years.

However, once Alomar came to bat in the top of the first inning of Game 1, civility reigned. There was the deafening chorus of boos and signs galore ("ALOMAR IS DE'SPIT'ABLE" was the first one the NBC cameras picked up) but no violence. Nothing Alomar hadn't seen over the past weekend in Cleveland.

But the brotherhood of umpires continued to get their quiet revenge when Alomar was in the batter's box, as occasionally a seventeen-inch-wide plate magically expanded to two feet. Take for example this moment, his first at-bat of the series when Alomar worked the count to 2-2 against New York's young lefty Andy Pettitte. On the 2-2 offering, Pettitte tossed a breaking ball that landed a good three inches off the plate. Called strike three. The 56,495 fans erupted as an expressionless Alomar softly laid down his bat, batting gloves, and helmet. Contesting the call would have been pointless, yet anyone with a shred of impartiality watching knew that if the batter had not been Alomar, home plate umpire Larry Barnett would have likely kept his hands on his hips.

Alomar had a quiet Game 1 (a 5–4 Yankees win in extra innings), going 1–6 with three strikeouts. The man crouching behind the plate for most of those at-bats was New York catcher Jim Leyritz. What does he think—was there one strike zone for Alomar and one for everyone else? "Not really," responds Leyritz when asked in a 2020 interview. "From what I remember, I don't remember him being singled out as somebody who would get a different strike zone than we would."[19]

For the sanctity of the game, one could hope that was the case. But it's worth noting that Alomar, a .328 hitter in the regular season, didn't just

struggle in Game 1 but finished the ALCS batting .217. While the poor performance can't solely be attributed to a more pitcher-friendly strike zone at
times—after all, there was considerable mental strain on Alomar as he dug in
against New York's all-star pitchers David Cone, Jimmy Key, and Pettitte—
it's certainly possible that the umps were a contributing factor.

Certainly, it seemed the New York media and umpires were still absorbed
in the Alomar-Hirschbeck soap opera. Veteran umpire Jim McKean went on
record as saying, "We've had bumpings, we've had fights, but I've never really
seen a ballplayer try and directly spit in an umpire's face. Only animals spit
in people's faces."[20] However, players on both teams had mostly moved on.
Leyritz recalls,

> By then, it didn't necessarily blow over, but just as far as the players go, we
> didn't really think much of it. We had an opinion as far as what we thought
> about what happened. It really wasn't the news. I think more of it was Cal Rip-
> ken and everything he had been through and [how he] had finally gotten back
> to the playoffs. I think that was the bigger news, more so than the incident that
> happened earlier.[21]

(Interestingly, one player who did articulate his belief that Alomar had
erred in judgment was Mariano Duncan, a fellow Latino and Alomar's
counterpart at second base for New York. As Duncan remarked at the time:
"What Robbie did is wrong, wrong, wrong.")[22]

At this point, Alomar wasn't complaining about being in Ripken's shadow.
Ripken was still the most popular player in the game and the fact that he was
back in the postseason for the first time since 1983 was an above-the-fold
story. Plus, the Iron Man was also thirty-six years old, and his team was four
wins from the World Series, so it was certainly possible that this was his last
chance for a title. While the New York writers relentlessly pressed Alomar for
juicy quotes (he did apologize again at the beginning of the series), the glaring
spotlight on Ripken provided a welcome distraction.

During Game 1, an even bigger distraction came courtesy of Jeffrey Maier,
a twelve-year-old boy from Old Tappan, New Jersey, who had just celebrated
his bar mitzvah. The Orioles were ahead 4–3 in the bottom of the eighth inning when Derek Jeter lofted a fly ball to the right field warning track. As
Tony Tarasco lifted his mitt to snag the ball, Maier reached over the wall and

robbed the Baltimore outfielder of the putout. Umpire Rich Garcia gifted the Yankees a game-tying home run—it was clearly fan interference, but there was no instant replay so the call couldn't get overturned—and a few innings later, center fielder Bernie Williams led off the bottom of the eleventh with a walk-off homer to end one of the all-time strangest postseason games.

After the game, a throng of reporters tracked down Maier. The *New York Post* was preparing a front page ("Angel in the Outfield") showcasing the kid's deed. There was already talk of him doing the late-night talk show circuit.

While Maier may have been the toast of the Big Apple, in Baltimore, he had instantly become the biggest enemy since Bob Irsay, the Baltimore Colts owner who had surreptitiously moved the team to Indianapolis. The Orioles faithful didn't find the adolescent reaching into the field of play so cute. He had robbed the O's of the second out of the eighth inning and a chance to escape with a 4–3 win. Undoubtedly, it would have been unsafe for Maier to travel a few hours south and attend the upcoming weekend's games at Camden Yards.

Even the most ardent, unabashed Yankee fans had to admit Baltimore got screwed by Maier and the *right field* umpire Garcia. (In the postseason, umpires are also stationed in the outfield.) Slow-motion television replays provided incontrovertible evidence that Maier had reached at least a couple of feet over the wall and interfered with play. This was an illegal act and had Maier been an adult, he probably wouldn't have emerged as an instant folk hero across the Tri-State Area; rather, he likely would have been spending the night in prison.

For at least one evening, Alomar was not the most polarizing figure in baseball.

Once the ALCS shifted to Games 3 and 4 in Baltimore (the Orioles stole Game 2, 5–3), the Alomar-Hirschbeck narrative became even more of an afterthought. Alomar was no longer playing in front of fans threatening to inflict bodily harm on him. However, he was playing in front of fans who were coming to the slow realization that Ripken was damaged goods, and that he could not lead the Orioles to a pennant. Batting in the six-hole, Ripken finished the series with a .250 average and didn't drive in a single run. In the decisive Game 5 (a 6–4 win for the Yanks), the living legend went 0–4 with two punch outs.

Alomar also received less attention in this series because Ripken's counterpart at shortstop, Derek Jeter, was coming into his own. The eventual AL Rookie of the Year followed up his sparkling rookie season by hitting a robust .417 in the ALCS. In the pressure crucible of October baseball, the twenty-two-year-old kid from Kalamazoo, Michigan, catapulted New York to its first World Series since 1981. Charming and handsome, Jeter was the most eligible bachelor in NYC and a teen heartthrob across America. And now he loomed as the heir apparent to Ripken as the face of Major League Baseball.

The final play of the series perfectly symbolized the passing of the torch: in the bottom of the ninth inning of Game 5, Baltimore was down two runs. On a 2-2 pitch, Ripken hit a one-hopper deep in the hole at short that Jeter backhanded and fired across the diamond to first baseman Tino Martinez. Barreling down the line, Ripken left his feet and dove headfirst into the bag . . . only to look up and see first base umpire Rich Garcia pump his right fist in the air.

This time, Garcia made the right call. Jeter had indeed thrown Ripken out to clinch New York's first pennant in fifteen years.

While the Yankees were set to face the Atlanta Braves in the Fall Classic, the Orioles' World Series drought would now drag into the late 1990s. And they would be starting the next season without the services of their best player in Alomar, who would finally serve his suspension.

In hindsight, some of the lowest moments from the Alomar-Hirschbeck feud did not actually involve the ballplayer and umpire themselves. It was such an emotionally charged, drama-filled incident (or series of incidents, rather) that a few unfortunate developments went largely unnoticed in the aftermath of the spat.

Consider, for example, the scene in the Baltimore clubhouse following the penultimate game of the regular season that clinched a playoff berth for the Orioles. While players were standing up on training room tables, dousing one another with champagne, spraying baby powder in the air, just trashing the place, there were a few spitting beer at each other—a blatant gesture to belittle Alomar's act and mock the outraged public for supposedly overreacting.

Three days later, on the afternoon of Tuesday, October 1, during the introductions before Game 1 of the American League Division Series, the crowd at Camden Yards gave Alomar a boisterous ovation. While the Baltimore faithful standing behind their man was homerism personified, the ugly reception given to the six umpires converging at home plate during the pre-game exchange of lineup cards was baffling. What had they done to deserve the taunts and catcalls? Was it because they were colleagues of Hirschbeck? (He was not working the postseason.) Irrespective of the exact motive, the booing was insensitive to say the least given Hirschbeck's personal situation and the fact that this had been a brutal year for the men in blue: the season began with longtime umpire John McSherry collapsing on the turf of Cincinnati's Riverfront Stadium before dying of a massive heart attack and ended with the humiliation of Alomar not being fairly punished.

Certainly, Alomar's teammates and fans proved unfailingly loyal, but the person who most notably rushed to his corner was his boss, Orioles principal owner Peter Angelos. For it was Angelos ("There must be some pressure on him [Alomar] to act that way") who had summoned manager Davey Johnson for a meeting following the postseason-clinching win in Toronto.[23] Present were two attorneys who wanted Johnson to sign an affidavit stating that he had heard Hirschbeck call Alomar a vile name. If they could provide sworn testimony that Alomar had been provoked, that he was a good Catholic boy defending his mother's honor, perhaps Major League Baseball would feel more inclined to let Alomar play in October. However, Johnson refused to oblige. There were quite a few choice words flung back and forth and it was impossible to confirm with 100 percent certainty that one particular term was used. A couple decades later, in his memoir *Davey Johnson: My Wild Ride in Baseball and Beyond*, the skipper acknowledged: "Angelos, who had no proven baseball competence, was continuing a pattern of meddling in the affairs of our team that had begun at the start of the season."[24] Angelos was not only a meddler but the chief enabler of Alomar and, of course, ultimately got his wish even without Johnson's cooperation.

8

Saving Face

Things could not have worked out better for Roberto Alomar and the Orioles. With their franchise player finally serving his five-game suspension during the first week of the 1997 regular season (Alomar was still paid but donated his earnings to charity), the O's managed to go 4–1. Meanwhile, for Alomar personally, the downtime was a blessing in disguise as he had extra time to rehab a severely sprained ankle at the team's spring training complex in Florida. (Over the winter he tripped and fell on stairs in his Baltimore apartment building and then aggravated the gimpy ankle before spring training in a charity hoops game.) Even if there hadn't been a suspension, it was quite possible that Alomar may have sat out some, if not all, of the first week of the season.

On Monday, April 7, when he was eligible to return for Baltimore's afternoon tilt against the Kansas City Royals at Kauffman Stadium, Alomar was indeed batting second, playing second. Judging by the pregame atmosphere, it seemed that the folks in KC were going to be more polite than fans in Cleveland and New York had been in October. Shortly before the O's were slated to begin batting practice, the autograph hounds spotted Alomar coming out of the visiting dugout. Over the course of nearly ten minutes signing a couple dozen baseballs, Alomar heard hardly any references to last year's incident. The fans couldn't have been more gracious ("I appreciate your taking the time, Mr. Alomar!") or respectful ("Thank you very much, Mr. Alomar!").[1]

However, once the game started later that afternoon, it was apparent that the throng of fans jockeying for signed souvenirs during BP didn't represent how the majority of the 40,052 ticket-holders felt.

It was now Kansas City's turn to continue making life miserable for Roberto Alomar.

When his name was announced over the public address system during the player introductions, a shrill cacophony of anger and resentment sliced through the chilly early spring air. The jeers only intensified when Alomar strolled to the plate for his first at bat and continued until he was retired on a sacrifice bunt, only to resume every time he fielded a ball or came up to the plate again. In the top of the eighth, Alomar led off with a line-drive single to right field for his second hit of the game. As Jeff Reboulet popped out of the Orioles dugout and trotted toward first to pinch-run for Alomar (his heavily taped bum ankle was still nagging him), the hooting and hollering reached a fever pitch—a scene that would become all too familiar for Alomar as his Orioles visited ballparks across America that spring.

"It was unique," remembers Scott Kamieniecki, a former starting pitcher for the Baltimore Orioles. "I mean the first couple weeks, when they booed him, it was kind of odd that it lasted that long. There was a lot of negativity."[2]

There certainly was. And it didn't just last until mid-April. Every time Baltimore made its first trip to a different city in 1997, a new segment of the population got the chance to roast Alomar. Even the clubhouse didn't provide much relief as the baseball writers in every city—from New York to Anaheim— would creep over toward Alomar's stall during batting practice before a series opener and ask about last September's incident. The answer was invariably the same. ("Let's talk about baseball. I want to leave it at that.") But it didn't deter a new crop of reporters from asking the same tired questions every time Alomar was in their presence. The routine grew especially irksome when the Baltimore writers would desperately try to glean new insight into Alomar's lingering feelings over the matter. The ballplayer had been on good terms with the beat writers during his first year in town (win or lose, he wouldn't duck a question during the postgame sessions), but heretofore casual exchanges often became tense.

On the evening of Tuesday, April 22, there was actually a newsworthy development in the Alomar-Hirschbeck soap opera. The Orioles were playing the Chicago White Sox at Camden Yards. Starting at second base was Alomar and less than 90 feet to his left was first base umpire John Hirschbeck. For the first time since last September, they would have to be on the same field together—an inevitable situation that both men had dreaded all winter.

The Orioles, undefeated at home thus far, rode an 11–4 record into the two-game set with Chicago and had staff ace Mike Mussina on the hill. But naturally, the considerable buzz leading up to the game had nothing to do with box scores or standings. Pregame chatter revolved around one simple question: would there finally be a public reconciliation between Alomar and Hirschbeck? Last fall, Alomar had issued "his" written apology and Hirschbeck had declared it was time to move on, but recent attempts by the MLB Players Association to arrange a meeting or generate a joint public statement by the two proved unsuccessful. It was anyone's guess as to whether the player and umpire would kiss and make up or just ignore each other.

It turned out to be the first scenario. In one of his finest moments as a young adult, Roberto showed initiative when he jogged out to take his position in the first inning and went over to greet Hirschbeck in shallow right field. As the two shook hands and exchanged a few seemingly pleasant words, the Camden Yards crowd applauded. (Only minutes earlier many had booed Hirschbeck during the pregame introductions.) After Baltimore's 3–2 win, Hirschbeck told reporters, "I considered it over long before we came to town, but this makes it final. I hope you will let it go, too. I just wanted to go to Baltimore, do my job and move on."[3]

Unbeknownst to the public, neither man really moved on. This was supposed to be the moment of contrition that the nation had long desired (and it was certainly a good look for Alomar), but as Hirschbeck would later admit to *Sports Illustrated* in 2013, "It was staged. Phony. Nothing in my heart changed in that moment."[4] The evening after the handshake, Hirschbeck was behind the plate and every time Alomar came to bat, Hirschbeck wouldn't look at him. Later in the spring when Hirschbeck was the second base umpire in games Baltimore played, he would move away from his traditional perch behind the bag so he didn't have to be near his nemesis.

The two baseball lifers could publicly state there was closure, but on the diamond nothing had changed. And the reality was that neither Alomar, being a twenty-nine-year-old ballplayer, nor Hirschbeck, being a forty-two-year-old umpire, was leaving baseball anytime soon. In short, there was no end in sight to the acrimony and awkwardness.

Although the nagging questions from reporters and nasty taunts from fans didn't disappear following the public embrace in Baltimore, Alomar, as usual, showed no ill effects on the diamond. On April 26 against the Boston Red Sox, Alomar had a career day, going 4–4 with three homers and six RBIs; he followed up a solid first couple months of the season by hitting .348 in June; in the field he was literally perfect for the first six weeks, not committing a single error until May 16. That Roberto was continuing to play at an elite level in all facets of the game (while nursing a strained left shoulder that forced him to bat exclusively from the left side) certainly provided a distraction, at least at some level, from the lingering aftermath of the Hirschbeck ordeal.

In spring 1997, there was another welcome distraction courtesy of Cal Ripken sliding over from shortstop to third base to make room for the newly acquired Mike Bordick. Ever since Davey Johnson took over as manager before the 1996 season, he had plans to move Ripken, who broke into the majors as a third baseman, over to the hot corner. In 1996, Ripken begrudgingly shifted over to third after Johnson insisted on a young, dynamic prospect named Manny Alexander playing short for an extended period of time. While the experiment lasted all of six games as Alexander was quickly ruled a bust, Ripken broke down defensively in the ALCS against the Yanks and GM Pat Gillick started contacting free-agent shortstops right after the World Series. So, when the O's signed Bordick to a three-year, $9 million deal to be their new shortstop, there was (understandably) great speculation over how well one of the game's legacy players would handle the transition to a new position this late in his career. To his credit, Ripken made himself into a very serviceable third baseman, but there was drama along the way as on more than one occasion, Johnson had to remind Ripken, who still believed he was the best shortstop in baseball, that he was the manager. The episode represented one of the very few blemishes on Ripken's Norman Rockwell–esque career in Baltimore.

By mid-season, Alomar, batting over .300 and putting on a nightly defensive clinic, was a no-brainer selection to start at second base for the American League in the All-Star Game in Cleveland. Even though many fans still weren't able to forgive and forget, Alomar received a whopping 1.65 million all-star votes, nearly double the total for his closest rival at second base, Chuck Knoblauch of the Minnesota Twins.

All-star week was full of mixed emotions. While Sandy proudly joined Roberto on the AL squad, which marked the fifth time the brothers played in the same All-Star Game, only days earlier their ninety-five-year-old grandmother who had been bedridden for three years after breaking her hip in a fall had died. The All-Star Game festivities prevented Roberto and Sandy from attending the funeral, but the brothers did dedicate the game to her, each pinning a black ribbon to the other's jersey, right over the heart, prior to the game.

Somewhere, Grandma Toni, as the boys liked to call her, was smiling. The night belonged to Sandy (he went into the break riding a thirty-game hitting streak while pacing the American League with a .375 average), as he clubbed a two-run, seventh-inning homer that propelled the American League to a 3–1 win. As Sandy dazzled in becoming the first all-star MVP in his home ballpark, Roberto had an uneventful evening, going hitless in two at bats. But at least he was able to live vicariously through his older brother.

"It couldn't have worked out better for the family," Roberto told *USA Today Baseball Weekly* after the game. "I've had some great moments in baseball, but to me, you can put this in that category. It was a great day for the Alomars."[5]

Roberto didn't have a great performance, but, more importantly, he had a great experience at Jacobs Field—certainly in comparison to last October's ALDS. At the very same ballpark in which he had been ruthlessly shamed nine months earlier, Roberto received a mostly cordial reception this time around. While there was a smattering of boos when Roberto took batting practice the day before the All-Star Game and when he was introduced the next day during the pregame ceremonies, the decibel level was markedly lower than it had been all season.

Speaking to the media following Monday's workout, Alomar acknowledged, "It's hard not to hear the crowd when you're on the field. You try to concentrate and stay focused on what you're doing, but it's impossible to block out everything from the stands, the good or the bad."[6]

Finally, it seemed as though the fans, through electing Alomar to start the All-Star Game and then tapering down the in-person booing, were acknowledging it was time for closure.

Roberto Alomar was not in the conversation for 1997 American League MVP. When the final votes were tallied in November, twenty-one players finished ahead of him. He was looking up at a couple downright unremarkable players (reliever Doug Jones, first baseman Tony Clark), three Baltimore teammates (relief pitchers Arthur Rhodes and Randy Myers and first baseman Rafael Palmeiro), and his brother.

Anyone who saw a glimpse of Alomar's play that season, particularly in the second half, knew this was an injustice—not just to Alomar, but to the game of baseball. After the all-star break, Alomar had torn the cover off the ball, posting a .384 average (albeit in limited action due to injuries). With six errors all year, Alomar was arguably the game's best infielder, never mind second baseman. The only conceivable explanation for Alomar not getting much love from the voters is that he missed fifty games with the aforementioned shoulder ailment and later a pulled groin (along with the short suspension) which naturally deflated his power numbers (fourteen homers and sixty RBIs). Otherwise, it was rather obvious that Alomar was the MVP of his division-winning team and no less worthy of accolades than the eventual AL MVP, Ken Griffey Jr.

"In my opinion, looking back, he was probably our best all-around player," reflects Scott Kamieniecki. "He was probably one of the best in the game. I don't think anybody on our team brought more to the table than him. He made it look so easy too."[7]

"Robbie was almost so good, that he was bored with the game," acknowledges Jeff Reboulet.[8]

This is hardly hyperbole. When the Orioles took infield practice before games, Robbie was seldom challenged: it was more likely that he would bring up the spitting incident with reporters than boot a grounder or make an errant throw during pregame warmups. Tired of going through the motions during the pregame routine, Robbie got creative in summer '97. Reboulet recalls double play drills when he was playing shortstop and a one-handed Alomar would use his glove to flip the ball over to the second base bag from thirty feet out. When that got old, there were circus catches and behind-the-back shuffle throws to master. What was the point of working on fundamentals? It's not like he could get any better.

B. J. Surhoff says,

I can't sit here and come up with one play defensively and say, "Wow!" But what I can tell you where I said, "Wow!" was watching him take groundballs before a game. He had a special pair of hands. He would take a groundball with his left hand and all in one motion, it would go around his back to whomever he was flipping the double play with. It would come out of his glove, and he would never use his hand. What people didn't understand was how fundamentally sound he was, which enabled him to do that.[9]

Throughout the course of his twelve-year career, Reboulet played with some of the game's most feared sluggers in Kirby Puckett and Gary Sheffield. He played with Ripken in Baltimore and Adrian Beltre in Los Angeles. All were Hall of Fame-caliber players, but none of them could impact the game in as many ways as Alomar could. "In general, people have asked me who is the best player you ever played with," says Reboulet. "To this day, I still believe the best player that I have ever played with, and/or probably against, was Robbie Alomar. His talent level was exceptional. Like he is the most talented guy that I probably played with. The reality was he was a five-tool guy."[10]

Reboulet played with Alomar for two years in Baltimore (1997–1998). The countless clutch hits and breathtaking plays blend into one highlight reel. Like most former teammates of Alomar's, the former journeyman infielder struggles to identify one play as being particularly noteworthy. But eventually, one memory comes to mind and, ironically, it happens to be Alomar's second inning at bat during a ho-hum late-season game against the non-contending Toronto Blue Jays. It was September 23, 1997, and Baltimore was riding a comfortable four-game division lead into the season's final week. Not exactly a high-stakes situation. Reboulet recalls,

> We're in Toronto. Roger [Clemens] is pitching. Sometimes, you're just kind of rolling through the motions and Robbie was no different than anybody else. He would be cruising through a game. For whatever reason, in the second inning on a 2–2 pitch, Roger tried to take Robbie's head off. Robbie hits the deck, and he gets up and now he's pissed. So, they're screaming at each other. They're really going at it verbally. It woke Robbie up, and he was determined to make him [Clemens] feel that. Roger threw a high fastball and he [Robbie] ripped one off the right centerfield wall. By the time the ball hit the wall, he was already on second base. He was flying. He was almost thinking about an inside-the-park-homer. It's because Roger basically challenged him. Robbie was as talented as they come. So, when he was into the game, there was nobody that was going to stop him from being successful in that at bat.[11]

Understanding what kind of a player Alomar was during the Baltimore years is easy—his immense, versatile talents were on display every time he took the field. What is not so easy is understanding what kind of teammate Alomar was during this middle portion of his career. None of Alomar's former teammates in Baltimore has anything bad . . . or exceptionally good to say about his character. Alomar simply remained too much of an enigma in his own clubhouse for most guys to gauge his personality.

"I didn't really hang out with him," says Scott Kamieniecki. "It wasn't like I would go out of my way or he would go out of his way. We were teammates, but we weren't close."[12]

Pitcher Doug Drabek, who came over to Baltimore in 1998 to wrap up a solid and lengthy career, echoes a similar sentiment: "I didn't really hang out off the field. We lived in different places. On the road, we didn't really do anything together. As far as I can remember, he wasn't the guy that would stand up and yell and be very vocal."[13]

Surhoff says,

> I got to know Robbie, but I wouldn't tell you we were close off the field. I had four kids, and I lived here [in the suburbs]. He was single. I think he lived downtown. Professionally and in the clubhouse, I feel like I got along very well with him. I thought we had a mutual respect in terms of being teammates. He wasn't a real vocal guy. He really kind of kept to himself. His locker was next to Raffy [Rafael Palmeiro]. I would say he was probably closest to Raffy because of their lockers. Raffy, obviously being from Cuba originally, was fluent in Spanish. So those guys would talk in Spanish a lot.[14]

"He was pretty quiet," adds Reboulet. "He would kind of do his thing and play. He wasn't very boisterous. I think he had to get to know you a little bit before he was personable."[15]

While the reserved demeanor could border on standoffishness at times, there were very few times during the 1997 season when Alomar went out of his way to cause trouble for anyone. Back in early April, Alomar blew off a team luncheon and was subsequently fined by Davey Johnson. A few months later, he had no use for playing in a midseason exhibition game against Baltimore's minor-league affiliate in Rochester; naturally, another unexcused absence—and subsequent fine—followed. While neither episode reflected well on the organization (or made life easy for Johnson), this was certainly not unusual behavior for an athlete of Alomar's renown. And especially this year, there was an underlying sense of appreciation and respect for Alomar as he battled through a litany of injuries to his ankle, shoulder, and groin. Robbie may not have played every game with bumps and bruises like Ripken (who else did?), but he was not that guy who couldn't get out of the trainer's room.

"Robbie never appeared to me to be walking with a limp or having a bandage wrap or some kind of heating pack on him," remembers Rick Krivda. "When we showed up at three o'clock for BP, he was always game ready. Nothing would hinder him at all."[16]

The 1997 season was, by far, the most injury-plagued of Alomar's career. From July 30 to August 26, he was on the DL with a pulled groin. In September, the left shoulder started barking again (he initially injured it during a May 31 game against Cleveland), forcing him not only to sit out several more games but also to give up hitting right-handed. The latter issue was particularly worrisome for the eventual AL East champion Orioles, who were slated to face the Seattle Mariners—and their indomitable southpaw ace Randy Johnson—in the ALDS. Casting a menacing seven-foot shadow from the mound, Johnson featured a wipeout slider and blistering fastball that were absolutely devastating to lefties, but often fairly manageable for righties. From manager Johnson's perspective, an exclusively left-handed hitting Alomar (even one who batted .500 in September) was damaged goods against The Big Unit.

In Game 1 at Seattle's Kingdome, the right-handed hitting Jeff Reboulet was penciled in as the starting second baseman; thus, Alomar's duties would be limited to pinch-hitting or serving as a late-inning defensive replacement. The move backfired, as Reboulet went 0–2 and was lifted for Alomar in the sixth. Ultimately, it made no difference who was playing second as the rest of the Orioles lineup pounded The Big Unit for five runs on seven hits en route to a breezy 9–3 Game 1 win. After the teams split the next two games, Baltimore was gearing up for another Johnson start in a potential closeout Game 4 back at Camden Yards. Once again, the O's skipper viewed Reboulet and his thirteen career homers as a bigger threat than a left-handed hitting Alomar, who only had two hits so far in the series. Whether it was a stroke of genius on behalf of Davey Johnson or just dumb luck, the plan worked to perfection: in the first inning, Reboulet, using his short and compact stroke, rocketed a

97 mph fastball into the left-field bleachers, setting the tone for Baltimore's 3–1 series-clinching win that sparked the franchise's first champagne-flowing postseason celebration at home since 1970.

For good measure, Baltimore was able to win the ALDS by defeating Johnson twice without Alomar having to overexert himself. (He came in as a late-inning defensive replacement in Game 4 and later singled in his only at bat against Johnson in the series.) Indeed, Alomar spent nearly half the series reclining on the bench—a timely rest considering his full-time services would be needed in the upcoming ALCS against his brother's Cleveland Indians, a team with no imposing left-handed starters.

The Orioles and Indians may have been battling for the AL pennant, but the high-stakes competition didn't prevent the Alomar family from having a re-union of sorts during Columbus Day weekend in Cleveland where the ALCS shifted after the teams had split the first two games in Baltimore. With Game 3 set for a 4:17 p.m. start on Saturday, the plan was for Roberto to leave the ballpark, presumably in the early evening, hop into his older brother's silver Audi (on loan for the weekend) and drive over to Sandy's house in Westlake, Ohio, to enjoy some postgame pizza with his parents, brother, sister-in-law, and their two kids.[17] Unfortunately, Game 3 of the 1997 ALCS, which Cleveland won 2–1 in the twelfth inning when center fielder Marquis Grissom stole home on a botched squeeze play, turned out to be the longest postseason game in baseball history, taking nearly five hours to complete. As such, this would have to be a quick family get-together. After all, Sandy Jr. had young kids and Game 4 was on Sunday.

As Roberto walked out of Jacobs Field and into his brother's sports car, he appreciated that he didn't have to hail a cab to make the twenty-minute drive down I-90 to the suburbs. But he knew there was a catch. There was *always* a catch with his brother. Surely, Sandy Jr. had something in mind. So, Roberto was frustrated, but not surprised, when he turned on the ignition and saw the gas gauge flash empty. This was downtown Cleveland so there was no shin-ing beacon of gasoline in sight. Would he have enough in the tank to make the fifteen miles? It was almost 10 o'clock—would a gas station be open now? Where even was the nearest gas station? No such thing as GPS or iPhones back in 1997.

Once he got on the highway, Roberto started clutching the wheel with sweaty palms. It was slowly approaching midnight and the thought of breaking down on a highway was nerve-racking, to say the least. Finally, there was a sign for a fuel station a mile away. After exiting the interstate, Roberto pulled up to a self-service pump, filled the car with $25 worth of gas, signed an autograph on a receipt slip for a shocked customer (*Roberto Alomar is really stopping for gas this late at night?*), and climbed back into the driver's seat. Now, he was able to laugh at his brother's prank.

Once Roberto arrived, the gathering at Sandy's Westlake mansion was not the least bit awkward—everyone accepted the fact that the Alomar Championship Series was going to be bittersweet for the family: one brother would go on to play in the World Series; the other would be watching it on television. While sitting down on the couch to catch Game 3 highlights, the boys and their dad conversed loudly in Spanish and English between bites of pizza. No one felt shy about providing impassioned commentary because hardly any of the highlights involved Roberto and Sandy—a trend that was continuing throughout the series.[18]

Going into the ALCS, aside from the inevitable hoopla surrounding Ripken possibly playing in his last postseason, the matchup between the Alomar brothers was the storyline getting the most airtime. But the fraternal rivalry was now becoming a sidebar as the Alomars were struggling mightily, having gone a combined 1–16 in Games 2 and 3. After being named All-Star Game MVP, posting a thirty-game hit streak, and slugging a pivotal home run against the Yankees in Game 4 of the Division Series when the Indians were four outs from elimination, Sandy was hitless thus far in the ALCS. Roberto's bat was not completely silenced (two-run homer in Game 1), but he had already committed a pair of errors.

By the time Robbie left his brother's house shortly before 1:00 a.m. and drove back toward the team's downtown hotel, the attention had shifted toward Mike Mussina, the Game 3 starter. His masterly performance (fifteen strikeouts, all within the first twenty-one batters faced) was even more impressive as it came at the expense of Cleveland's stacked lineup featuring veterans Manny Ramirez, Jim Thome, Matt Williams, and David Justice.

Mussina's postseason run this October—he had been lights-out against Seattle in the ALDS—grew even more newsworthy because he hailed from the bucolic central Pennsylvania village of Montoursville, a place haunted by the fairly recent TWA Flight 800 tragedy. Watching Mussina dominate this fall provided a morsel of relief to the townsfolk still reeling from the plane accident that had killed twenty-one residents, sixteen of whom were members of the local high school French Club. Without question, no community in America had been so devastated by the horrific tragedy as Mussina's hometown. But here was Mussina, a constant presence at high school football games and engaged to a local girl, silencing Cleveland's potent lineup after beating Randy Johnson twice in the ALDS and giving the grief-stricken town something to relish.

The city of Baltimore was also resting its hopes on Mussina's golden right arm. After splitting the next two games at The Jake, the Orioles turned to Moose (on three days' rest) for a must-win Game 6 at Camden Yards. Pitching with a greater purpose than just getting the O's to the World Series, Mussina tossed eight shut-out innings while fanning ten. However, the Orioles were unable to plate a single run and the game remained scoreless heading into extra frames.

In the top of the eleventh, Cleveland's Tony Fernandez hit a solo-shot to give the Tribe a 1–0 lead. In the bottom half, Baltimore was down to its final out when Brady Anderson singled to right. Up next was Roberto, with a chance to extend his club's postseason run . . . and put an end to a personally frustrating postseason series. On the mound was Cleveland closer Jose Mesa, the pitcher Roberto hit the game-tying single and go-ahead home run against during the decisive game of last year's ALDS. Behind the plate was brother Sandy. It was a gritty at bat with Robbie working the count full after fouling off a couple mid-90s fastballs. As he geared up for the payoff pitch, Robbie did his trademark routine of pinwheeling the bat and leaning in. After an exceptionally long pause (Cleveland skipper Mike Hargrove was so nervous he literally looked away), Mesa finally delivered the 3–2 pitch, a cut fastball inside. Rather than swinging, Robbie lunged out of the way to sell the pitch as a ball inside that was headed toward his chin; his brother, however, was more convincing in framing the pitch as a strike that caught the inside corner.

As the Indians streamed out of their dugout to celebrate their second AL pennant in three years, Roberto, in utter disbelief, hopped up in the air and turned to home plate umpire Mike Reilly. But that was the extent to which he disputed the questionable call. What was the point of being any more demonstrative or, gulp, aggressive? It would only give the haters (and there were still quite a few) further ammunition.

"We had the right guy up," says Kamieniecki. "We were very confident. We didn't like the call. I think Jose Mesa got away with one on that. I thought it was a ball. Whether it was over the plate was irrelevant to me, I thought it was high. Today it's not high, but back then it was."[19]

For the second consecutive October, the Orioles fell short of the AL pennant—not exactly what owner Peter Angelos had in mind when he had opened up his checkbook to bring aboard Alomar and the other splashy free agents two years earlier. Or when he had hired Davey Johnson as manager that winter.

A couple of weeks after the ALCS, Angelos aired his dirty laundry. For months he had been frustrated with the manner in which Johnson had punished Alomar back in July. Alomar, as previously mentioned, had skipped an exhibition game without notifying anyone. (He later claimed it was in order to return to Puerto Rico to attend his grandmother's funeral, which he ultimately did not do.) Angelos was comfortable with Johnson levying a $10,500 fine (ultimately, Alomar avoided paying it) but was livid when he learned that the monetary sum had to be paid to a foundation of which Johnson's wife, Susan, was managing director. Once Angelos's grudge became public, Johnson felt it was time to leave. Even though he had one year remaining on his three-year, $2.25 million contract (and was about to be named AL Manager of the Year for navigating the team to the league's best record), Johnson was more than happy to offer his resignation on November 5.

Angelos was not exactly crestfallen in accepting the resignation. In fact, it is quite possible that although the O's had finished 98–64, falling two wins shy of the World Series (all four ALCS losses were decided by a single run), he may have simply fired Johnson had the manager not left on his own terms. While Johnson may have been baseball's winningest active manager, there were signs that he was starting to lose the clubhouse. At the very least, it seems fair to say that Alomar was not the only player who had a contentious relationship with the skipper. Rick Krivda explains,

I liked Davey [Johnson]. I think a lot of the guys thought he was different. I remember times where [guys would ask] "Where's the lineup?" I remember some guys would come into the clubhouse at two o'clock or so, and you would see the lineup card, and it wasn't there [filled out]. A lot of times Davey would play golf until four o'clock, and he would come in and then put up the lineup card. I think that made a lot of guys mad.[20]

The lineup guessing game was particularly annoying to Chris Hoiles and Lenny Webster, who were splitting the catching duties in 1997 and would have appreciated knowing in advance who was starting an afternoon game following a night one. (During the 1996 season, Johnson's lineup shuffling also sparked controversy when Cal Ripken's little brother Billy, who had joined the club briefly as a utility player, grew sour toward his manager for not consulting with Cal on the temporary move to third.)

Less than a week after Johnson was named AL Manager of the Year, Ray Miller, who in 1997 had served as Baltimore's pitching coach, a post he had previously held for the club from 1978 to 1985, was named the new manager.

As far as Alomar was concerned, preparing for a new manager was business as usual: he hadn't even played a full decade in the majors and was now onto his sixth manager. And, truthfully, with everything Alomar had going on this winter, the managerial switch was probably not at the forefront of his mind. Shortly after the season had ended, he underwent arthroscopic surgery on his left shoulder; with free agency a season away, rumors of a trade to the Yankees or Indians started heating up; by January he was a certified globe-trotter, accompanying his girlfriend, tennis pro Mary Pierce, to tournaments throughout Europe as well as to the Australian Open.

Once the 1998 season got underway, there must have been times when Alomar wished he had stayed overseas. After barely playing .500 ball in April, Baltimore had a dreadful May, going 11–17 while suffering a nine-game losing streak. With the underwhelming start, Baltimore started fading out of contention in the AL East and talk began swirling that the front office was looking to unload Alomar and first baseman Rafael Palmeiro to the New York Mets in an apparent salary dump. The increasingly widespread reports (which ultimately proved to be false) were not falling on deaf ears: by Memorial Day weekend, it was painfully obvious that Alomar, while still hitting over .300, showing occasional pop, and playing his usual Gold Glove defense, was merely going through the motions nearly every time he stepped on the diamond. As *Baltimore Sun* scribe Ken Rosenthal wrote at the time,

"Manager Ray Miller has repeatedly defended Alomar, but club officials evidently are fed up with a player who looks as if he would rather be anywhere but Baltimore."[21] Despite Alomar's unprofessional demeanor, Miller, at least through the first couple months of the season, did indeed stand up for his player—both to ownership as well as to the remaining pockets of spiteful fans.

Back in early May the Orioles were visiting the expansion Tampa Bay Devil Rays, which meant a new city would have an opportunity to remind Alomar of his past sins. And it certainly got ugly at Tropicana Field when fans sitting near the Baltimore dugout blistered Alomar with vicious taunts throughout the weekend series. In The Trop's dome environment (as always far from a sell-out), the jeering was particularly conspicuous, so much so that it became a primary focus of the three-game set. When asked about the reception in his post-game media session, Miller remarked, "Is he [Alomar] supposed to turn all his money over to a convent? Give it all to charity? What sways people? Maybe he needs to talk more, become more public, become more personable. I don't know."[22]

One could interpret the comments as Miller expressing frustration over an injustice that many were uncomfortable discussing: if Roberto were white, the fans would have moved on by now. Several months earlier, during a late-season "Monday Night Football" game, Denver Broncos linebacker Bill Romanowski, a white man, spat in the face of San Francisco 49ers wideout J. J. Stokes, a Black man. After Romanowski apologized profusely and paid his $7,500 fine, the incident magically faded away. In fact, just a month later when the Broncos were gearing up to play the Green Bay Packers in Super Bowl XXXII, the linebacker's (recent) despicable act was not a hot topic of conversation. Of course, Roberto's case involved more than just a wad of saliva: his insensitive post-incident comments toward Hirschbeck regarding his late son were still fresh in the minds of many baseball fans and perhaps accounted for the lingering pockets of hostility.

Following the Tampa series, the home crowds at ballparks across America continued to grow incrementally less hostile toward Alomar—they had their chance in 1997 to express outrage and that was enough. However, that didn't make the season any more bearable. The losses kept mounting and by the end of June, Baltimore's record stood at 37–46, a dismal mark considering the club's sky-high payroll. The Yanks were running away with the division and the Wild Card was a two-horse race between the Red Sox and Blue Jays. A raft of injuries started crippling the Orioles' roster. (Roberto suffered a sprained pinkie in July that forced him to go on the DL for a brief time.) What was supposed to be a World Series or bust year was turning into a season from hell.

"That was a challenging year," admits Doug Drabek. "I think the expectations were there at the beginning and then you have injuries and guys with off-years. All kinds of things going on."[23]

Former *Baltimore Sun* sports columnist John Eisenberg offers a more macro perspective on the debacle that was the 1998 season when he says, "It was a very disappointing season. The team wasn't that good. There was a fall-off there and that always breeds discontent in the clubhouse. They were right on the precipice of falling off a cliff and being really bad for a long period of time."[24]

The adversity didn't exactly bring out the best in Roberto. His contract was set to expire at season's end, and he soon realized that no offers for an extension were forthcoming. (Interestingly, GM Pat Gillick had a similar contractual situation that summer and would soon meet the same fate as Alomar.) After being named MVP of the All-Star Game at Coors Field in Colorado, he hit only .271 in the second half. During the final week of the season, one club official told the *Baltimore Sun* that Alomar "decided to lay down about a month ago."[25] As Reboulet says,

If Robbie was in a comfortable situation where he liked his teammates, Robbie was going to be motivated to play. If there were some disruptive things going on, whether it would be some issues with teammates or something going on in the background that he wasn't comfortable with, then it was probably going to show in his game. For whatever reason, he was not comfortable there.[26]

As is often the case in a veteran-laden club that is vastly underachieving, the new manager was the sacrificial lamb, the guy taking a disproportionately large slice of the blame pie. Reboulet also recalls,

I think Davey [Johnson] was more of, "Throw the balls and bats out there. Let the guys play for seven innings and then I'll mix and match with the pitching. And there we go." I think Ray [Miller] managed situations more and [was] kind of controlling some of those situations. I think as a veteran group of players, that may not have gotten across very well. I think that kind of affected it [the team's record] a little bit. It was just not a good year in '98.[27]

"Ray was a phenomenal pitching coach, but I think he was a little out of his element as a manager," acknowledges Scott Kamieniecki. "I give him credit for trying, but I didn't think it worked out well for him. I didn't think he was the right guy for the managerial job at that time."[28]

Indeed, the front office's desire to promote from within backfired. Miller had won a World Series with the O's back in 1983 when he was on their coaching staff and had presided over a solid pitching staff during the 1997 AL East-winning season. He was quite familiar with the organization, but not with managerial work, as he hadn't served as a big-league skipper since September 1986 when he was let go by Minnesota. Managing ballplayers of the modern era—in particular, Baltimore's roster full of star-studded multi-millionaires—was simply too much to ask of Miller.

While Alomar was far from the only established veteran butting heads with Miller, his relationship with his boss proved to be particularly toxic down the stretch. On August 26 in Chicago, Miller tore into his guys for their sloppy play in a 6–4 loss to the White Sox the prior evening. The heavily maligned manager was especially peeved at all the mental mistakes and felt inclined to single out Alomar, who was allegedly out of position on a bunt play. With the whole team watching, Miller came over to Alomar's locker and mocked his effort. Immediately, Alomar popped out of his stall and started screaming in his manager's face, leading to an ugly confrontation that nearly became physical before teammates eventually intervened.[29]

Similar to last year's situation with Davey Johnson at the helm, it was pretty clear that Alomar and Miller couldn't share the same workspace. But unlike Johnson, Miller, despite skippering the team to a 79–83 mark, had the backing of the Baltimore front office and wasn't going anywhere. Translation: Roberto (once again) would have to find a new home.

"I really don't know what happened," says B. J. Surhoff. "I don't know if he wasn't happy anymore there. I would have much rather . . . he stayed and played with us."[30]

9

Rockin' in Cleveland

When Roberto Alomar and the Baltimore Orioles played the Cleveland Indians during the 1998 season, Alomar had told Cleveland shortstop Omar Vizquel that he would love to play for the Tribe.[1]

While unabashedly forthright, Alomar wasn't exactly divulging a shocking secret.

For nearly everyone in the Baltimore Orioles organization, it was pretty obvious that Alomar's days in black and orange were numbered given not only his acrimonious relationship with manager Ray Miller but also the imminent rebuilding efforts to purge the roster of high-priced vets. On the other side, Cleveland seemed like a natural fit. He could reunite with big brother Sandy (they only played in eight games together in San Diego back in the late 1980s), form a double-play combination for the ages with Vizquel, a fellow Latino who hailed from Venezuela, and bolster an already potent lineup—yet one still in need of his services.

When a still-in-his-prime thirty-year-old Alomar became a free agent in November 1998, Cleveland jumped. Since the franchise's 1994 renaissance season, the Tribe had contended (four AL Central titles and two pennants) despite lacking a serviceable second baseman ever since Carlos Baerga had been dealt to the New York Mets. Since the Baerga trade, the position had been a gaping black hole, as fifteen second basemen had come through the turnstile. And as Joey Cora went 1–17 during the 1998 postseason, the

Cleveland front office realized the club wasn't going to win its first World Series in a half-century without a top-flight second sacker. So, although Cleveland general manager John Hart had to satisfy the demands of fiscal responsibility mandated by owner Richard Jacobs, who had an eye on selling the team, the GM didn't blink in offering Alomar a $32 million, four-year contract, one to which he eventually agreed. As Alomar had been on Hart's radar screen for years, this move was extra gratifying for the executive on a personal level.

Going into the 1999 season, the Indians already had great offensive talent with the likes of Jim Thome, Manny Ramirez, David Justice, Travis Fryman, and Kenny Lofton, but, with Roberto, the club had a player who truly excelled in all facets of the game. When the team began training in Winter Haven, Florida, in February, manager Mike Hargrove (he actually had played with Alomar's father, Sandy, for the Texas Rangers in 1977) challenged his guys with an empirical goal: win over 100 games. Soon, his message of urgency found its way onto T-shirts some players started wearing under their game-day uniforms:

100+
GO HARD OR GO HOME[2]

Since the mid-1990s, Hart had felt that his team coasted through the regular season as the perennially weak AL Central posed virtually no challenges. With the postseason a foregone conclusion, it seemed that the players themselves got bored and complacent by early August—whether they finished with 90 or 100 wins, October baseball surely awaited. As starting pitcher Charles Nagy remarked at the onset of the 1999 season, "The last couple of years we've glided into the playoffs. It seemed like we were lethargic, like we didn't care. . . . I've always felt you should go into the postseason sprinting."[3] Meanwhile, Hargrove, aware that he would likely be dismissed if his loaded team did not break the World Series drought, went public with the challenge.

(In his 2019 autobiography *Mike Hargrove and the Cleveland Indians: A Baseball Life*, Hargrove recalled how his boss wasn't too pleased that he didn't keep the message private: "John [Hart] was pissed. Oh, he was pissed. He said to me, 'What are you doing?' I said, 'I've tried everything in the world.

Let's try this, and see what happens.' He was upset with me, that I came out publicly and stated that.")[4]

It seemed reasonable to believe that Alomar could be the difference-maker in catapulting Cleveland over the defending champion New York Yankees, who had recently acquired Roger Clemens, for the AL pennant en route to a World Series title. However, there were some observers (i.e., national baseball writers) who found it surprising that Alomar was at the epicenter of Hargrove's hard-core campaign given his final season in Baltimore. After all, Alomar, who posted a .229 average in September 1998, had been accused of not hustling to back up first base on bunt plays and not running out grounders and pop-ups, among other acts demonstrating his apparent nonchalant attitude.

Once the regular season started, Alomar's unceremonious ending in Baltimore was all but forgotten. The relentless lineup started drawing comparisons to those of the Ruth-and-Gehrig-led Yankees teams. Jim Mecir, pitching for the Tampa Bay Devil Rays at the time, remembers how with Cleveland's starting nine, "number eight was like an all-star. It was insane facing them. There were no holes in that lineup."[5] Cleveland raced out to a 29–10 start, a mark that was not only the best record in Major League Baseball but also the best start in franchise history. And no one was more responsible for the offensive outburst than Alomar, whether he was clubbing home runs, spraying line drives into the gaps, dropping perfectly placed bunts down the third base line, or swiping bases at will.

Certainly, in spring 1999, no one felt that Alomar was assuming an air of indifference when he stepped onto the diamond.

"He showed up to play hard every day," recalls Mike Jackson, who was Cleveland's closer in the late 1990s. "Even though he knew he was the best in his position, he came out and showed up to play every single day."[6]

It wasn't just the on-field hustle. Realizing that 1999 was shaping up to be a career year that could pad his Hall of Fame credentials (indeed, his final numbers, a .323 batting average, twenty-four home runs, and 120 RBIs, were nothing short of spectacular), Alomar took great pride in being a student of the game. Whereas many teammates would kill time before the first pitch playing table tennis or PlayStation in the clubhouse, Alomar often sat quietly in front of his locker, poring over scouting reports on opposing pitchers.

Meticulously researched reports that he would later reference in the late innings. Jackson says,

> I remember one particular game we were down, and we needed a big hit. I was in the clubhouse—it was early in the game, maybe the fifth or sixth inning. I used to stay in the clubhouse around that time. Robbie came in and looked over notes about different pitchers. Next thing you knew, he went out there, and the guy must have thrown what he had charted in his scouting report because Robbie hit a home run to win the ballgame for us.[7]

"He just was so far ahead of everybody mentally," recalls Jim Ingraham, who served as the Indians beat writer for the *Lake County News-Herald/Lorain Journal* at this point in Alomar's career. "It was like watching an adult playing the game with children. He was a step ahead of everybody on every play, offensively, defensively. He just seemed to see the game better than everyone else."[8]

While Robbie certainly won many ballgames for Cleveland that year, his brother's impact was far less substantial, as he only played in thirty-seven games due to a career-threatening left knee injury. Even though Sandy's on-field contributions were minimal, his clubhouse presence, even more so than that of any of the team's stars, was immense. Particularly when he could inject some levity into a locker room full of guys grinding through the inevitable injuries and slumps that comprise a 162-game season.

One of Sandy's batterymates, right-handed starter Dave Burba, has never forgotten how Sandy liked to masquerade as a fan on a series of prank calls from an unknown number. Burba recalls,

> I would be driving home after a game, and I would get this phone call. And this weird person on the phone would tell me what a great job I did and how proud Cleveland was. I couldn't figure out who it was. I never asked, "Who is this?" I just said, "Thanks." This goes on every time I would pitch a good game. Somebody was messing with me. I couldn't figure it out. It took me about half the season, and I happened to be walking through the clubhouse, and I heard Sandy say something, and I stopped dead in my tracks and I said, "You're the dude that keeps calling." And he just started laughing.[9]

While Sandy could be a barrel of laughs, he was also a consummate professional who made Hargrove's life easier by keeping guys in line—including his hotshot younger brother. Back in spring training, when Robbie had tried to brush off a reporter asking for a few minutes of his time, Sandy grabbed Robbie's shoulder and gently said, "Do it now."[10] This wouldn't be the only time that the naturally extroverted Sandy, who was unfailingly polite to the media, tried to serve as a role model for his little bro.

"He [Roberto] was a star and he knew he was a star," says Paul Hoynes, longtime Indians beat writer for the *Plain Dealer*. "He was kind of a diva a little bit. He carried himself like regally almost. There was a little bit of an edge to him."[11] Toward both his happy-go-lucky teammates and reporters stressed by deadlines. Jim Ingraham remembers,

> Like a lot of stars, he had a pretty good opinion of himself. He was never humbled by the game, which you can't say about many other players. He had a little prima donna in him. I always had the feeling that he was kind of on his own little island at times when he was with the Indians. I don't think he was ever really that close with a lot of the players on the team. I think Robbie had understandably an inflated sense of himself. There were times when you had to wait overly long by his locker. He knew how great he was. He thought nothing of making others wait for him.[12]

Nevertheless, Roberto's reserved, standoffish demeanor was hardly concerning to Hart and Hargrove, who, as the season progressed, realized that a Cleveland lineup with him in the three-hole could easily account for over 100 wins.

Shortly after Alomar had signed with Cleveland back in November, John Hart remarked, "It would be worth the price of a ticket just to watch Omar and Robbie turn a double play."[13]

For those fans lucky enough to score tickets to Jacobs Field during summer 1999 (the ballpark was continuously selling out every night) they didn't feel cheated in this regard. Whether such fans were old enough to have seen Charlie Gehringer and Billy Rogell or too young to have memories of Lou Whitaker and Alan Trammell, there was a growing consensus among baseball enthusiasts—both in northeast Ohio and across America—that Alomar and Vizquel comprised the best double-play combo in the game's history.

At times, they looked more like acrobats, even trapeze artists, than middle infielders. Alomar diving into shallow right field to snag a scorching one-hopper, then shoveling the ball to Vizquel from *twenty-five feet* out; an airborne Vizquel making the glove-to-hand transfer in one fluid, effortless motion before firing to first base; Alomar making a diving backhanded stop on a hot shot up the middle before calmly flipping the ball to the bag; Vizquel catching the ball barehanded, tapping second base, leaping over the onrushing baserunner to fling a strike to first. While the acts of beautifully synchronized athleticism were astounding, the range covered by Alomar and Vizquel in the middle of the diamond was, quite simply, unprecedented.

"When those guys are on your team, you get to see it every single day," says Mike Jackson. "You get to see these guys make plays that a lot of major-league players could not make. I knew when I was out there on the mound, if I could keep the ball on the ground, in the infield, I knew that those guys were going to make some plays."[14]

Former shortstop Nomar Garciaparra was playing for the Boston Red Sox during the entire time Alomar and Vizquel were double-play partners. Decades later, he can still recall one particular twin killing:

> Literally the ball was hit and he [Alomar] did not move his feet. It looked like he just grabbed the ball with his hand and before you knew it, it was in his glove and it looked like he shuffled it to second without even looking. Still hasn't moved his feet. After he shuffled, he went back to kind of stretching as Omar was completing the double play. And then the first baseman threw it back to him and he still didn't even move his feet. He just kind of threw it back to Omar as they threw the ball around after they finished the double play. His feet never moved the whole time. It was so perfect. He just flicked it, like not even looking to second base. He knew it was a perfect toss. Omar was going to finish it and he was getting ready for the first baseman to throw back to him. It was one of the coolest things I've ever seen on a baseball field.[15]

Robbie and Omar weren't just middle infielders; they were artists with impeccable attention to the most minute detail. The infield wasn't just an arrangement of dirt and grass—it was a canvas requiring meticulous care. Otherwise, it wasn't worthy of their presence.

Fenway Park's notoriously choppy infield was a prime example of what irked Alomar, who was so paranoid about playing on unsmooth infields that he refused to wear his spikes during pregame infield practice. Garciaparra remembers the following story:

> I really liked to watch the way guys took groundballs, the way they practiced. So when we would go to Cleveland, they [the Indians] took batting practice first and the visiting team took it second. Well, I wanted to get there early and I would go out in the dugout and I would watch the way Omar Vizquel and Robbie would take groundballs to see if I could just pick up stuff. I mean their hands were amazing.
>
> And then when they would come to Fenway, they would hit second, so I'd go do my batting practice and I'd come back out to watch them take groundballs because I'd want to see how they positioned, just different things even at Fenway. Well, they didn't take groundballs. I was like, "I just missed them. I must have missed their time to take groundballs or they're taking them before even we take batting practice."
>
> So then in the offseason in passing I would see Robbie working out [Garciaparra and Alomar went to the same trainer in the offseason] and I said, "Hey Robbie, you know what's crazy—I come watch you take groundballs at batting practice [at Jacobs Field] but at Fenway, I come to look at you and I want to watch you take groundballs in practice. But do you not take groundballs there or do you take it at a different time?" He goes, "Oh, no, no, no. Omar and I never take groundballs there for batting practice. We like our space too much. Worst infield. That infield's so bad. No way. No thank you. We don't know how you do it every day."[16]

(Interestingly, the Fenway Park infield was one of the very few places where Alomar would regularly put his knee down on a routine grounder.)

By mid-season, as the narrative of Alomar and Vizquel forming the all-time greatest double-play partnership gained more traction, *Sports Illustrated* was interested in doing a cover shoot of the two Hispanic teammates, one that could fittingly encapsulate this historic development.

Apparently, Robbie had no interest in participating.

As double-play partners, Alomar and Vizquel may have left fans, teammates, opponents, managers, reporters, groundskeepers, batboys, and peanut vendors slack-jawed, but, unbeknownst to the public, theirs was an

often-frosty personal relationship. While they could (usually) coexist peacefully with one another, the reality was that Alomar didn't particularly care
for what he perceived as Vizquel's insouciant approach toward the game.
According to some reporters, Alomar felt that Vizquel, who was very fond of
late-night partying, coasted on his prodigious talents, that the game almost
came too easily to him. (Talk about irony.)

Paul Hoynes, who has been covering baseball in Cleveland since the days
of typewriters and Western Union transmissions, recalls,

> I don't think they [Alomar and Vizquel] were enemies, but they didn't go out
> together. It's not like they went out to dinner after games and stuff. Robbie
> was kind of late to the party here because Omar had been in Cleveland for ten,
> eleven years. Fans loved Omar. If he made an error, he was forgiven. He could
> do no wrong. I think Robbie kind of wanted that same affection from the fans.
> It's not like they didn't like Robbie, but he just hadn't been there long enough.
> He was a great player, but he didn't have his roots in Cleveland, like Vizquel
> did. They were kind of different personalities. Vizquel was a fun guy, he was
> always joking around in the locker room. He was easy to talk to. Robbie was a
> little more guarded.[17]

It should be noted that while Vizquel broke into the majors with the Seattle
Mariners, it was in Cleveland where he blossomed into an all-star.

"They clearly were not best of friends," adds Ingraham. "Neither one
wanted to give ground to the other one as far as the accolades they thought
they were entitled to. I don't think either one would have been unhappy if the
other one hadn't been on the team at that particular time. [But] I don't think
that whatever friction that might have been there ever manifested itself during a game on the field."[18]

Even Mike Hargrove later acknowledged in his autobiography, "They
[Alomar and Vizquel] didn't pal around, but they worked well together."[19]

A former teammate's perspective on an allegedly strained relationship:

"I don't remember anything negative or positive. Robbie was kind of a
quiet guy," says Cleveland starting pitcher Dave Burba, who, admittedly,
never spent much time outside of the clubhouse with either Alomar or
Vizquel.[20]

By leading a subdued and private baseball-centric life, Robbie was in many
ways the polar opposite of Omar. Indeed, Cleveland's shortstop was an en-

gaging, charismatic guy and a true Renaissance man whose off-field hobbies included playing the drums and painting. But his act wasn't for everyone. In addition to Alomar, there were other teammates who grew weary of Vizquel's brash attitude and showboating antics. In particular, former Cleveland closer Jose Mesa would later resent Vizquel after the shortstop called him out for blowing Game 7 of the 1997 World Series in the beginning of his autobiography, *Omar! My Life on and off the Field*. On more than one occasion, the Cleveland front office got calls from the state patrol or local police force citing complaints of Vizquel speeding in his Canary Yellow Porsche to the ballpark. And going into the 1999 season, Vizquel had been very outspoken in his displeasure with his current financial situation: with Alomar aboard, he was now the lowest-paid infielder in Cleveland. This didn't exactly endear him to his new teammate from the start.

(When cataclysmic mudslides wreaked havoc on Venezuela in December 1999, Vizquel phoned over a dozen current and former teammates to solicit donations in support of his countrymen. Alomar, despite being one of the wealthiest Cleveland players, was not one of them.)[21]

While off the field, their egos may have clashed at times, it was overwhelmingly indisputable that on the field, Alomar and Vizquel maintained a highly professional relationship.

Although the Indians failed to eclipse 100 wins, Hargrove's preseason challenge still achieved the desired result. After dropping its final three games, the club finished 97–65, winning the AL Central by a whopping 21.5 games. Most importantly, the ball club stayed engaged down the stretch, going a combined 34–22 in essentially meaningless August and September games. The resultant ninety-seven wins matched the mark set by the 1948 Tribe team that had captured the franchise's last World Series.

Going into the 1999 American League Division Series, Cleveland was expected to breeze past the Boston Red Sox, a team whose fortunes largely hinged on the right shoulder of ace Pedro Martinez. At least on paper, Boston's suspect lineup (young catcher Jason Varitek, coming off a .269 regular season, was Boston's number three batter, while Cleveland countered with Robbie Alomar in the three hole) and lack of pitching depth appeared vastly overmatched by an Indians team whose juggernaut lineup had scored over a thousand runs in the regular season. When a strained back forced Martinez to depart Game 1 after four innings, the 45,182 fans at The Jake let out a collective sigh of relief knowing that Boston's greatest asset, Martinez, who went 23–4 with a 2.07 ERA during the regular season, was shelved, perhaps for the balance of the series. After Cleveland bested Boston 3–2 that evening and then cruised to an 11–1 laugher the following afternoon with Alomar going 3–4 with a couple RBIs, an ALCS rematch against the vaunted Yankees appeared imminent.

But when the series shifted to Fenway Park over the weekend, the Red Sox, whose World Series drought was three decades longer than that of Cleveland, looked like a different team. Despite missing Nomar Garciaparra with a leg injury, Boston's lineup erupted in Game 3, staving off elimination with a 9–3 win.

The following evening, Mike Hargrove opted to go with workhorse ace Bartolo Colon on three days' rest (he had pitched eight innings in Game 1) to prevent the series from returning to Cleveland for a winner-take-all Game 5. The decision ultimately spelled the end of his decade-long managerial run in Cleveland.

Colon never gave his team a chance, as he got rocked for seven runs in the opening two frames before Boston's offense miraculously plated sixteen more runs to rout Cleveland by a football-like 23–7 score.

For Cleveland, what transpired publicly on the field was humiliating; what happened in the privacy of its dugout was apparently worse.

In the bottom of the seventh inning with his team down a dozen runs, Hargrove replaced Roberto with Enrique Wilson at second base. Reportedly, soon thereafter, a disgusted Alomar left his dugout seat and made his way to the toasty clubhouse, this time not to review scouting reports but, rather, to check out for the evening. Upon realizing Alomar's intent, third baseman Travis Fryman chased Alomar down the tunnel to the clubhouse and barked at him to get back to his teammates.

Fryman may have been a gentle soul, a guy who, while hunting in the offseason, would make painstaking efforts not to shoot a deer from farther than twenty yards away, out of fear that he wouldn't be accurate enough to kill Bambi instantly.[22] But he was no softie when it came to tolerating prima donna behavior. As a four-time all-star and one of the game's most highly respected and grittiest veterans, Fryman wasn't afraid to stand up to Alomar for ditching his teammates. In the tunnel, a profanity-laced argument ensued (shouts of "Fuck you, Fryman! Fuck you, Fryman!" were audible in the dugout) before Sandy stepped in. Once separated from Fryman, Roberto nestled into the clubhouse for the evening while the on-field bloodbath continued.[23] (Several months later, when Roberto arrived in Winter Haven for spring training, he found his locker next to Fryman's and promptly requested that his stall be relocated. Alomar's wish was granted, and he was moved next to Vizquel. When Vizquel arrived and learned whom his locker was next to, he requested a move.)[24]

Despite getting outscored by a 32–10 margin in Games 3 and 4, the Indians came home to a booming Jacobs Field for Game 5 on Columbus Day. (Today, it would be the Guardians playing on Indigenous Peoples' Day.) Since the mid-1990s, the ballpark had been rocking with excitement every time the Indians took the field, but tonight the crowd was extra jazzed. No way was an inferior Red Sox team going to derail the Tribe's curse-busting mission.

"Going over there in Cleveland, I remember how loud it would be," recalls Nomar Garciaparra. "Jacobs Field was one of the loudest places to play in baseball. It was so loud. I loved it. It was unbelievable. This was the time when they kept count of how many sell-outs [in a row they had]. There was a lot of playoff energy atmosphere even during the regular season, and then in the postseason it was a whole other level."[25]

Unfortunately, some fans did not represent northeast Ohio with dignity and respect this evening.

After three innings, Cleveland was leading 8–7 after pounding Boston pitchers Bret Saberhagen and Derek Lowe. Despite nursing a sore back, Pedro Martinez volunteered to (more like, demanded to) pitch. As the eventual '99 AL Cy Young winner walked out to the bullpen between innings, he was greeted by a "Fuck You, Pedro!" chant. Once he started doing his warm-up exercises in the visiting bullpen, the taunting grew more intense. One fan referred to the Boston ace as a "beaner," a slur referring to the diet of Latinos, while another deranged ticket-holder leaned over the bullpen railing and barked, "Pedro, if you get out there to pitch today, you're going to get shot!"[26]

Ultimately, the jeers and cowardly threats had no ill effect on Martinez. If anything, they provided further ammunition as he capped a remarkable regular season by tossing six no-hit innings. At 11:30 p.m. EST, when Martinez fanned Vizquel for his eighth strikeout, Jacobs Field was largely hushed: Boston's wounded ace had just silenced Cleveland's all-world lineup on the way to his team's series-clinching 12–8 win. Now, at the dawn of the twenty-first century, the Indians were ending their first century of existence with still only two World Series titles (1920, 1948).

While Alomar had a quiet Game 5 (1–4 with a double), he finished the series hitting .368, continuing to cement his legacy as a clutch postseason hitter. And for Cleveland, with Alomar in the middle of its ferocious lineup, one that promised to remain largely intact through the winter, there was a strong likelihood that it would contend again in 2000.

But not with the same manager.

The offseason leading up to the 2000 campaign was an eventful one for Roberto. In fact, he hardly had any time to dwell on the recent collapse against Boston. He was now engaged to tennis pro Mary Pierce and was accompanying his fiancée on tour stops in Europe, Hong Kong, and Australia. (The two celebrity athletes had been introduced to one another by a mutual friend in Sarasota several years earlier when Alomar was undergoing rehabilitation exercises.)

While Robbie was traveling the globe, the Indians were getting accustomed to a new manager, the first time they had to do so in a decade. As expected, Mike Hargrove had been fired shortly after the postseason debacle and would go on to manage Alomar's former team, the Baltimore Orioles, in 2000. This left the door open for hitting coach Charlie Manuel. The Indians quickly settled on Manuel to be their next skipper as his lineup had bludgeoned opponents at an astonishing rate in 1999. Still, John Hart knew the move would face some ridicule.

Despite his well-deserved reputation as a hitting guru, the laid-back Manuel was often derided as a country bumpkin because of his thick Appalachian drawl. In fact, the man was born in a car resting alongside a West Virginia byway and, along with ten siblings, raised in a three-bedroom house in backwoods Virginia. There were also significant concerns about his precarious state of physical health, as over the past decade, he had suffered two heart attacks, the latter of which necessitated quadruple bypass surgery. Manuel may have only been fifty-six years old, but with his underlying heart condition, not to mention weather-beaten old face and snow-white hair, he looked more like an elderly man than a middle-aged one.

Unfortunately, Manuel's health only took a turn for the worse in February 2000 when his colon ruptured, prompting emergency surgery to remove eight inches of the organ. While he had hoped to postpone a second operation, one that would reattach his colon, until the all-star break, Manuel felt compelled to have the procedure done in early May.

When a still-healing Manuel returned later in the month—he had to wear a colostomy bag under his uniform for several weeks—the Indians' on-field play didn't exactly ease Manuel's recovery. After playing .500 ball in May (which included a six-game losing streak), the Indians went 13–16 in June. As the team had virtually the same lineup as last year's edition and was not hit by the injury bug, the so-so start was particularly disappointing.

As was Roberto's growingly divisive clubhouse presence.

During a June 18 game against the Detroit Tigers, Alomar got beaned in the third inning by Willie Blair. Afterward, he was expecting Manuel to instruct either his starter, Jaime Navarro, or reliever, Justin Speier, to retaliate—especially considering this was the second consecutive year he had gotten plunked in the head by Detroit. However, Manuel, hesitant to do anything that would spark a Detroit rally, one that could have potentially jeopardized the eventual slump-busting 9–4 win, ordered no such vengeful act. So, Alomar went public with his postgame grievance following his team snapping another six-game skid.

"I give my heart and soul to this club," said Alomar to reporters hovering around his locker. "I play hurt all the time. I've been hit two times in the head by these guys. I don't think he [Blair] did it on purpose. But if we get hit in the head, they've got to get hit in the head."[27]

When asked if he had directed Navarro or Speier to retaliate, Alomar responded, "That doesn't come from me."[28]

While Alomar was certainly not the first or last star ballplayer to ever throw his manager under the Fung Wah, his dismissiveness toward Manuel was simply too egregious to ignore. At least from the perspective of writers who covered the team every day.

"I think Robbie always kind of fancied himself [as] the manager," acknowledges Hoynes two decades later.[29]

This sentiment was shared by other Cleveland scribes as well. In June 2002, when Roberto returned to Cleveland during his first year with the New York Mets, Chris Assenheimer of the *Chronicle-Telegram*, in reexamining

Roberto's brief time in Cleveland, wrote, "Alomar criticizing his manager [Charlie Manuel] wasn't a surprise. He publicly ridiculed former Orioles manager Ray Miller and had little respect for Manuel and his coaching staff. He was proud to say he didn't listen to any of them."[30]

A few weeks after the Detroit incident, Robbie's ongoing whining over inadequate protection finally backfired on him. During the last game before the all-star break on a sultry afternoon in Cincinnati, he got nailed by reliever Danny Graves in the top of the ninth inning. In the bottom half, with a runner on first and one out with his team up 5–1, Cleveland reliever Steve Karsay, knowing there would be hell to pay if he didn't retaliate, hit Reds catcher Eddie Taubensee.

Everyone assumed Alomar would be satisfied that his teammate stood up for him—especially considering the hit batsman helped the Reds rally for two runs in the ninth before the Indians escaped with a 5–3 win.

That was not the case, however.

Convinced that Karsay's method of exacting revenge didn't send a strong enough message, Robbie called out his young teammate minutes after the team had settled into the clubhouse.

Immediately, Sandy jumped to Karsay's defense. He did more than call out his little brother; he tore into Robbie, lambasting his selfishness. A few weeks earlier in Detroit, Sandy had sided with his sibling. But not this time. Even though Robbie was a devoted brother and uncle, one who had built a large house in the Cleveland suburb of Westlake for the express purpose of hosting his large family on holidays, Sandy couldn't stomach Robbie picking on an innocent teammate while continuously disrespecting the manager, who, in addition to battling colon issues, had recently been diagnosed with kidney cancer.

In this sense, Sandy continued serving as the team's de facto captain.

"There wasn't really a guy who was the voice for the team per se. If anybody, I would say Sandy Alomar," mentions Dave Burba.[31]

His voice was heard loud and clear this afternoon. Typically, the clubhouse doors swing open to the media approximately fifteen minutes after the last pitch. Today, it was closer to a half-hour. And with the only recognizable English words shouted back and forth being F-bombs, the reporters awaited entry, clueless as to what was transpiring. Paul Hoynes explains,

Robbie felt it [the pitch from Steve Karsay] didn't hit him hard enough or didn't hit him in the right spot. This is old Riverfront Stadium, and we're standing outside the clubhouse, and we hear these two guys *screaming* at each other in Spanish. We have no idea what's going on. It was loud and went on for about ten or fifteen minutes. I think Sandy was really, really upset with Robbie because he [Robbie] called out his teammates and just for acting the way he did.[32]

Eventually, third base coach Jim Riggleman intervened before punches were thrown. When the media was finally ushered in, the entire club remained tight-lipped about the fracas. In fact, it wasn't until later on that the root cause of the incident was leaked to the writers, who, for the sake of not wanting to burn their sources, chose not to write about it.

According to one longtime Cleveland Indians beat writer who wished to remain anonymous, the incidents in Detroit and Cincinnati were not isolated ones.

"Robbie called his teammates and manager out all the time off the record. Truth be told, dude was a jerk—from what I'm told. Not many of his teammates liked him, outside of his brother and that was iffy."[33]

While Robbie had his moments with teammates and could come across as the Lone Ranger of the clubhouse, he may not necessarily have been universally loathed within the walls of Jacobs Field. Largely because he was so damn talented and easily one of the American League's most valuable players every year that he donned a Cleveland uniform.

"He [Roberto Alomar] was a Hall of Fame–type caliber player, and we knew this guy was a Gold Glove on defense and just made our team much stronger," says Mike Jackson. "He's an RBI guy, average guy, he was very difficult to strike out. He didn't talk that much. He went out there and did his stuff on the field."[34]

Writers covering the Indians on a daily basis didn't feel inclined to publish reports about Robbie's repeated off-field incidents primarily because his superlative play was invariably the compelling narrative for the next day's paper. "Even though he was only with the Indians for three years, he was the best all-around player I've ever seen," says Jim Ingraham. "He never did the wrong thing on the field. He had every possible skill necessary to be a Hall of Famer."[35]

Paul Hoynes concurs. "He is the best overall player I have ever covered. I have been covering baseball since 1983. He was so smart defensively. He knew the game so well. He played in Cleveland three years, and I thought he could have been the MVP every year."[36]

The closest Alomar ever got to being named American League MVP was in 1999, when he finished third behind fellow Latin stars Ivan "Pudge" Rodriguez and Pedro Martinez.

As was the case throughout his career, even when Alomar was on the pine, his off-the-charts baseball IQ garnered respect from anyone within earshot.

When asked to recall his memories of Robbie, Dave Burba says,

> He just went about his business. Got to know him a little bit, sitting next to him on the bench. Some of the things that really stood out to me, he would sit there and tell me what the pitcher was going to throw. He started talking to me about how he figured it out or what he saw, and I thought that was quite amazing. He was so intelligent that he would sit there and he would have fun picking the pitcher apart, telling us what the pitches were going to be. A lot of times I sat next to him just so I could see if I could figure out how he was doing it. I just couldn't see what he saw. No wonder he was a Hall of Famer. I certainly enjoyed watching him play, having him as a teammate, and listening to him talk about the game.[37]

Most importantly, the off-field incidents did not prevent Alomar from having another sterling year in 2000. Undoubtedly, the extracurricular activity was merely a sidebar to Alomar's offensive production (.310, nineteen home runs, eighty-nine RBIs) and sparkling defense. Especially with Manny Ramirez as a teammate.

One of the game's most feared sluggers who had anchored the imposing Cleveland lineups of the 1990s, Ramirez had infuriated management during the 2000 season when he took his sweet time coming back from a hamstring injury. When Ramirez returned from a forty-four-game absence, he belted twenty-five homers in the final seventy-one games, but it wasn't enough to help Cleveland, which finished with a disappointing 90–72 record, overtake the Chicago White Sox for first place in the AL Central. Peeved that Ramirez's inexplicably prolonged DL stint may have cost the Tribe a postseason berth, the Cleveland front office let him walk as a free agent.

To compensate for Ramirez's departure, John Hart signed two-time American League MVP Juan Gonzalez to a one-year, $10-million contract for the 2001 season. (Ramirez signed with Boston for $160 million over eight years.)

No one was more excited about Cleveland acquiring the mustachioed slugger, who was coming off a miserable, injury-plagued season in Detroit, than Robbie. The two Puerto Rican natives had known each other since the late 1970s when they were Little League teammates. As a sign of his rosy outlook, in spring training, Robbie predicted that a happier and healthier Gonzalez would be good for 170 RBIs in 2001. While Gonzalez didn't make fans forget Manny Ramirez—starting in 2001, Jacobs Field was no longer selling out every night—he did knock in 140 runs by season's end, so Alomar's projection wasn't ridiculously off-base.

Even with Gonzalez onboard, Alomar was not particularly happy about playing another season for Charlie Manuel—it didn't help that Sandy was now playing for the White Sox—but the second baseman was healthy, and his continually brilliant five-tool play was reason alone to go up to the ticket window on game day and grab seats. By early July, Alomar was again in the running for American League MVP and was selected to his twelfth consecutive all-star team. During the Midsummer Classic at Safeco Field, Alomar (as well as everyone else in uniform) was once again eclipsed by Cal Ripken Jr., who, after having declared that 2001 would be his final season, was once again the center of attention. When Ripken jogged out to third base in the top of the first inning of his nineteenth and final All-Star Game, shortstop Alex Rodriguez came over and suggested they swap positions, a gesture meant to pay homage to Ripken's past life as a shortstop. In the bottom of the third inning, Ripken connected on a first-pitch batting practice fastball from Chan Ho Park for the game's first run. When Alomar entered the game in the sixth inning to replace starter Bret Boone, Ripken, who was later named game MVP, was taken out for Troy Glaus. In the late innings, Alomar went 0–2, but hardly any viewers nationwide were paying close attention once Ripken had exited.

For Alomar, Ripken's nineteen all-star nods were a tall order to match. At this relatively late stage of Alomar's career, it was hard to envision him getting selected seven more times. Still, no one foresaw the thirty-three-year-old future Hall of Famer playing in his last All-Star Game this evening.

After finishing the 2001 regular season with a career-high .336 batting average, Alomar fizzled in the postseason. In the American League Division Series against a 116-win Seattle Mariners team, whom the Indians had staged an epic twelve-run comeback win against back in August, Alomar batted .190.

During Game 5 in which Cleveland lost 3–1, Alomar had arguably his worst game of the season, as he went 0–4 while hitting into two double plays, neither of which he hustled to beat out.

Shortly after the ALDS, Cleveland's new GM, Mark Shapiro (Hart had gone to the Texas Rangers), informed Alomar, who was making $8 million per year while approaching his mid-thirties, that he was under orders from the front office to shed salary. Alomar responded by articulating his strong desire to stay in Cleveland. While delighted by this response, Shapiro couldn't promise a trade wouldn't materialize, but he did mention that Cleveland would have to be blown away with the return haul. Alomar left the meeting fairly confident he wouldn't be dealt, or if he were, there would be ample notice.

At 8 a.m. on December 11, Alomar received a call from Shapiro notifying him that he had been traded to the New York Mets. In the end, Alomar was the one blown away, as he was not only caught off guard by the sudden announcement, but also by the fact that the Indians received not one high-profile player in return. In exchange for Alomar *and* a couple prospects, the Mets only had to trade outfielder Matt Lawton, who was coming off a .277 season, middle-reliever Jerrod Riggan, outfield prospect Alex Escobar, and minor leaguers Billy Traber and Earl Snyder. "It was not a pleasant departure," recalls Paul Hoynes.[38]

A few months later when he was starting spring training with the Mets, Alomar told reporters, "He [Shapiro] told me if something was going to happen, he was going to let me know. He didn't let me know. That's it."[39]

Robbie was not the only one left feeling betrayed. Underwhelmed by the return package, Cleveland fans realized that management was clearly prioritizing profit margins over box scores. For new principal owner Larry Dolan, the bottom line was simply . . . the bottom line. Unsurprisingly, Shapiro left the winter meetings in Boston exclaiming he would have to wear a bulletproof vest upon returning to Cleveland. Trading away the franchise player would spark the dreaded talk of his team rebuilding.

Meanwhile, Alomar was bracing for his third different team in five seasons—while no longer competing in the American League.

But Alomar's career wasn't the only thing changing in his life.

He would be heading to the Big Apple as a bachelor after splitting up with fiancée Mary Pierce just before the holiday season.

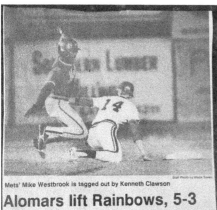

Mets' Mike Westbrook is tagged out by Kenneth Clawson

Staff Photo by Wade Spees

At the beginning of the 1985 season, neither Roberto nor Sandy was eighteen years of age, yet both contributed to the Charleston Rainbows' 78–61 record that summer. *Ken Clawson*

Alomars lift Rainbows, 5-3

By RAY COX
Post/Courier Reporter

The Charleston Rainbows injected a double dose of Alomar into the Columbia Mets Saturday night in College Park and came from behind to take a 5-3 victory.

When it wasn't Sandy Alomar Jr., who won't turn 19 years old until June 16, hustling a single into a double, it was just turned 17 Roberto Alomar, his brother, smacking two hits and driving in two runs. Roberto had the game-winning RBI in a three-run sixth inning.

"Nothing they do surprise me," said Rainbows manager Jim Skaalen. "Roberto is just a great athlete. He has the tools and he knows how to use them on the field. Sandy just made a good aggressive turn and made it into a double."

Sandy's hustling play opened the sixth. He hit a soft liner that Columbia starter and loser Doug Barba appeared to just snag with his throwing hand. It died in short center field.

While Mike Westbrook nonchalantly fielded the ball, Sandy never stopped running and with a Pete Rose headfirst slide into second set the tone for the inning. But the uprising had to wait about five minutes while Sandy recovered from a faceful of dirt, Skaalen said.

"I just started running and I saw him not running hard to get the ball and I said, 'Hey, I got a chance,'" said Sandy, whose fisher reached first

base for the Rainbows. The elder Alomar had a 15-year major-league career.

Kenneth Clawson, in a rare start at shortstop, followed with a sharp single up the middle with Sandy holding at third. Reliever Marion Hubbard sacrificed Clawson to second and set the stage for the switch-hitting Roberto Alomar.

Batting from the right side for the first time in the game, Roberto slapped a grounder in the hole between first and second on the first pitch for two RBI. He then stole his second base of the game and advanced to third on a wild pitch. He scored on a groundout by Rodney McCray.

The two Alomars were a combined 4-for-9 with four runs scored and one RBI. The other led off with hits in the three innings in which the Rainbows scored.

Roberto is off to a fast start with a team-leading 18 hits for a .563 average. Skaalen said Sandy had the best spring training average on the team but has yet to "start swinging it like he's capable."

"I did hit a lot stronger in the spring," said Sandy. "I'm in a slump and I get so anxious to hit. I just have to slow down and do my best.

"My brother is a good hitter and good fielder. I think he'll be one of the best in this league and any league."

Hubbard, who pitched four innings in relief of starter Robert Greenlee,

got his second victory. He gave up but two hits and struck out seven. Rusty Ford finished the ninth for his fourth save. The trio struck out 14 Mets.

NOTES
● The Rainbows conclude the three-game series with Columbia tonight at 7:30 at College Park on Family Nite. They go on the road to Florence for three games before returning home on Thursday for a six-game homestand.

During the Padres' spring training in 1986, a bunch of prospects were selected to go to Mexicali to play Mexico's All-Star team from the previous year. From left to right are Ed Puig, Joey Cora, and Roberto Alomar. *Ken Clawson*

Alomar posing for a photo before a game against the St. Louis Cardinals at Busch Stadium in 1990, which would turn out to be his last year in San Diego. *Ron Vesely*

From 1991 to 1995, there was arguably no more popular pro athlete in the entire province of Ontario than Roberto Alomar. *Ron Vesely*

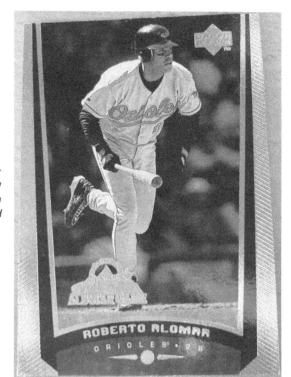

An Upper Deck baseball card of Roberto Alomar, circa 1999—when few players, if any, had more impressive numbers on the back of theirs. *David Ostrowsky*

The 1998 American League All-Star team. This All-Star Game would be the last Midsummer Classic in which Roberto (second row, far right) and Sandy (back row, standing next to teammate Jim Thome) played together. *Colorado Rockies*

Roberto would go on to win MVP of the 1998 All-Star Game at Coors Field by virtue of going 3–4 and scoring a pair of runs. *Colorado Rockies*

Even as he approached his mid-thirties, Roberto Alomar remained one of the most athletic middle infielders in the game. *New York Mets*

One of the best contact hitters of his generation, Roberto never whiffed more than ninety-six times in a single season. *New York Mets*

One of his rare moments of enjoyment as a New York Met. *New York Mets*

Roberto was a staunch advocate for the New York Mets hiring interpreters so that young Hispanic ballplayers, such as Jose Reyes, his one-time protégé, could feel more comfortable speaking to reporters. *Carly Goteiner*

For a short while, it appeared that Roberto had revived his career for a young D-backs team in spring 2004 before a Ben Sheets fastball broke a bone in his dominant hand, sending him to the DL. *Norm Hall/Arizona Diamondbacks*

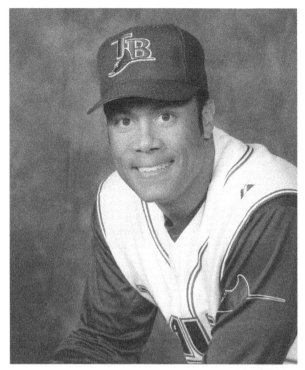

Roberto's time playing for the Tampa Bay Devil Rays was so short-lived that many fans struggle to recall the Hall of Famer playing for Lou Piniella's annual AL East cellar dwellers. *Tampa Bay Rays*

There are strong parallels between Carlos Beltran and Roberto Alomar: both switch-hitting Puerto Rican ballplayers had overall disappointing careers in Queens, not to mention well-publicized lapses in judgment (the Astros sign-stealing operation for Beltran, the spitting incident for Alomar) that forever tainted their respective legacies. Perhaps most importantly, however, both Alomar and Beltran were strong advocates for every MLB team being required to employ a Spanish-language interpreter, a development that finally came to fruition in 2016. *Carly Goteiner*

Pitcher of Fame Bert Blyleven was inducted along with Roberto into the Hall in 2011. Blyleven, pictured here signing an autograph for a fan during the Parade of Legends as part of HOF Induction Weekend in July 2017, is a regular at the annual festivities . . . unlike his former co-inductee, Alomar. *David Ostrowsky*

Whether it has been serving as Cleveland's bench coach, interim manager, or first base coach, Sandy Alomar Jr. has followed in the footsteps of his father, Sandy Alomar Sr., who enjoyed a lengthy coaching career after retiring as a player. *David Ostrowsky*

10

Back in Queens

When New York Mets manager Bobby Valentine picked up the phone on the evening of December 10, 2001, he didn't know whether to be angry or shocked. On the line was his boss, GM Steve Phillips, claiming the Mets had acquired Roberto Alomar, the .306 career hitter and ten-time Gold Glove winner.

Was this a prank?

Valentine was in no mood for pranks. A year removed from winning the NL pennant, his Mets had grossly underperformed in the '01 season, going 82–80. He wasn't about to get fired, but a slow start in the upcoming spring would trigger people calling for his head. He knew how the Big Apple worked.

He also got to know the Big Apple on a very personal level over the past three months, which was why he was still grieving. After one of his dear friends, a smokejumper called to duty when the twin towers collapsed, lost his life on 9/11, Valentine made it his business to get involved in relief efforts, whether it was consoling families at Ground Zero or stopping by funerals and firehouses across the New York metropolitan area.

And now he had to hear about the Mets (*the Mets?*) landing Alomar— pretty much the ideal player to stabilize the team's infield and provide a spark at the top of the order? It was a pipe dream for which he had neither time nor patience.

But this was no fantasy: Roberto Alomar was the newest member of the New York Mets. Nearly twenty years later, Bobby V. recalls how it all went down:

> I got a call late at night. I was in bed, and I picked up the phone. It was my GM [Steve Phillips]. He said, "We just got Robbie Alomar." I said, "Why would you wake me up with something like that? It's got to be bullshit." And he said, "No, it's true. It's done. He will be here tomorrow." I was in total disbelief. I think I then said, "What's wrong with him?" or something like that. But he [Phillips] said, "No, he has got a clean bill of health, everything is okay."[1]

At the time, Robbie Alomar and the New York Mets seemed to go together like peas and carrots: Alomar was familiar with Queens, having lived there for part of his childhood; his old man had played with Valentine, albeit briefly, on the Texas Rangers; several Latinos were on the team and quite a few Puerto Ricans lived in New York City; supposedly, there were worse cities than NYC to live in as a single guy—especially when you could look forward to luxuriating in a penthouse suite at the Avalon Riverview in Long Island City.

Ultimately, none of this mattered. For one and a half maddening seasons at Shea Stadium, Alomar endured the wrath of Mets fans and tabloid writers while Maria, back on the island, worried that her son was lonely living by himself in the big city.

Alomar struggled from Day One in Flushing. He finished April hitting .267 with eighteen strikeouts. In the season's opening month, he had more GIDPs (three) than stolen bases (two). Roberto never snapped out of the early-season funk and finished '02 with a .266 average (which tied a career low, set during his rookie season) while only slugging eleven homers (his lowest season total since the strike-truncated 1994 campaign). For the first time since 1989, he was not named to the all-star team.

When asked to recall what stands out from his one year managing Alomar with the Mets, Valentine responds, "How heartbroken I was almost every time he was playing."[2]

The saving grace for Alomar was that his teammates were hogging the back pages of the tabloids. It started in May when Valentine declared that baseball was ready for an openly gay player. In a New York minute, *New York Post* gossip columnist Neal Travis pounced on the opportunity to suggest a Mets star (most likely Mike Piazza) was gay. Subsequently, the Mets were forced to hold an official press conference whereby Piazza vehemently denied the rumor. A few weeks later Roger Clemens returned to Queens for the first time since the infamous bat throwing incident during the 2000 Subway Series. Naturally, there was a lot of hype for the interleague series. *How would the Mets get their long-awaited revenge?* (Mets starter Shawn Estes failed to deliver the ultimate payback when Clemens batted during his start in the middle game of the three-game set.) For good measure, right before the all-star break, pitcher Mark Corey acknowledged that he had been smoking dope with Tony Tarasco shortly before he had a seizure and collapsed on a street near Shea Stadium after a recent game. As the Mets went a combined 24–30 in May and June, it grew apparent that this year's club bore little resemblance to the 2000 squad that won the NL pennant or even the '01 edition that represented NYC with such great dignity after 9/11.

However, these sideshows eventually did fade away, and Alomar's inexplicable struggles became more exposed. While there were certainly other high-priced vets, such as Mo Vaughn and Jeromy Burnitz, having down years, it seemed that the fans were most demonstrative in taking out their frustration on Alomar. As far as New Yorkers were concerned, there were no excuses for why their new $8 million-a-year acquisition had morphed into a pedestrian ballplayer seemingly overnight. No one cared that he was adjusting to a pitcher-friendly home ballpark in a new league. Or that Valentine was moving him around in the batting order. After all, Alomar was on the right side of thirty-five and not battling any significant injuries. Not to mention, trading for Alomar meant that wildly popular second baseman Edgardo Alfonzo had to adjust to a new position at the hot corner. As the summer wore on, nearly every time Alomar strode to the plate at Shea a thunderous chorus of boos rained down on his handsome head. Alomar, of course, was no stranger to unruly cacophony directed toward him—provided that it was on the road.

Was it a bit too much from the Shea faithful?

"Yeah, I thought it was too much," answers Valentine.[3]

Of course, the New York media didn't help. The more Alomar scuffled, the more reporters from the *Daily News, Post, Newsday, Star-Ledger,* and *Journal News* reminded Mets nation that he wasn't even living up to the standards set by one of his predecessors, fellow countryman and good friend Carlos Baerga, who played for the Mets several years earlier. Granted, Baerga was in his prime when he played for the Mets, but couldn't Alomar at the very least hit .281 like Baerga had done during his 1997 season in Flushing? Valentine admits:

> Probably the biggest problem was that he [Alomar] followed Carlos Baerga. Carlos was not the player that Robbie was for his entire career, but for a couple years, he kind of was. He [Baerga] was a switch-hitter who would get close to 100 hits from both sides of the plate, hit with power. They both came from Cleveland. They were both terrific people. And yet the fans had a sour taste in their mouths from the expectation and how it compared to the performance. There were a lot of sportswriters and sports talk show hosts who quickly would conjure up the comparison, and I thought that was so unfair. They weren't looking at Robbie as a stand-alone entity. They were looking at him mixed in with the image of Carlos. I fought off those questions from the first month of the season.[4]

Particularly from the right side, Robbie was virtually an automatic out, batting just .204 with only nine extra-base hits, one of which happened to be his 200th career home run on August 24 at Coors Field. (At this point, it was impossible to deny his legacy as a five-tool star.) There was even slippage on defense with eleven errors committed. Valentine says,

> His smile was still there, but it always had a little sadness to it. Because he just wasn't the same player that he was a couple years prior. It happens sometimes when Father Time just turns that page. He was always impeccably dressed, and [there was] a wonderful presence to him. His look was that of someone who stepped off the cover of a magazine. He never shied away from a tough moment, and he had some tough moments. He was just always a great stand-up person.[5]

There were some troublemakers on the '02 Mets, but it does not appear that Alomar was one of them. In addition to the aforementioned marijuana incident involving Mark Corey and Tony Tarasco, there was outfielder Roger Cedeno getting arrested for driving under the influence. During a fan appreciation day in September, reliever Armando Benitez and shortstop Rey Ordonez refused to sign autographs. Several days later, Ordonez continued taking out his frustration on Mets fans by making a comment to the press in which he referred to them as "stupid." After a brief pregame dugout scuffle with Cedeno back in June, Alomar went about the season minding his own business—just as he had done for *most* of his career.

However, after maintaining a pleasant and fairly subdued presence throughout his first season in New York, Roberto felt inclined to speak out during the offseason about an issue near and dear to his heart. With so many Mets players hailing from Latin America (Cuba, Venezuela, Dominican Republic, and Puerto Rico were all represented) and not one Spanish-speaking coach or front office executive, Alomar made a public request for ownership to hire a liaison to counsel his fellow Latin American teammates and provide language interpretation services. As Alomar told ESPN's Bob Klapisch in January 2003, "Guys are afraid to speak because of the language problems, and that's not right."[6] Unfortunately, the Mets, under principal owner Fred Wilpon, made no such hire for the upcoming '03 season.

It was hard not to shame the club here. This seemed like a perfectly reasonable request—why not spend an extra $50,000 a year to make some of your core players more comfortable? It was also a thoughtful move on behalf of Alomar, who had been playing in the United States for over a decade yet still found the English language challenging to master. Unlike pretty much everything on the diamond, demonstrating fluency in English did not come easily to him. (Following Toronto's series-clinching victory in Game 6 of the 1993 Fall Classic, Alomar was asked about his club's pitching staff and responded by saying that he was "happy about them.") Thus, he could empathize with younger Latino ballplayers who had even more limited English proficiency and were tasked with answering reporters' rapid-fire questions in the postgame group interview sessions. Why should they come across as unsophisticated or insensitive or selfish just because they hadn't yet grasped the nuances of a new language?

While the Mets didn't respond favorably to Alomar's suggestion this offseason, his taking the initiative did lay the groundwork for significant institutional changes: a couple of years later, the team hired the game's only Hispanic general manager in Omar Minaya and added two Latino coaches to the staff. Meanwhile, Puerto Rican outfielder Carlos Beltran, who would join the Mets as Minaya's marquee free-agent acquisition before the 2005 season, picked up where Alomar had left off by eventually spearheading MLB's first-ever Spanish-language translator program, whereby each club would be required to hire one full-time interpreter.

Similar to how he addressed ballpark security matters, Roberto Alomar seemed to be ahead of his time on this critical issue as well.

The Mets opened camp in 2003 by welcoming aboard yet another Hispanic player: journeyman shortstop Rey Sanchez. For Alomar, the acquisition was especially meaningful because Sanchez's hometown was Rio Piedras, Puerto Rico, meaning he was now part of the first-ever all–Puerto Rican starting double-play combo.

"It's something to be proud of," Alomar said during spring training. "It's an accomplishment to be the first to do something. It's an honor just to be playing with Rey, and this will be an even greater honor, to be the first from Puerto Rico."[7]

Not only was Sanchez a native Puerto Rican, but he was also a mature, respectful professional—unlike Robbie's erstwhile double-play partner, Rey Ordonez. To help alleviate some of the toxicity that had seeped through the clubhouse the prior summer, the Mets acquired two other classy veterans, Tom Glavine and Mike Stanton, in the offseason. The club was also under fresh leadership as Valentine, after a seven-year run in Flushing, was supplanted by Art Howe. And it certainly was music to Alomar's ears when the new skipper vowed to maintain a more consistent lineup on a daily basis.

While newfound optimism pervaded the Mets' camp as Opening Day approached, there was the lingering concern for Alomar that a contract extension did not appear imminent. Despite the subpar 2002 season and resultant harsh reaction from fans and reporters, Alomar made it clear that he enjoyed playing in Queens and expressed interest in staying with the Mets beyond 2003. (It wasn't like he was the first guy to struggle during Year One in New York.) But the feelings weren't mutual. In addition to Alomar, there were five other Mets who had seven-figure salaries set to expire in October 2003, and Steve Phillips was eyeing a drastic roster overhaul. Ownership, in particular Fred Wilpon, liked Alomar, but it was hard to commit to a thirty-five-year-old likely headed toward the back nine, if he wasn't there already. Furthermore, the upcoming free-agent class was stacked with enticing names including Vladimir Guerrero, Andy Pettitte, and Miguel Tejada.

Once the season got underway, it appeared that Phillips had made the right call by not extending Alomar.

If anything, Alomar showed signs of regression from 2002. By the end of April, he was hitting .240 without a single bomb, demonstrating his days as a power threat were long gone. He was also no longer a threat on the base paths, as he had but two steals in the first month. In fact, he wasn't running much at all on the diamond, as he rarely sprinted down the line on routine grounders.

While it was a dismal first month to his second season in the Big Apple, Alomar upped his game during the most personally meaningful series, one against the Montreal Expos at San Juan's Estadio Hiram Bithorn. Playing in front of legions of his fellow countrymen, Alomar had a couple multi-hit games during the four-game series spanning April 11–14. As was the case throughout his career, when Alomar was motivated and happy, like he was in San Juan, his natural ability took over. But unfortunately, as this season dragged on (the Mets got off to an 11–17 start), Alomar was neither motivated nor happy.

There were myriad problems in Queens in 2003. On offense, the Puerto Rican duo of Alomar and Sanchez turned out to be a complete bust—even more so because of the latter's performance. Sanchez not only struggled to hit over .200 that spring, but he also did not live up to his reputation of being a consummate professional as he reportedly left the dugout for a clubhouse haircut during the fifth inning of a 13–4 loss to the St. Louis Cardinals on April 30. When word leaked out to the press about Sanchez's disappearing act, the humiliating incident served as a microcosm of the club's dysfunctionality. (Sanchez would get dealt to Seattle later that summer.) In addition to Alomar, there were other players (most notably veteran Cliff Floyd) who didn't exactly break a sweat trying to beat out grounders. Closer Armando Benitez was blowing saves seemingly on a nightly basis. Mike Piazza, the beloved face of the franchise, was essentially becoming a defensive liability behind the plate. Ailing first baseman Mo Vaughn was getting paid north of $17 million to play in twenty-seven games and hit .190. The end result was a trainwreck of a season in which the Mets swiftly nosedived toward the cellar of the NL East.

Alomar knew his days in New York were numbered. With the Mets going nowhere, the front office was looking to shed payroll and Alomar's $8 million salary was certainly not commensurate with his production. It was a foregone conclusion that by the July 31 trading deadline, Robbie would (once again) be wearing a new uniform.

Alomar's refusal to hustle between the lines and apathetic demeanor were undeniable. It was, quite frankly, inexcusable behavior for a professional athlete. But, unknown to the fans and even many writers, was Alomar's behind-the-scenes work mentoring younger teammates such as Ty Wigginton, Jeff Duncan, Joe McEwing, and, in particular, hot prospect Jose Reyes. This was a "Do as I say, not as I do" scenario. While Alomar was going through the motions for nine innings each night, he helped educate the quartet of youngsters through pointing out the game's nuances while demonstrating keen attention to detail.

"I was a young guy, and Robbie was toward the end of his career," says Duncan, who had a brief stint playing centerfield for the Mets in 2003. "He and I connected really well. He kind of took me under his wing. If we were on the road, he would take me to lunch, and I would pick his brain. One of the brightest baseball minds I have met along the way in my journey of baseball."[8] (During the prior season, Robbie had a similar influence on Roger Cedeno. As Bobby Valentine says, "I thought that Robbie helped unlock some of his [Cedeno's] treasure, his ability to be a switch-hitter who could steal bases and take over the game much the same as Robbie did most of his career. He helped him to the point that when they were separated, I think that Roger's progress was retarded.")[9]

Even with his professional demise imminent, Alomar's passion for baseball hadn't dimmed. And this unconditional love for the game didn't go unnoticed by some of the impressionable kids on New York's roster. Even with the losses mounting and boos amplifying, here was a guy who, at least some days, still got pleasure from his craft. Perhaps even more impressive was that amid the 24/7 distractions lurking in New York City, as well as on the road for that matter, Alomar maintained his laser-sharp focus on the sport—just as he had done as a curly-haired boy growing up along the southern coast of Puerto Rico. Duncan adds,

He [Alomar] wasn't in the limelight. [Mike] Piazza, he was a very popular figure in New York City. He was at the time the bachelor guy. You would see him in magazines. Tom Glavine wasn't as popular in New York City, but he had that Major League Baseball popularity and a lot of respect from a lot of people. Tom did a lot of other things too, like golfing. He was a big hockey player. He had a lot of balance. He had a family. Whereas for Robbie, baseball was his life.[10]

Robbie could have used a diversion this summer. Although his defense had improved considerably from the prior season, it wasn't enough to mask his offensive woes. For the month of June, he hit a quiet .250 and had three times as many strikeouts (nine) as walks (three). He didn't go deep once and drove in only three runs. In all likelihood, had Alomar not come with such a hefty price tag, a benching would have been in the cards.

That Alomar's best days were behind him was only natural. He was, after all, thirty-five years old and had broken into the big leagues while the Berlin Wall was still erect. Declining power numbers and slower bat speed were par for the course at this late stage—when one was not on performance-enhancing drugs, that is. While Alomar's career was representing the natural progression at this point, it was, quite literally, unbelievable how some of his contemporaries in their mid-thirties (Javy Lopez and Gary Sheffield come to mind) were suddenly posting the best offensive numbers of their careers. Later in the decade, a parade of MLB players would be associated with the steroid era that ultimately marked a sad chapter in the game's storied history. But by all accounts, there is not a single shred of evidence suggesting Alomar crossed over to the dark side. In this sense, he carried himself with dignity during his final days as a big leaguer. Even if Alomar didn't respect the game's integrity by blatantly refusing to hustle, he showed some regard for the sanctity of baseball by not committing the cardinal sin of cheating.

On July 1, Alomar got a head start on the upcoming holiday weekend celebrations when he was called into interim GM Jim Duquette's office (Steve Phillips had been let go a few weeks earlier) and told he was no longer part of the moribund Mets organization. Robbie, now a certifiable journeyman, was handed a one-way plane ticket to Chicago where he would be playing for the contending White Sox (his third team in three seasons) at hitter-friendly U.S. Cellular Field and in the familiar American League Central. For good measure, his brother was Chicago's backup catcher.

The Mets were in full rebuild mode. Leading up to the 2003 season, the plan was to supplement an aging core of players with free agents. That plan, of course, failed miserably, and now it was time to unload such veterans. For weeks, if not months, everyone in Queens had known that Alomar was a goner. While the trade was the furthest thing from a surprise, the end result was still a letdown for the Mets, as White Sox GM Ken Williams, coincidentally a former teammate of Alomar's, would not part with any serious prospects and only had to deal a trio of unexciting minor leaguers (pitchers Royce Ring and Edwin Almonte and infielder Andrew Salvo). Williams also refused to overpay for Alomar's services, only agreeing to fork over $150,000, the prorated share of the major-league minimum, while the Mets were still on the hook for $3.75 million of the remainder of Alomar's 2003 contract. Alomar was destined for Cooperstown, but the White Sox—like the rest of baseball—knew that he was now damaged goods and, more importantly, understood the Mets' predicament.

When the news broke, the New York writers were like great white sharks in the water smelling blood. The ink-stained reporters had been riding the club hard all season ("The media was all over us. There was a lot of negative media," recalls Jeff Duncan)[11] and Alomar, more so than anyone else, had been a human piñata for them. They weren't going to let up now. This was the writers' last opportunity to remind fans in the Tri-State Area that for the past couple seasons their hard-earned money had gone toward the lavish salary of a seemingly apathetic player whose performance had fallen drastically short of expectations.

A few of their parting shots:

Jack Curry of the *New York Times*: "Alomar was supposed to be one of the reasons they [Mets] contended, and, of all the players who have failed the Mets in the last season and a half, he was as big a failure and as much of an excuse-maker as anyone."[12]

Joe Gergen of *Newsday*: "Within hours after he was dealt to the White Sox, there was no trace of the man in the clubhouse. The locker he never fully occupied, at least not in body *and* soul, was bare before the Mets embarked upon the second half of a lost season. The memories he left behind were scant, even among teammates. Rarely, if ever, has an acknowledged superstar departed with less fanfare."[13]

Paul Schwartz of the *New York Post*: "Nary a tear was shed when news spread through the Mets clubhouse; his former teammates reacted with the sort of indifference Alomar often was accused of spreading."[14]

Before leaving for LaGuardia Airport to catch his short flight to the Windy City, Alomar went up to Duncan and reliever Dan Wheeler. With not a flashbulb or digital recorder in sight, the twelve-time all-star invited his less-heralded teammates to move into his Avalon Riverview penthouse suite for the rest of the season. For a nominal fee (less than what they were currently paying in rent), Duncan and Wheeler settled into the palatial unit, while enjoying high-end amenities and a spectacular view of the East River and Manhattan skyline.[15] Alomar didn't have to do this. He could have just terminated the lease (and saved a bundle in doing so). But he knew that neither guy had the funds to live in the Avalon Riverview at the time—Wheeler and Duncan were staying at a no-frills hotel near Shea Stadium, so the Avalon was an upgrade.

But Mets fans didn't know about Alomar's random act of kindness. They only knew that he was one of the biggest busts in franchise history and had appeared like a zombie every time he had stepped onto the diamond since April 2002. Indeed, when the trade went down, legions of passionate fans—from Staten Island to Long Island—let out a collective sigh of relief: they no longer had to watch Roberto Alomar pretend to care about the fortunes of the New York Mets.

In hindsight, it's a shame that Roberto Alomar and the Mets weren't a good combination. Had he played to his full potential and emerged as a cornerstone of the franchise, Roberto could have represented a beautifully sculpted bridge from Mike Piazza to David Wright.

End of the Road

On the evening of July 1, 2003, the Chicago White Sox acquired outfielder Carl Everett from the Texas Rangers after trading for Roberto Alomar in the afternoon. In the next morning's edition of the *Chicago Tribune*, noted sports columnist Rick Morrissey cracked, "Roberto Alomar and Carl Everett on the same day? This is like famine and pestilence strolling arm in arm into town, isn't it?"[1] Yes, in the span of several hours the ChiSox landed the two most notorious umpire baiters in recent memory (Everett had infamously head-butted umpire Ron Kulpa back in 2000), so lumping them together in this fashion was all too easy for the Chicago writers, who apparently were just as ruthless as their counterparts in New York.

Aside from the wisecracking Chicago media already on Alomar's case, playing for the White Sox promised to be a better experience than playing in Queens. The club's reputation hadn't been tarnished by off-field buffoonery. Highly esteemed veteran skipper Jerry Manuel was in charge and, similar to Roberto's favorite manager, Cito Gaston, he had a laissez-faire approach to managing. (As former White Sox reliever Mike Porzio recalls, "I think in some ways his [Manuel's] strength was that he put good people around him, and he let the good people do what they know how to do. That's what happens in a lot of big-league clubhouses, you assemble the best club you can, and then you just stand back and watch them play.")[2] The core of the roster was comprised of veterans Frank Thomas, Magglio Ordonez, Paul Konerko,

Bartolo Colon, Esteban Loaiza, and older brother Sandy, so the thirty-five-year-old Roberto fit right in. With Chicago in a dogfight for the AL Central, the next three months would be packed with meaningful games. There'd be pressure, but with the more popular crosstown Cubs also in the running for the postseason, not every inning of White Sox baseball was going to be dissected.

The early returns were encouraging: the White Sox went 17–9 in July and entered August only one game back of the surprising Kansas City Royals for first place in the AL Central. And Roberto, still nursing a sore left hip flexor that compounded his struggles batting right-handed, was contributing, albeit in a limited capacity. While starting against southpaws was pretty much out of the question, Alomar was still a threat versus righties. Against Tampa Bay's burly righty Victor Zambrano back on July 4, Alomar went 2–3 with two RBIs. The next evening, he cracked a couple more hits; the season average was creeping closer to a respectable .270. On July 12, a few days before the All-Star Game, which the White Sox happened to be hosting, Robbie, who Manuel acknowledged "could be kind of winding down," got on base three times with a pair of walks and a single.[3] Were these pennant race–altering performances? Not exactly, but Alomar was proving to be more than an eighth-inning defensive replacement, a role that some pundits had predicted would be his primary function in Chicago. Perhaps even more importantly, he was showing signs of life at the plate by no longer giving up on at bats early in the count and swinging halfheartedly at breaking balls in the dirt.

On a personal level, Alomar had something to prove. For one, he was slated to become a free agent in November. An improved second half could translate to one final seven-figure contract. Nothing wrong with that. Secondly, in the days following the trade, the New York media continued ripping him. One such example: Mets radio play-by-play man Gary Cohen went on a Chicago radio station and called Alomar "a disgrace from the day he arrived."[4] Above all else, Roberto did not want to be a "disgrace" in his new hometown, perhaps his final one as a ballplayer.

The only downside to joining a pennant contender such as the White Sox was that the club was not full of impressionable young rookies hungry for a future Hall of Famer's advice. In the spring in Queens, it seemed like every week there was a new twentysomething prospect strolling into the clubhouse to replace a soon-to-be-departing thirtysomething veteran—as well as the occasional "Four-A" player having a cup of coffee with the big-league team and eager for any pointers that might improve his chances of staying up. That was just the nature of being on a rebuilding team. But the 2003 White Sox were not rebuilding. They were very much in the hunt for a postseason berth and had no interest in shipping off their longest-tenured players. With no one coming up to his locker asking for bunting tips or how to properly execute the hit-and-run, Roberto didn't feel inclined to go out of his way to be anyone's big brother.

"He kept to himself," recalls Mike Porzio. "He did his own thing to prepare but it wasn't as interactive, in my experience, with all of the other people on the team. Robbie was going to get his work done. Not that he wouldn't help, of course he would. He was more, 'I'm going to get myself ready and do my part to be the best player I can be to help the team.'"[5]

Just like it had been in Cleveland a few years earlier when they were sharing the same clubhouse, Robbie's introverted nature stood in stark contrast to Sandy's gregariousness and joviality. If anything, it was an even more pronounced difference now, as Robbie was so new to the team while Sandy had been there since 2001 (although he did play for Colorado briefly in 2002) and had a well-established presence. Porzio adds,

> I think Sandy was more optimistic about things and definitely more outgoing. I think he made a good effort to lead the team in the right direction and be uplifting to teammates. I enjoyed his presence. He wasn't just all about himself. He cared about his teammates. Robbie, he was more reserved, whereas Sandy was more, hanging around the batting cage and shooting the shit with people. Not in any way a negative thing, it was just different personalities.[6]

It's very hard to glean insight into a teammate's personality when said individual is not only fairly reclusive but also only around for a few months. Nevertheless, one characteristic about Robbie that was strikingly obvious to Porzio, and presumably everyone else on the Chicago bench, was the guy's prescient ability to foretell what was about to transpire between the lines.

Porzio, who likens Alomar's keen intuition to that of slugger Larry Walker, another former teammate now in the Hall of Fame, says:

Some talented players see the game differently, and he [Alomar] had an unbelievable ability to know which pitches people were going to throw. It was really his ability to pick up pitches which I found uncanny. It was remarkable how often he could do that, because obviously major-league pitchers are pretty good at being deceptive and not tipping their hand at what they throw. I don't know if his vision was that good or it was just so many years of watching pitchers that he had every little nuance down. I was just fully in awe of how well he could do that. Things he did as a student of the game were amazing to me.[7]

In terms of becoming a true baseball savant, what really helped Alomar—in addition to being a hawk-eyed baseball lifer—was, in fact, his reticent nature. As teammates would make small talk about any number of things over the course of nine innings, Alomar mostly stayed quiet while maintaining his trademark laser-sharp focus on opposing pitchers. In doing so, he noticed the most subtle patterns in a pitcher's routine, whether it was someone tilting the glove a fraction of an inch closer to the chest for a fastball or lifting the front leg a half-second slower for a breaking ball. In turn, this information was disseminated throughout the dugout for the betterment of the team. So even though Alomar's on-field production was obviously limited at this late stage, he was able to contribute in other ways, namely by channeling his baseball acumen toward enlightening others.

Ultimately, both Roberto Alomar and the White Sox fizzled down the stretch of the 2003 season. The team went 29–25 over the final two months while fading out of the AL playoff picture. For Robbie, things got progressively worse after the all-star break. Following a subpar August (.235 average, nearly twice as many strikeouts as walks), he was relegated to part-time duty in September while posting a .221 average for the month. His second half in Chicago (.253 and seventeen RBIs) proved to be even worse than his first half in New York (.262, twenty-two ribbies). While he was still an above-average defensive second baseman, Alomar was inching closer to being an automatic out every time he strode to the plate. It literally seemed that dropping down a textbook bunt (a vastly overlooked skill that Robbie had mastered earlier in his big-league career) was his best offensive weapon at this point. That only two years earlier Alomar had hit for a career-high .336 made his current situation seem even more bleak.

And yet, despite the downward trajectory, Ken Williams and the rest of the White Sox brain trust expressed a strong interest in re-signing Roberto, even going so far as to offer a one-year, $2.5 million contract in December. But Roberto, with the firm backing of his agent, Jaime Torres, who insisted that his client only accept a two-year deal, passed. This turned out to be poor advice. No one was willing to commit to Roberto beyond one year—certainly not after the last two seasons. There were other suitors, namely the Los Angeles Dodgers, Montreal Expos, St. Louis Cardinals, and Colorado Rockies, but no franchise was budging on its one-year ultimatum. And these NL clubs weren't floating around the same kind of money that the White Sox had been discussing. Not to mention that Torres's hardline stance seemed to sour the relationship between Alomar and the White Sox, as the team's front office believed Roberto's camp was continuing to be unreasonable. (The White Sox contended that back in August, Williams and Alomar had a private conversation in which they had verbally agreed to a one-year deal worth $3 million. When Williams reached out to Torres to go over the details, the agent, already peeved that he had not been consulted initially, remained adamant that the contract be for two years—just like his stance now.) After the White Sox and Alomar decided to go their separate ways, Williams told the *Chicago Tribune*, "I'm disappointed that it didn't work out, but I'm even more disappointed that Robbie felt that at some point he was disrespected or not communicated with. This he said/she said thing is not worth my time. I'm not going down that road."[8]

By early January 2004, a new potential employer, the Arizona Diamondbacks, entered the picture. This was an enticing option. The D-Backs were coming off an 84–78 season and needed a new starter at second, as they had recently dealt Junior Spivey to the Milwaukee Brewers. In other words, this wasn't just a chance to platoon or serve in a utility role. Furthermore, joining Arizona meant reuniting with Carlos Baerga. So, when Arizona offered Alomar $1 million ($350,000 of which would be deferred without interest until 2009) to try to revive his career during the upcoming 2004 season, the superstar-turned-journeyman ballplayer couldn't decline. While the offer was a little disheartening—the salary was not even half of what Chicago had promised—Alomar had already made over $70 million in his major-league career (in addition to endorsement deals) so losing out on an extra one or two million was not exactly life-altering. Plus, as his agent Torres remarked at the time, "Robbie has saved enough in his career to live off the interest."[9]

Torres knew what he was talking about here. Even when he had started making serious money back in the early 1990s, Robbie, ever cognizant of his father's past financial struggles stemming from failed business endeavors, remained relatively thrifty. And as tens of millions of dollars flowed into his bank account in the ensuing years, Robbie, unlike many other prominent professional athletes of his generation, didn't go hog wild with extravagant purchases or loans to long-lost friends. Now, as retirement loomed, he could focus his attention exclusively on baseball—which is exactly what he did over the next six weeks before spring training got underway.

After settling into his new home in the Phoenix area, Robbie spent his days getting into tip-top shape at a state-of-the-art health club in Tempe. By mid-February, he had put on eight pounds of muscle and was leaner and meaner than he had been in years. He had good reason to bust his hump this off-season: there was a fairly strong chance it would be his last. In all likelihood, Arizona represented the final opportunity to revive his sinking career. While Cooperstown was pretty much a given, being a first-ballot Hall of Famer was not. Knowing that there were already writers who couldn't forget the Hirschbeck incident, he didn't want the recent debacle in Queens to serve as other scribes' lasting memory of his career.

But when baseball activities began in earnest during spring training, Alomar looked like a thirty-six-year-old who had devoted more than half his life to pro ball. He struggled advancing from first to third on a single. His range up the middle was quite limited—groundballs he used to snag with ease were now whistling past his glove. But the Diamondbacks, under manager Bob Brenly, weren't overly disappointed. They had invested very little in what was essentially a long-shot of a reclamation project.

While the team's fortunes weren't resting on his ability to play a serviceable second base and perhaps hit .280, there was the expectation that Alomar could lend his expertise to others. After winning the World Series in 2001, the Diamondbacks were trying to rebuild, as the clubhouse was now teeming with prospects. Alomar's wealth of knowledge, coupled with his willingness to mentor young guys, which he had recently demonstrated in New York, made him a true asset. At least, theoretically.

Corner infielder Shea Hillenbrand, who, in 2004, was embarking on his first full season with Arizona, says,

> It's so crazy how someone of Robbie Alomar's caliber, how they perceive the game, how they envision it. Their perspective is so much different. I think a lot of guys didn't take advantage of that. I think we were at the point where the game had shifted to where you have the rookies and you have the young kids that are entitled. I think that might have rubbed Robbie the wrong way. Younger players really didn't choose to take advantage of opportunities to be in the presence of someone that great. You'd be an idiot if you didn't utilize him as a resource to do everything you could to better your game.[10]

Hillenbrand certainly did. To this day he raves about Alomar and, quite frankly, is unable to say enough nice things about him. The former two-time all-star adds,

> I always found myself at his locker, picking his brain. I always went over there, first and foremost to talk about baseball. At this point in his career, he had accomplished so much, and he was at the tail end of his career to where now a guy like that, they're really approachable. I was never afraid to approach a guy like that in the clubhouse, but, most importantly, Robbie always made you feel welcome. His passion for people and the passion for the game were really contagious. I think his passion for helping other people was above and beyond his passion for playing baseball. Baseball is in his DNA because he is an Alomar, but what stood out was how he took that time to be present and to help you and to not make you feel like you were a distraction or an annoyance. Whenever I went over there to talk about how to field a groundball, or how to throw a baseball, or how to hit, it always seemed like the conversation took a detour to life. About being a man, about how to navigate off the field.[11]

Once the regular season began in April, Hillenbrand opened up to Alomar about a rather unusual personal problem. In the midst of an early-season slump, Shea would return home to situations straight out of the film *Poltergeist*. As he recalls, the oven would turn on out of the blue (yes, this could have been quite dangerous); the radio would change stations on its own; lights would randomly flicker on and off. Upon explaining his predicament to Alomar, he was delighted to hear he wasn't the only ballplayer alive who had ever experienced a brush with the supernatural.

"I had ghosts in my house, so I thought," explains Hillenbrand. "I had things that were going on crazy in my house in Arizona, and he [Alomar] sent me to one of his friends and told me how to navigate to get these ghosts or spirits or whatever they were out of my house."[12]

Hillenbrand recalls getting in touch with Alomar's go-to paranormal investigator, who asked to see pictures of the supposedly ghostly rooms. Shortly thereafter, Hillenbrand's suspicions were confirmed when he heard back that there was an apparition of a man with a top hat, striped shirt, and blue jeans in the family room and another one of a small child in an upstairs room. The subsequent advice was straightforward and simple: burn sage in each room and open up all the windows and doors and all the spirits will leave, and when you close the windows and doors you put certain types of seeds over each door so the spirits can't return. Hillenbrand dutifully followed the instructions and, ultimately, didn't have to ask for a refund.

"Apparently, it worked because after I did this seance in my house—I'm opening the windows and burning sage and I think my neighbors probably thought I was smoking marijuana or doing some kind of satanic ritual—nothing happened after that. That's the crazy thing—it worked. I'm glad social media wasn't around back then."[13]

Perhaps it was merely coincidental, but Hillenbrand's season took off after he had performed the cleansing rituals. After hitting .184 in April, he was good for a .304 average in May and went on to have a career year at the plate.

The Diamondbacks got off to a 4–9 start due in part to Alomar's ongoing struggles. During the first two weeks of the season, he hit .222—a regression from even the past couple downright mediocre seasons—and was demonstrating significantly limited range at second, just as he had during spring training. The erstwhile all-star was never expected to be the linchpin of Arizona's lineup or reemerge as a Gold Glove recipient, but, even so, this was a rather underwhelming start.

On the evening of April 20 when the D-Backs visited the Milwaukee Brewers for the opener of a three-game series, young hurler Ben Sheets drilled Alomar in the right hand with a fastball in the top of the sixth inning. After learning that he had suffered a broken bone in his dominant hand and was likely shelved for at least a month, Alomar acknowledged, "It's going to be tough to deal with, and at my age it's [tougher]. I'm already 36, and in the game of baseball you never know when it's going to be over. . . . I'm going to try and deal with it the best I can, and I'm going to try to be there for my teammates."[14]

There was no guarantee the starting job at second would still be his upon returning from the DL. There was gritty twenty-six-year-old second baseman Matt Kata coming off a solid rookie year and eager to prove he could be an everyday big leaguer. Alomar's absence also meant that the club's top prospect, Scott Hairston, a career .323 hitter in the minors, was likely to get called up for an extended time.

Would Alomar accept a bench role for a noncontending team? Even if he could return in a starting role, was there really a point in pushing forward given his limitations? It seemed like a serious possibility that Roberto Alomar had played in his final major-league game.

"It [Alomar's injury] was so disheartening," Hillenbrand says. "I hated it, probably more so than he did, because having a guy like that in the lineup—regardless if he produces or not—having him in your presence and on the field is just magical. When we lost Robbie in that situation, I was just like, 'Okay, here we go.'"[15]

Robbie showed some grit and determination here. The easy thing to do would have been to hang 'em up. He had nothing left to prove on the diamond. He was a legacy player who was a shell of his former self with his eyesight, reflexes, and agility declining by the day. But he chose not to step away from the game he had been playing for a third of a century. He had made a one-year commitment to Arizona, and he wasn't going to renege on his promise.

After a two-month rehab, Robbie rejoined a Diamondbacks team that was seventeen games under .500. He wasn't exactly entering a high-stakes pennant race, and that wasn't necessarily a bad thing—especially after last year when he was playing for big-market teams with high expectations. And he wasn't the everyday starter at second either, as the rookie Hairston had demonstrated considerable potential since the call-up. For one of the precious few times in his professional career, Robbie would have to accept being a platoon player.

Apparently, the role didn't bother him because he started hitting the cover off the ball by the end of June. In fact, in just over a week, from June 30 to July 8, he collected twelve hits and drove in a handful of runs. After cooling off a bit over the next few weeks (pinch-hitting just wasn't for him), Robbie had his best offensive game in years on August 4 against the Florida Marlins: 4–5 with three RBIs. He even cleared the fences in the sixth. Perhaps this was shaping up to be a career-reviving season in the desert: his average stood at .309, and he was displaying more than warning-track power; the defense was solid—only three errors thus far; with the broken hand behind him, there were no significant injury concerns; his candidacy as a first-ballot Hall of Famer even got a recent boost, as he had just reached 2,700 hits—suddenly, 3,000 didn't seem so farfetched.

Alas, it was not to be. On the morning of August 5—literally hours after his banner night against the Marlins—Arizona traded Roberto to the Chicago White Sox for a player to be named later (it was eventually minor-league reliever Brad Murray, who would quit baseball soon after he landed in Arizona in February 2005) and cash.

Through no fault of his own, Roberto had little value to the Diamondbacks, who were headed for their worst season ever (far worse than their inaugural 1998 campaign) and thinking only in the future tense. The club was unloading veterans—they had just parted with graybeards Steve Finley and Brent Mayne a week earlier—and was focused on development. If anything, Roberto's recent production had exceeded expectations, but the rebuilding franchise couldn't justify keeping a player nearing retirement who was taking at bats away from up-and-comers like Matt Kata and Scott Hairston.

"[Robbie and I] were the two most experienced players on the team," recalls Randy Johnson, still the most iconic player in franchise history. "The 2004 team, I think we lost 100 games. [It was actually 111.] It was the franchise's worst year record-wise. Overall, I don't think we need to open up that can of worms again."[16]

A team that loses over one hundred games is bound to have considerable turmoil, and the 2004 D-Backs were no exception. Perhaps the emblematic moment of said turbulence occurred on July 9—a week after manager Bob Brenly had been canned—when outfielder Luis Gonzalez dropped a fifth-inning fly ball in San Francisco that led to three unearned runs. Johnson later confronted Gonzalez in the dugout, and the two veterans got into a brief altercation that nevertheless went public. The Big Unit continues,

That was an extremely hard year, but it was a transition year for the organization. We had won a World Series three years before, and they were transitioning into a much younger team then. If nothing else, 2004 was a one-game highlight [he threw a perfect game that May]. I have been retired now for eleven years, and I have so many other interests now. My memories are so foggy [with] it being so long ago.[17]

It's hard to blame Johnson for having a selective memory. Likewise, it's hard to blame Roberto if he wasn't heartbroken about leaving a team nosediving toward a 51–111 finish. Who would want to (potentially) close out his career in that manner? And getting traded back to the White Sox wasn't the worst-case scenario. It wasn't like the Diamondbacks had jettisoned him to Milwaukee or Oakland. Roberto was actually quite comfortable and familiar with the Windy City. The ChiSox still had his big brother, and their first-year manager, Ozzie Guillen, was a fellow Latino who hailed from Venezuela. Meanwhile, getting reacquired by Chicago was a confidence booster—for the second consecutive summer Ken Williams thought his services could be helpful in overtaking the Twins in the AL Central.

But unlike last summer, the AL Central race was not really a race at all. The White Sox were slightly worse, and the Twins were slightly better, resulting in the latter taking the division by nine games. Over the course of eighteen virtually meaningless late-season games (Roberto sat out the last few weeks with a sore back), he hit a soft .180 while reportedly struggling with his vision—a rather disturbing sign for a hitter, akin to a chef with impaired taste. Unsurprisingly, less than a week after Chicago's ho-hum season concluded, the front office declined to offer Alomar arbitration, and he was subsequently granted free agency.

But after his mini-resurgence in Arizona, Roberto wasn't done with baseball—not when he was a couple of half-decent, injury-free seasons away from 3,000 hits. But was baseball done with him? Would there be any takers this coming winter? He was in an awkward predicament. For most ancient players trying to hang on the solution is simple: leave the mitt at home and make yourself into a semi-productive DH. But Roberto's situation was the opposite. His ability to produce offensively was the wild card (painful to acknowledge for a lifetime .300 hitter), but he was still fairly reliable with the glove, as he had only made one error down the stretch for Chicago.

While American League clubs had hardly any extra incentive to sign Roberto because he possessed little value as a DH, the Tampa Bay Devil Rays were willing to take a flier on him. Not wanting to outbid themselves, the Devil Rays offered Alomar a lowball one-year contract worth $600,000. The only other team remotely interested in Roberto's services was the St. Louis Cardinals who, unlike Tampa, couldn't offer him a chance to be the starting second baseman. Thus, Alomar was headed to the Devil Rays, his eighth big-league team and fourth in the past two years.

It didn't take long for Roberto to feel out of place in Tampa Bay's spring training camp. It was an exceptionally young roster, which, this being the mid-2000s, meant that the clubhouse was packed with tattooed millennials consumed with their iPods and flip phones. How things had changed since the mid-1980s when he first started reporting to training camps and mullets and Walkmans were in vogue.

Once day-to-day activities got underway, it grew even more apparent that Roberto was of a different generation than most of his teammates. He had to be extra mindful of taking care of his thirty-seven-year-old body and, to his credit, made a concerted effort to do so. When workouts ended at the team's training complex in St. Petersburg, most guys would hit the showers, dress, and then bolt to the links, fishing charters, or strip clubs. Roberto was the only one who consistently stayed late for more stretching, exercising, and icing. (He was still experiencing lingering soreness in his lower back.) There were many afternoons when the only people left in the clubhouse were the twelve-time all-star and a few clubhouse workers cleaning jockstraps and scraping dirt off cleats.

A week into camp, Alomar sat down with Tom Jones of the *St. Petersburg Times* and was quite candid in explaining the source of his heightened motivation:

"I think if it takes 3,000 hits to get the Hall of Fame, I'm going to try to get there. It's big. Not a lot of players get the chance to get there. Now that I'm close, it would be a treat."[18]

Roberto was (relatively) close—276 base knocks away from the sacred milestone. And he wasn't *that old*, still a few years shy of turning forty. He felt confident that he had two or maybe even three more seasons left in him, even though his performance over the last three summers suggested otherwise.

And deep down, Alomar knew there really was no pressure in pursuing 3,000 hits: if he fell short, enshrinement in Cooperstown was still inevitable.

By early March, it was painfully obvious that Alomar had no chance of playing another couple seasons. With the stiff back forcing him to miss a string of exhibition games, Alomar was relegated to hitting off the tee and jogging for a solid week. When he did resume taking infield practice, his mobility and range were notably poor. Slightly errant throws from shortstop Julio Lugo or third baseman Alex Gonzalez were invariably finding their way to the outfield. Bending down to glove a grounder became a laborious task. And his ability to get around on a big-league fastball had completely vanished—he was still searching for his first hit all spring. It seemed like a foregone conclusion that Jorge Cantu, a twenty-three-year-old kid previously presumed to be Alomar's backup, was now the club's Opening Day second baseman.

Even as Roberto continued struggling in all facets of the game, Devil Rays manager Lou Piniella, a former teammate of his dad's back in the 1970s in New York, remained loyal to his veteran. On March 18, he was even penciled in as the starting second baseman against Toronto.

Fortunately, it was not a nationally televised game whose outcome actually mattered.

In the top of the first, the erstwhile Gold Glove winner made a pair of errors. Two errors in one inning? In his glory years, Roberto wasn't accustomed to making two errors in one month. After striking out in the bottom half, Roberto went over to Piniella and excused himself from the rest of the game.

It was time.

His body—from his eyeballs down to his ankles—was failing him. He wasn't half the player he had been merely four years ago when he had hit .336 and driven in 100. And the honest truth was that he probably wasn't even half the player he had been as a slender teen roaming the sandlots of Puerto Rico. He had made a valiant effort to stage a comeback—it wasn't like he had quit in the middle of the hellacious 2003 season—but now realized the game had passed him by.

During the next day's press conference at Progress Energy Park in St. Petersburg, Alomar remarked, "I played a lot of games and I said I would never embarrass myself on the field. I had a long career, but I can't play at the level I want to play, so it's time to retire."[19]

By all accounts, Roberto never resorted to performance-enhancing drugs to prolong his career. Just a couple of days earlier in the week, some of his contemporaries—Rafael Palmeiro, Mark McGwire, Sammy Sosa—had been grilled about their alleged steroid use during a congressional hearing. Roberto was never suspected of using PEDs to artificially rejuvenate his career—no small accomplishment during the steroid era when dozens, if not hundreds, of other aging players turned to chemists instead of trainers and magically saw their careers take off. Indeed, because Roberto abided by the rules and honored the integrity of the game, his career followed the natural trajectory. Which meant it was time to walk away.

12

Trouble in Paradise

For the first four years of retirement, everything had gone according to plan for Roberto Alomar. He was enjoying a quiet and private life. Occasionally, he would play in a celebrity golf tournament or make a public appearance for the Toronto Blue Jays, whether it was gladhanding fans and sponsors during the team's annual Winter Fest or throwing out the first pitch before a random game, but for the overwhelming majority of his post-playing days, he stayed at arm's length from the public. Just the way he liked it. While his primary residence was in the tony Whitestone neighborhood of Queens, Alomar also spent time back home in Puerto Rico as well as in Tampa and Toronto. No one was keeping tabs on his whereabouts now that his celebrity status was fading.

All that changed on Wednesday, February 11, 2009.

As America was in the throes of its worst economic downturn since the Great Depression, a cringeworthy story involving Roberto's sex life hit the newsstands. Ex-girlfriend Ilya Dall, whom Roberto had started dating when he was playing for the Mets, filed a lawsuit in federal court alleging that over the past several years, he had insisted on engaging in unprotected sex while suffering from HIV. The thirty-one-year-old Queens resident had previously lived with Alomar (along with her two children) and was now demanding $15 million in punitive damages for Alomar exhibiting "gross and wanton negligence" in constantly refusing to undergo testing even while developing symptoms associated with HIV such as white spots on his mouth and throat, a yeast infection, and shingles.[1]

In response to the disturbing allegations, one of Alomar's attorneys, Luke Pittoni, told the *New York Times* in a phone interview, "We believe this is a totally frivolous lawsuit. These allegations are baseless. He's healthy and would like to keep his health status private."[2] (Alomar, himself, would only make a terse statement echoing his lawyer's message that he was healthy and the lawsuit was full of lies.)

Alomar's current lover, Puerto Rican swimsuit model Maripily Rivera, stood firmly behind her man when she told a Puerto Rico TV station, "It's not true. When you're on the side of truth, you have nothing to hide. I support him and I love him more than ever. They want to destroy him, but they won't be able to."[3]

According to the lawsuit, Alomar allegedly "lied and purposefully misrepresented his physical condition" and "was endangering the health and well-being of [Dall] by continuing to have unprotected sexual relations with [her]."[4]

Clearly, someone was lying. Was it Alomar's camp? Or was it Roberto's old flame, Dall? Either way, once details of the allegedly unhealthy relationship emerged from the seventeen-page lawsuit, Roberto was beyond humiliated. Dall claimed that in April 2005, a month after Roberto had retired, he began showing the aforementioned signs of having contracted the virus, yet he refused to submit to HIV testing. As referenced in the lawsuit, the ex-ballplayer claimed that he had already undergone multiple tests yielding negative results. Per the suit, once Alomar reassured her that he was not a carrier of the sexually transmitted disease, she resumed having unprotected intercourse with him . . . until February 6, 2006, when the couple learned that Alomar had indeed tested positive for HIV. There was more. Weeks later, the lawsuit continued, a physician advised the couple that Alomar, now too weak to walk and foaming at the mouth, was infected with full-blown AIDS, which was allegedly confirmed by a spinal tap. Perhaps the most gruesome detail in the lawsuit was Dell's allegation that in 2005, Alomar told her he was sexually assaulted by two men when he was seventeen—meaning he should have known he was at risk for HIV.[5]

Important issues regarding Dall's claims were soon raised. Dall had tested negative for HIV on multiple occasions, yet in 2009 she was still plagued by

"AIDS phobia," whereby she was supposedly in a perpetual state of fear that disrupted her eating and sleeping habits. Although symptoms can remain dormant for several years, the disease is typically picked up by blood tests from four to twelve weeks after possible infection. Then there was the claim that Dall's two children were put at risk because Alomar had kissed them and they had shared the same bathroom facilities. As medical professionals were quick to point out, it is highly unlikely for one to contract HIV from routine household exposure. And then the question was asked that if, in fact, Alomar had tested positive for AIDS in February 2006, why did Dall continue living with him until October 2008—especially considering how much she said she agonized over her health as well as that of her children?[6] (There were no indications that Alomar ever threatened violence against her if she decided to leave, and Dall even acknowledged that he never laid a finger on her.)

Alomar and his attorneys claimed that he was healthy but, at least initially, his attorneys didn't explicitly state that he wasn't infected with HIV. (Eventually, Roberto would steadfastly deny being HIV-positive, though he never would provide proof of his negative status.) Roberto's father, Sandy, the bench coach of the New York Mets at the time, told the *New York Daily News* he had never before heard rumors of his son having AIDS. He claimed that whenever he had seen Roberto over the past year, his boy appeared as healthy as ever. With so much conflicting information present, it seemed like a messy and lengthy legal affair was imminent.

It turned out to be the exact opposite. Less than three months after the allegations were made public, Alomar scored a legal victory when Dall withdrew her original $15 million civil suit. Reportedly, Alomar and his exgirlfriend reached a private settlement, the financial terms of which were not announced.[7]

It seemed that Roberto's public image, which he had worked so hard to restore since 1996, was not going to take another beating. The scandal quickly faded from the public's conscience. As spring bled into summer, it was like it never happened.

Roberto moved on from the imbroglio pretty quickly. By summer 2009 he was married to Maripily Rivera, dubbed in gossip circles as the Paris Hilton of Puerto Rico. (They were officially married on June 1 before a judge in Puerto Rico without any pomp and circumstance.) The celebrity couple was preparing to move into an 18,703-square-foot mansion in the gated Avila community north of downtown Tampa where, surely, they could stay out of the public eye. Which meant, as far as Roberto was concerned, the days of being the subject of ignominious tabloid headlines were over.

Or so he thought.

August 2010. Barely a year after tying the knot with Roberto, Maripily obtained a temporary injunction for protection against domestic violence against her now-estranged husband. According to Maripily, over the past several months Roberto had assaulted her on three separate occasions, including one incident in which he threatened her with a knife. Roberto subsequently denied said claims and filed for divorce, alleging that Maripily had previously threatened divorce unless she received partial ownership of the Tampa mansion. The court gave Maripily the benefit of the doubt and ordered Roberto to vacate their home while only affording him a tiny window to collect some of his valuables, most notably his Ferrari and Rolls-Royce. He was also ordered to not get within five hundred feet of Maripily and was forbidden from trying to contact her.[8]

How did this new relationship turn so toxic in less than a year? Well, as it would turn out, Ilya Dall wasn't Roberto's only former partner claiming that he had insisted on not using a condom during intercourse despite his (allegedly) knowing that he had HIV. After settling with Dall in May 2009, Roberto soon faced a $6 million lawsuit filed by noted merengue singer Giselle Ortiz on the grounds that Roberto's alleged HIV-positive status was causing her severe emotional duress. Yet another former girlfriend, pro tennis player Meghann Shaughnessy, soon raised similar claims of duress caused by Alomar's alleged HIV-positive status and subsequently engaged in settlement talks with Alomar's attorneys.[9] (Shaughnessy's legal team drafted, but never filed, a lawsuit seeking unspecified punitive damages that was ultimately mailed to Alomar for settlement purposes. Per the legal draft, Shaughnessy claimed that she and Alomar had been in a romantic relationship in 2004 and 2005, although at the time she did not know that Alomar was living with Dall. In the legal draft, Shaughnessy alleged that Alomar would neither confirm nor deny whether he had HIV. She also said that he refused to provide her with his medical records for confirming or denying that he carried the virus.)[10] That multiple women started coming forward seeking money from Roberto naturally caused significant tension between the newlyweds, hence the heated arguments leading to Roberto's alleged acts of domestic abuse. It is worth noting that Maripily claimed to have believed Alomar's denials about the other women's HIV claims until she learned of the financial settlements that he had reached with them.[11]

By late 2010, Maripily wasn't just seeking a restraining order against Roberto: she was gearing up for her date in court. The model wanted financial compensation for not only the physical abuse Roberto inflicted upon her but also for the mental anguish stemming from his false reassurance that he was healthy enough to have unprotected sex. "Prior to the marriage," the lawsuit said, Alomar informed her "he had been tested for sexually transmitted diseases and the tests were negative." However, after the wedding in summer 2009, she "learned from conclusive proof" that he was indeed HIV-positive.[12] (Her attorneys supposedly possessed a paper trail identifying medications used by Alomar to treat HIV; however, by this point he had explicitly declared he never had the virus.)[13]

One factor working in Roberto's favor was that Maripily, just like Dall and the other accusers, did not test positive for HIV. But Maripily's situation was different from the other womens' situations. She felt that, on multiple occasions, Roberto had posed a direct threat to her life. Per court records in Hillsborough County, Florida, the following incidents occurred: in April 2010, Roberto pulled out a knife and threatened Maripily; two months later, the couple got into a yelling match that ended with Roberto chest-bumping his wife to the ground (deputies were dispatched, however, a report wasn't filed); on the evening of Sunday, August 1, 2010, deputies responded to the Alomar residence when Maripily alleged that her soon-to-be-ex-husband got within inches of her in an aggressive manner; a day later, Maripily reported to the sheriff's office that Roberto had shoved her several feet, causing her to fear for her life, an allegation that finally warranted the domestic violence injunction.[14]

When court proceedings occurred a few months later in a downtown Tampa courthouse, Maripily said the following via a translator:

> Anytime I would question him about settlements he has made with other women and problems that came from that, he would get very aggressive, get in [my face and scream].
>   He would chest bump me. Ever since I have been married to him, I have been the victim of aggression and manipulation, in the sense he has told me if I

said what I know that there will be very serious consequences against me. That he is Roberto Alomar and they will believe him and not me. And he can pay whoever he wants to say whatever he wants them to say. And he can destroy me and my family.

I feel disillusioned, destroyed. I have a broken heart. I am angry at myself that a person used me. And [told] so many lies.[15]

After one court appearance in early November, Maripily, with the aid of her attorney serving as an interpreter, told ESPN senior writer Mike Fish that Roberto had used his marriage to her "so he could return to fame and look like a family man. He is raising a child, my child [by a previous relationship]. . . . I feel he used me for all this. He mistreated me. He took whatever he wanted. And he lied to me."[16]

While Maripily was providing soundbites to the media—she was even giving interviews to *Super Xclusivo*, Puerto Rico's No. 1 TV show, one featuring a puppet—Roberto was, predictably, hiding behind a wall of silence. On multiple occasions, he turned down interview requests from ESPN.com while his attorney, David Maney, failed to respond to at least five telephone messages from reporters. After being badgered for several consecutive days by the media, Roberto politely said he would speak when the case was over while adding, "I heard you're talking to the other party [Maripily]. Talk to them. You don't need me."[17]

The journalists onsite felt otherwise. They wanted to hear his side of the story in vivid detail. Aside from his February 2009 statement that Dall's lawsuit was filled with falsities and his subsequent dismissal of the HIV allegation, Roberto had remained tight-lipped for the past couple of years. And he certainly wasn't changing course during this current legal affair. Throughout the 2010 court proceedings, the former MLB star was often seen walking out of the courtroom stone-faced, shaking off interview requests, before huddling quietly with his lawyers outside the judge's chambers—a stark contrast to his estranged wife regularly holding court with a throng of reporters.

At times, the proceedings turned quite bizarre. In the courtroom, Maripily's attorneys not only detailed the alleged domestic violence while the couple was married (Roberto denied these allegations in court) but also claimed that when their client got exclusive use of the nine-bedroom estate as part of the temporary injunction, the lights, TV, and radio would turn on and off at random, presumably because her ex could control the house's electronics from afar on his iPhone. Such psychological warfare, as her legal counsel tried to reason, left Maripily feeling petrified to be home alone.[18]

(While developments in the months-long legal battle may have constituted breaking news in Puerto Rico, the trial received scant coverage stateside. Outside of ESPN and local papers in Tampa and St. Petersburg, hardly any other major American media outlets provided coverage. Maripily Rivera was a fairly anonymous figure in the United States and Roberto, as a retired professional athlete, was not the celebrity he had been earlier in the century. By the early 2020s, the vast majority of hardcore baseball fans couldn't even recall this unfortunate chapter of Roberto's life. One has to do some pretty extensive googling to unearth any legitimate archival material.)

From Roberto's perspective, the priority was retaining sole ownership of his sprawling mansion, one that had originally been solely in his name but was now under both his and Maripily's. It was a stunningly lavish property that he had recently acquired at a recession-driven bargain price of $2.4 million. Sitting on 3.4 acres, the estate included an indoor pool, home movie theater, eight-car garage, outdoor sports court, and five fireplaces. Undoubtedly, it was an asset destined to appreciate in value over the coming years and become an integral part of his wealth portfolio. His dream team of high-priced attorneys couldn't let Maripily walk away with even partial ownership. In the meantime, because his spouse was still residing in the house, Roberto asked the judge to prohibit her from "removing, using, dissipating, encumbering, disposing of, damaging or destroying" any of his personal possessions, including jewelry and baseball memorabilia.[19] It was inevitable that Maripily was going to get a nice lump sum; as far as Roberto's camp was concerned, they were in damage-control mode as the trial neared the finish line.

After months of legal wrangling, on July 12, 2011, unbeknownst to practically everyone outside of Puerto Rico, the divorce was finalized, and the drawn-out legal affair concluded with the parties reaching a private financial settlement. Meanwhile, Roberto retained ownership of his residence at 901 Palacio De Avila.

Less than two weeks later, he was headed to Cooperstown for his Hall of Fame induction ceremony.

13

Second Time Around

To understand just how meaningful the afternoon of July 24, 2011, was to Roberto Alomar you have to revisit the morning of January 6, 2010. For it was on the latter date that Roberto was told he was not yet worthy of the Hall of Fame. In his first year of eligibility, Roberto received 73.7 percent of the votes, falling eight votes shy of the requisite 75 percent. Roberto, despite being one of the three or four best all-around players of his generation, was denied access to the Hall while Andre Dawson, a career .279 hitter who belted 438 homers and drove in 1,591 runs while displaying a howitzer of a throwing arm in right field, along with manager Whitey Herzog and umpire Doug Harvey, heard their names called.

Ironically, even before the news broke about Alomar narrowly missing the cut, John Hirschbeck made a point of publicly stating that he *wanted* Roberto to get elected in his first year of eligibility. As the umpire told Peter Schmuck of the *Baltimore Sun* days before the 2010 class was announced: "If I could vote, I would vote for him. I would love to see him go in. . . . I don't think that one bad day in a person's life should be held against him forever. He has moved beyond that. I have moved beyond that. I hope everybody else has moved beyond that, too. . . . This is my 28th year in baseball and he is, by far, the best second baseman I have ever seen."[1]

(A decade later, Hirschbeck participated in an interview for this book and reiterated his belief: "The first time I had a lot of writers call me. And everybody called me, and I think that they were looking for a negative side. My answer was the same as the second time when he got voted in. I did every single sportswriter that called me. And my line about Robbie has always been, 'If that's the worst thing that he ever did in his life, then he's led a very, very good life.'")[2]

Hirschbeck was not the only MLB stakeholder who thought Roberto was a shoo-in for Cooperstown. An MLB Network crew was dispatched to Roberto's home in Queens on the morning of January 6, 2010, in order to record the big phone call from Baseball Writers' Association of America secretary Jack O'Connell. Roberto was one of the game's preeminent players in the 1990s, and MLB likes to have footage of these moments. But as the afternoon unfolded, there was no congratulatory call. By 2:00 p.m., the MLB Network crew had quietly packed up before the channel's live broadcast revealed the disappointing news.

After learning of his fate, Roberto, going on three hours of sleep, told *Newsday*'s Ken Davidoff, "I was shocked. It was shocking. Everyone's saying, 'You should be in there,' and you're not there."[3]

Who was everyone? Well, many of his fellow islanders for sure. After all, Roberto was, quite possibly, their most celebrated living athlete.

As Puerto Rico had only two native sons, Roberto Clemente and Orlando Cepeda, in the Hall of Fame at the time, this was supposed to be a special day for the baseball-crazed island, one that was in the midst of a crippling recession. The governor, Luis Fortuno, had been in touch with Roberto leading up to the results being announced. Roberto Clemente Jr. was anxiously awaiting the news. So, too, was his brother Luis and many of their friends and associates.

It wasn't just Puerto Rico that was tuned in—it was the entire region of Latin America. Among the dozens of fellow Latinos who reached out to Alomar in anticipation of good news were former all-star pitcher Luis Tiant, Mets general manager Omar Minaya, and Miguel Montas, the owner of El Nuevo Caridad, a Manhattan-based Caribbean restaurant popular among Hispanic ballplayers that was preparing to host a celebratory dinner for the Alomar family that evening.

From a personal standpoint, this seemed like the optimal time for Roberto to get elected. He had turned his life around, now married to Maripily Rivera after severing ties with Ilya Dall. The couple—weeks away from moving to

Tampa and months away from going through a messy divorce—was resting arm in arm on the living room sofa for hours leading up to the announcement. (In addition, his eight-year-old son, Roberto Jr., whom he had from a previous relationship, was alongside him.) This was supposed to be their first milestone celebration as a wedded couple.

But it was not to be. Election to Cooperstown is based on, among other factors, a player's "integrity, sportsmanship, character" (the "character clause") and apparently more than a few baseball writers (eight to be precise) thought that Roberto did not sufficiently embody such traits.

"A lot of the writers were still turned off by that one action [spitting incident] that people still talk about," says Roberto Clemente Jr., whose revered father was elected posthumously only several months following the tragic aerial accident. "There are a lot of purists. But you have people in the Hall that have been arrested, whatever the case may be. In the heat of a game, to do something like that [spit at Hirschbeck], I think it should have not held him back from being a first-ballot."[4]

Clemente's son has a point. The Hall of Fame that (initially) rejected Roberto is the same one that had made room for the notoriously hotheaded Ty Cobb; Cap Anson, the Chicago Cubs first baseman who so vehemently championed the game's color line in the 1880s; Commissioner Kenesaw Mountain Landis, who presided over baseball's segregationist policy for three decades; pitcher Gaylord Perry, who blatantly cheated through doctoring baseballs with foreign substances; Orlando Cepeda, who served ten months in prison after being arrested in 1975 for smuggling marijuana; and beloved Brooklyn Dodgers center fielder Duke Snider, who was charged with evading taxes on income from autograph signings and memorabilia shows.

"I wasn't shocked [that Alomar didn't get in the first time]," says longtime BBWAA member/Hall of Fame voter Barry Bloom. "My contemporaries held stuff against him. In the first year they just weren't going to vote him in on the first ballot, which is stupid."[5]

But a year later, to their credit, the BBWAA members voted overwhelmingly (as in 90 percent in favor) to send Roberto to Cooperstown. (Since 1966, no second-year candidate had received a higher percentage of the vote.) On July 24, 2011, Roberto was scheduled to take the stage, along with pitcher Bert Blyleven and executive Pat Gillick, to receive baseball's highest individual honor.

The 2011 Hall of Fame Induction Weekend was not the most well-attended weekend of festivities in the history of Cooperstown. Far from it, actually. In a decent year, upwards of thirty thousand seamheads pack into the charming lakeside village nestled in New York's Mohawk Valley. (Aside from the Iowa cornfields that Kevin Costner roamed, it is hard to ask for a more heavenly baseball setting than Cooperstown.) The 2011 HOF Induction Weekend barely drew half that number. This was in part because the 2011 class consisted of only two ballplayers, Alomar and Blyleven, but also due to the fact that neither inductee had such an ardent following. For comparison, the co-induction of Tony Gwynn and Cal Ripken Jr. in 2007 had shattered all attendance records with over eighty thousand fans on hand. (Alomar obviously had no interest in promoting the event considering that back in April he had kept his Hall of Fame orientation tour private by denying the media access.) By all accounts, the 2011 HOF Induction Weekend was a far more subdued affair—it did not sell out every hotel room within a fifty-mile radius, and fans didn't have to worry about suffocating in a crowd crush.

But what the weekend festival lacked in size it surely made up for with its global flavor. With his Puerto Rican heritage and storied career in Toronto, Alomar, along with his former boss Pat Gillick who hailed from California, had North America covered, while Blyleven, hailing from the Netherlands, provided a rare European presence in Cooperstown. (Born Rik Aalbert Blijleven in Zeist, Netherlands, in 1951, Bert Blyleven was the third child of Johannes Cornelius and Jannigje Blijleven, who had married when the nation was still under Nazi control and eventually fled war-torn Europe in 1954.)

"To have two players that had different heritages come in, I think that was really cool for baseball," says Bert Blyleven's son Todd, who was hanging around baseball clubhouses basically from the time he could walk and later played in the minors.[6]

The cultural pride was beaming vibrantly—particularly in honor of Roberto as thousands of his fellow countrymen descended upon central New York with their own red, white, and blue flags. Understandably so, as Alomar was only the third Puerto Rican and tenth Latin American native to be inducted.

Todd Blyleven adds:

I think that's what excites that whole Puerto Rican community is when you have people like the Alomar family that have given back, that are good people for the most part all the way through and through. I think his family portrayed the excitement and relief in a really positive way. They were super pumped and excited that he was there and really proud. I remember when he didn't get in that first year and some of the negative stuff that came out. That was not right, because players play with passion, and he always played with passion.

What you saw with Roberto Alomar on the field and what you saw on camera was him as this athlete. Off camera he is just a really nice, genuine guy. He doesn't stray far from the Alomar name in terms of what that means in the Puerto Rican heritage, and even in the United States. I never heard anything bad about him across the whole industry. I heard a lot, but he was always a guy you would never hear anything bad about.

He really appreciated everybody coming into Cooperstown to be there for him.[7]

Backdropped by rows of living legends including Hank Aaron, Yogi Berra, Johnny Bench, and Lou Brock, Roberto (looking trim and dapper with his leaden blue striped suit and baby blue tie) paid homage to his heritage by beginning his speech in Spanish (this segment included a beautiful tribute to Roberto Clemente and his family) before continuing in his vastly improved English. It was a thoughtful speech that fittingly captured how Roberto felt humbled by the honor. He covered all the bases by thanking the important people such as the BBWAA and Jane Forbes Clark, Chairman of the Hall of Fame Board and Museum, and acknowledged the unique privilege of being the first Toronto Blue Jay inducted into the Baseball Hall of Fame. But in the course of summing up his career, Roberto did make one eyebrow-raising statement by declaring: "To the New York Mets, the Chicago White Sox, the Arizona Diamondbacks, and the Tampa Bay Rays . . . I wore your uniforms with pride and dignity, and I want you all to know . . . I gave you my best, each and every time . . . I hit that field to represent you."[8] At least regarding Roberto's brief career in Queens—during which he hardly ever ran out grounders and pop-ups—it was simply untrue that he always put forth his best effort every time he took the field.

After mentioning all his prior teams and giving the customary recognition to former managers (he gave a special shout-out to Cito Gaston), coaches, teammates, and others, an admittedly nervous Roberto ended his brief remarks by expressing profound and heartfelt gratitude to his family. In the most touching moment of the ceremony, Roberto looked down at his mother, who was sobbing into a handkerchief, and said, "My mom is the most wonderful person in my life. She gave me love. She took me to the ballpark, even though I was a little boy running around, hanging around. Mom, thank you for everything that you have done for me. If I'm standing here today, it's because of you."[9]

While Roberto did not mention them in his speech, there were two notable guests sitting near his family up front. One was Spencer Miller, a young man restricted to a wheelchair by cerebral palsy since childhood, who had met and befriended Alomar during the Toronto years. The other was the new girlfriend, Kim Perks, who, as a former waitress in the SkyDome, had also met Alomar when he was starring for the Jays.

Blyleven's and Alomar's careers only overlapped for several years, from 1988 to 1992. (The "Frying Dutchman" played in the majors from 1970 to 1992 and had been on the HOF ballot for fourteen years before the baseball writers finally deferred to the advanced metrics supporting his case.) However, the Hall's two newest inductees shared a neat connection, as Blyleven and Alomar's fathers were teammates on the Texas Rangers in 1977. Similar to how Nolan Ryan took young Roberto under his wing earlier in the decade, Blyleven would occasionally pitch batting practice to a nine-year-old Robbie during the summer of 1977. Just over a decade later when Robbie was establishing himself as a big leaguer with the Padres and Blyleven was winding down his career with the California Angels, Robbie returned the favor by giving fielding lessons to Blyleven's tag-along teenage son Todd when their respective clubs crossed paths during spring training.

"It was really cool that my dad and Alomar got a chance to share that [Hall of Fame induction] together," says Todd Blyleven, who first met Alomar back in 1977 when their fathers were teammates in Arlington, Texas. "Especially with the history that my dad has had with the Alomar family. Those two guys [Roberto and Bert], they represented Hall of Fame baseball."[10]

(For the Blyleven family, this HOF Induction Weekend would take on greater significance years later when Todd nearly lost his life during the 2017 Las Vegas shooting, a nightmarish incident that still haunts him to this day.)

It was also quite fitting that Alomar got inducted alongside former Toronto executive Pat Gillick, whose career-defining moment was the December 1990 trade that had landed Toronto Alomar and Joe Carter. Had Alomar not blossomed into a Hall of Famer in Toronto, Gillick would not have either.

From catching up with former Toronto teammate (and fellow Hall of Famer) Paul Molitor to posing for a photo with an elderly Hank Aaron, who had known Roberto since he was a little tyke, the storybook baseball-centric weekend provided a much-needed diversion from the recent scandals. Back in the public spotlight, Roberto didn't have to face questions about his physical health. No juicy details of his sex life were being leaked out to the tabloids. For the first time in a long time, he was getting well-deserved attention for his professional accomplishments. Maybe now he would be known, first and foremost, as Roberto Alomar, Hall of Fame second baseman.

Once the Cooperstown festivities wrapped, Robbie hopped across Lake Ontario to his old stomping ground of Toronto where another ceremony awaited.

With Alomar's HOF plaque being the first to feature a Toronto Blue Jays cap, the franchise felt it was only fair to retire his No. 12. Alomar only played five years for Toronto, and typically teams wouldn't be inclined to retire the number of a player who had such a relatively short tenure. But this was a unique situation. Alomar was not only the first to enter the Hall as a Blue Jay, but he was also the single most responsible player for the back-to-back titles in the 1990s. Also, Toronto wasn't exactly running out of uniform numbers to assign, as no former Jay had ever seen his number raised to the rafters.

On July 31, a week after receiving baseball's highest individual recognition, Roberto was feted in a half-hour pregame ceremony prior to the Blue Jays' game against the Texas Rangers at the Rogers Centre, formerly known as the SkyDome. (This wasn't the first time the Jays had commemorated Roberto's career, as there had been a ceremony back in 2008 when he was inducted into the franchise's esteemed Level of Excellence.) Wearing a sharp navy-blue suit and red tie, Roberto, flanked by two red-clad Mounties, made his way down to the field through the stands. As the boisterous crowd gave him a standing ovation (hard to believe this was the same building where he had been ruthlessly jeered after the fight with Hirschbeck), he strolled to the center field stage where he was soon joined by former teammates Duane Ward, Devon White, Kelly Gruber, and Candy Maldonado, lifelong friend Carlos Baerga, one-time Toronto skipper Cito Gaston, and, of course, his awfully proud parents.

Speaking on behalf of the current Blue Jays was veteran utility infielder John McDonald, who grew up in Connecticut idolizing Alomar and later played with him in Cleveland.

"In 1994, I bought tickets to watch him play at Yankee Stadium, and I never thought that five years later we would be teammates in Cleveland," said McDonald. "Robbie is one of the greatest players to put on a Blue Jays—or any other—baseball uniform."[11]

It took the return of an all-time great to awaken such a dormant fan base as Toronto's. (Technically, Roberto had already returned to the Jays, as several months earlier he had been hired as a part-time special assistant in the baseball operations department in a low-key, largely behind-the-scenes role.) The Jays were a perennial .500 ballclub that hadn't been a true contender for a long time—really, ever since Alomar had left after 1995—and unaccustomed to playing at home in front of a packed house. That's actually putting it mildly. In the early 2000s, it was not uncommon for the team to perform in front of "crowds" consisting of no more than 15,000 fans. But this afternoon, Rogers Centre was uncharacteristically buzzing with 45,629 nostalgic fans. (The aggregate attendance for the series' first two games paled in comparison to the turnout for the ballyhooed finale.) This was not lost on Alomar, who acknowledged in his remarks, "I would love to see, every day, so many fans like I see today. Wow."[12]

Roberto finished his brief address to the Toronto faithful by saying, "When I was a little boy, I never expected to have my number retired. When I was traded to Toronto, I was blessed to come to play for a great city, a great organization, a great team, and, to me, the greatest manager that I have ever played for."[13]

It was no shocker that Roberto singled out Gaston, who was a year removed from his second and final stint as Toronto manager. As has been well documented, throughout Roberto's illustrious career he had his fair share of issues with managers. But his relationship with Gaston was consistently one of mutual respect and admiration (winning two championships together didn't hurt), a point that was clearly articulated that afternoon.

"Robbie is the best second baseman to play the game," Gaston exclaimed. "I'm pretty sure I can speak for the city of Toronto, our fans, the organization and myself—we'd like to thank you Robbie for all you've ever done for us."[14]

All of the speeches, in addition to the virtual tribute delivered by a host of former teammates including John Olerud, Jimmy Key, Dave Stewart, Joe Carter, and Tony Gwynn among others, were very thoughtful, but the most poignant remarks were delivered by Blue Jays' president and CEO Paul Beeston, who would later unveil Alomar's banner in center field that featured no. 12 with the Blue Jays retro logo and Hall of Fame insignia.

"There is going to come a time when a young generation of fans come into the ballpark and they're going to see that no. 12," predicted Beeston. "They're going to ask their parents, 'What does no. 12 mean?' And they're going to say, 'That's the number of Robbie Alomar, the greatest second baseman who ever played the game.'"[15]

14

A Most Improbable Friendship

After the Hall of Fame voting results had been announced on the afternoon of Wednesday, January 5, 2011, Roberto Alomar's fully charged phone became inundated with congratulatory calls, texts, and voicemails. The outpouring of support was much appreciated, but after a little while, the hundreds of calls and messages naturally started blending together. There were a few calls, however, that stood out, one of which came from John Hirschbeck. Alomar wasn't necessarily shocked to hear from the umpire (more on that later), but he was caught off guard by one comment in particular.

"We made it," Hirschbeck said. "We made it."[1]

We? A year earlier, Hirschbeck had gone on record advocating for Alomar's induction, leading the public to believe that they were on good terms. At the very least, by acknowledging Alomar's brilliant career in supporting his Hall of Fame candidacy, Hirschbeck was being professional. But, at this moment, by referring to himself and Alomar in the first-person plural, Hirschbeck wanted his former nemesis to know that he didn't just respect him on a professional level—he felt united with him on a personal level.

The story of reconciliation and, ultimately, an unlikely friendship began one morning in late November 1998 when Hirschbeck's thirteen-year-old son Michael, a die-hard Indians fan who was continuing his courageous battle against adrenoleukodystrophy, the insidious disease that torments the nervous system, burst into his parents' bedroom with some interesting news: Roberto Alomar was now a Cleveland Indian.

Of all the teams, it had to be Cleveland?

By virtue of residing in Poland, Ohio, Hirschbeck was regularly assigned to Jacobs Field and could now expect to cross paths with Alomar more frequently than he had been accustomed to. Occasionally during the 1997 and 1998 seasons, Hirschbeck and Alomar found themselves on the same diamond. These were awkward moments, both men deliberately ignoring one another, but they occurred once every couple months. Now Hirschbeck and Alomar would have to share the same workplace a couple times every month.

During Cleveland's homestand in May 1999, Hirschbeck left his house on the early side one afternoon to make the eighty-mile drive to work. With ample time to kill before the first pitch, he started shooting the breeze with longtime Jacobs Field locker room attendant Jack Efta. Hirschbeck trusted Efta's judgment, had a great working relationship with the man, and knew he was around the club 24/7. He couldn't help but wonder what Efta thought of Roberto.

The exchange, as Hirschbeck remembers it over two decades later, went as follows:

> Hirschbeck: "What do you think of him, Jack?"
>
> Efta: "John, you know what, he's one of the two nicest people I've ever met."
>
> Hirschbeck: "Really?"
>
> Efta: "And yes, you're the other one."[2]

It was interesting, even though Hirschbeck was inextricably linked to Alomar, at least from the public's perspective, that he didn't really know the ballplayer all that well. Even before their infamous moment, the two men had a respectful professional relationship but rarely engaged in conversation. What was Alomar really like when he wasn't at his worst? If Efta thought Alomar was a gentleman, maybe, just maybe, it was worth trying to mend fences.

"I kind of walked away, and I went over near my locker, and I thought about it," Hirschbeck recalls while trying to find decent telephone reception in a backcountry Ohio farmhouse during a November 2020 hunting trip.

"And I said, 'OK, enough is enough.' We [Robbie and I] liked each other before that incident, and it was time to try to move on.

"I'm sure he didn't want it to happen, and I look back and the pitch was outside. I wish I had just said, 'Ball Four!' But life doesn't happen that way. People do things."[3]

When Alomar and the Indians took the field in the top of the first inning that early May evening, Hirschbeck, who coincidentally was working second base, did not awkwardly shuffle toward the shortstop side of the bag to avoid making eye contact. Instead, he looked in Alomar's direction.

Hey, Robbie, how you doing?

That's all it took—five simple words—for the floodgates to open. Immediately, Robbie turned around, flashing a half-moon smile before starting up a nonstop conversation with the ump.

"My wife didn't go to a lot of games, but she was there that night," recalls Hirschbeck. "And she said, 'John, I was nervous they were going to hit the ball to Robbie because you guys were talking. It seemed like the whole game.'"[4]

The nationally televised handshake in Baltimore two years earlier was, according to Hirschbeck, "more of a representation of what had happened" while this (more or less private) hours-long exchange was "the real thing."[5]

The next day Roberto met with the entire Hirschbeck family—John, his wife Denise, and their three children, including Michael, who happened to be serving as an honorary bat boy for the Tribe on occasion that season. The all-star second baseman gave Denise a big hug and delivered a heartfelt apology to everyone. At long last, closure for both men. And the beginning of one of the most fascinating partnerships in the history of baseball.

In the days following the reconciliation, Roberto started treating Michael Hirschbeck like his little brother. The umpire's son, who was still reading and writing at a first-grade level because of ALD and continuing to go for regular checkups to monitor increased inflammation in his brain, maintained his infectious smile around the Cleveland clubhouse. Alomar was inspired by how Michael's passion for baseball hadn't dimmed even though he was battling a terminal illness. By early summer, Roberto and his brother/teammate Sandy started donating autographed jerseys for an annual fundraising auction held at a local golf tournament the Hirschbeck family ran to benefit ALD research. Framed together, the brothers' jerseys fetched $6,600, the most expensive item sold. This was just the beginning. A year later, Robbie purchased twenty-five specialized jerseys for his teammates to wear during an early-season game; afterward, each player signed the game-worn jerseys, which were then donated to the collection for Hirschbeck's charity auction. (Two decades later, Hirschbeck estimates that Robbie's donated memorabilia has accounted for charitable funds totaling over $200,000.)

As Alomar told *USA Today* in May 2000, "I want people to know that I care about people, especially kids. That's what it's all about. We're not here to hold grudges; we're here to help people. Someday a miracle will happen and we can find a cure for John's son. That would be the happiest day of my life, because I had helped somebody. Maybe God put us in this world to help somebody beat this disease."[6]

Michael would fight his entire life to beat a disease for which there is still no cure. Back in the early 1990s, he underwent experimental treatment during which he received a bone marrow transplant from his baby sister Megan, who was a genetic match. While the procedure certainly prolonged his life, he was never exempt from suffering. In addition to dealing with the aforementioned cognitive issues, Michael constantly experienced seizures that rendered him unable to drive a vehicle, live independently, or earn a living. While not destined to live a long life, Michael never complained and, even as a little boy, wouldn't ask his parents if he was going to die. His was an inspiring life, and Roberto went out of his way to provide companionship.

In all likelihood, had it not been for the spitting incident, Michael, who lived for all things baseball, would not have forged such a close bond with a future Hall of Famer.

On April 7, 2014, John was slated to work the Indians' home game against the San Diego Padres while Michael, then twenty-seven, was planning on serving as his favorite team's bat boy. Halfway through the drive to Progressive Field (formerly the ballpark known as "The Jake") the veteran umpire learned that the game had been postponed due to foul weather. No big deal. Father and son headed home, picked up their mother, and went on a joyride through the eastern Ohio countryside before settling in later that evening to watch the UConn Huskies capture the NCAA Division I Men's Basketball National Championship.

The following morning, Michael's parents were preparing to run a couple errands. Denise went up to Michael's bedroom to see if he wanted to tag along. From downstairs, John heard a blood-curdling sound. While accustomed to hearing his wife shriek when his son suffered a seizure, he knew this time was different. Indeed, it was. Michael's lifeless body was sprawled face-down on his bedroom floor. He had suffocated to death from a grand mal seizure.

When word got out that unspeakable tragedy had once again struck the Hirschbeck family ("winning the lottery in reverse," as Hirschbeck says), Roberto was one of the first people John heard from.

"After my brother passed away, he [Alomar] was very quick to reach out to my dad and extend his sympathies," says Hirschbeck's daughter Erin, a remarkable young woman who has toiled tirelessly to keep the spirit of her brother alive through spearheading fundraising efforts in his memory. "Anytime my sister and I have been around him, he always talks about the time that he spent around Michael. It means a lot to us. Ever since what happened back in the day, he has been so good to our family."[7]

Alomar's compassion toward the Hirschbeck family knows no bounds. He is aware of how much the family has suffered and has leveraged his resources toward supporting the "Magic of Michael Foundation," which was established in 2014 by a couple of the Hirschbecks' close friends to provide financial assistance to families of children suffering from a wide spectrum of disorders—including terminal illnesses such as ALD. (To honor Michael's legacy, the family's friends built on the Hirschbecks' ALD fundraising efforts by establishing this official organization that covers an even broader range of children throughout northeast Ohio.) Every year, a couple of weeks before the organization holds its marquee fundraising event—a star-studded golf tournament involving the likes of Joe Torre, Jim Leyland, Jim Thome, and Terry Francona, and an accompanying silent auction—a box of Alomar's game-worn jerseys and cleats arrives at the Hirschbecks' doorstep. No ballplayer, past or present, has done more for the organization in its efforts to purchase accessibility ramps, wheelchairs, and service animals.

"He [Alomar] has been more than willing to help in any way he can. And it's brought in a lot of money for us," adds Erin.[8]

For very different reasons, both Alomar and Hirschbeck have endured trying times in their middle-aged years. As if losing two young sons weren't enough, Hirschbeck has also had to deal with his own life-threatening issues. In 2009, a year after sitting out the entire 2008 MLB season after recovering from back surgery to repair a ruptured disk, he was diagnosed with testicular cancer. The tumor was removed, and physicians informed him the cancer had merely a 5 percent chance of recurring. Odds that were 95 percent in his favor apparently weren't enough. Just over two years later, in February 2012, John experienced agonizing pain in his lower back, prompting him to go to the hospital. The news was sobering: he was perilously close to renal failure as a massive, cancerous tumor was exerting pressure on his kidneys and for the next three days he would have to go on dialysis. Eventually, this new tumor was removed and thirty-two rounds of chemo later, his strong body remained undefeated against cancer.

While Hirschbeck battled one health issue after another, Roberto had his own issues with the allegations and subsequent lawsuits. It was beyond mortifying—the most intimate details of his sex life spilling out to the tabloids. Alomar's reputation was (once again) on the line, not to mention his life savings, but that didn't stop him from checking in on his friend to see if there was anything he could do.

Hirschbeck will not talk about the allegations and lawsuits Roberto has faced. In fact, he claims to be unaware of such developments and, given his recent string of hardships, it seems perfectly reasonable to believe that a celebrity sex scandal was never a matter of great importance for him. But when Roberto did have the professional setback in January 2010 upon learning that he was not a first-ballot Hall of Famer, one of the first callers was Hirschbeck, who told him, "I'm sorry. If what happened that day entered into this decision at all . . . I'm sorry. We'll get it next year."[9]

Truth be told, Alomar and Hirschbeck are friends, but not incredibly close ones. They do not talk regularly and rarely see each other. In part, this is due to the recent pandemic and the fact that Roberto moved from Tampa to Toronto in spring 2020. (Hirschbeck owns a winter home in Sarasota and when both were living on Florida's west coast, they met for dinner occasionally.) Hirschbeck, who has never visited Cooperstown, did not go to Alomar's HOF induction in 2011 (he was likely umpiring) and Alomar has never been invited to attend the Hirschbecks' annual fundraiser. As Hirschbeck acknowledges, "He's on my phone, and I hope I'm on his phone. If I went to Puerto Rico with my wife, I would make sure I gave him a call. Honestly."[10] But considering how the two men nearly killed each other back in September 1996, their casual friendship in which they reach out to each other during important times has been impressive.

Generally speaking, the now decades-long partnership has gone unnoticed. Back in spring 1999, some of the Cleveland papers ran stories of Alomar making amends with John and later apologizing in person to the entire family. The following year, *USA Today* ran a fairly lengthy piece chronicling Roberto's random acts of kindness toward Michael. Perhaps the most notable press the Hirschbeck-Alomar relationship has received came in 2013 when *Sports Illustrated*'s Albert Chen wrote a feature story in the magazine's annual "Where Are They Now?" issue. And on multiple occasions, both Alomar and Hirschbeck have gone on record saying they have long moved on from the infamous altercation. Yet those instances aside, the feel-good story of redemption and forgiveness has garnered very little publicity, which partially explains why, even to this very day, the spitting incident continues to leave an indelible mark on Roberto's legacy.

"My dad is the first one to say, 'He is a great guy. He made a mistake. Everyone makes mistakes,'" says Erin.[11]

In fairness, in the heat of the moment, John may have made a mistake, too. As Pat Gillick told the *National Post*, a Canadian daily, back in April 2008 when Robbie joined Toronto's Level of Excellence, "What he [Alomar] did certainly was not appropriate. I would never defend that. But I was sitting in the first row behind the batter's circle on the visitors' side, and I heard what Hirschbeck said to him. Let me put it this way. What he said to Robbie would get you very, very upset."[12]

Roberto may be thin-skinned, but he clearly dropped any grudges he had toward Hirschbeck a long time ago. The Hall of Famer not only embraced John and his late son Michael, but he has also been very pleasant around the umpire's lovely wife and daughters—especially when there are no flashbulbs or microphones around.

When asked to recall any personal memories that she has of being in Robbie's presence, Erin is quick to recall one time back in the early 2000s. During one school vacation, she and her mom flew down to visit John, who was staying at their Sarasota home for spring training. After landing at Tampa

International Airport, Erin and Denise went to The Cheesecake Factory downtown for a quick dinner. As they walked into the restaurant, a blue Rolls-Royce
with curtained windows pulled up. Out stepped Roberto, who, despite not
having seen Hirschbeck's wife and daughter for years, immediately recognized
them. He did more than come over and say a quick hello. He made Denise and
Erin feel like they were the most important people in his life.

"Most people coming out for dinner, they might be in a hurry or they might
not want to sit and talk with people," says Erin. "But he could not have been
nicer. He was so happy to see us. He asked all about how my dad was doing."[13]

John is doing fine these days. At least as well as anyone could be doing with
the hand he has been dealt. After forty-one years in baseball, thirty-four of
which were spent in the big leagues, he retired following the 2016 season—his
last assignment was actually umpiring the Cubs-Indians World Series. It was
quite a career, as he was behind the plate for Roy Halladay's 2010 postseason
no-hitter, Barry Bonds's record-breaking 756th career homer, and Mariano
Rivera's record-breaking 602nd career save. He doesn't regret walking away
at the relatively young retirement age of sixty-two. As any professional umpire will acknowledge, the constant travel and occasional verbal abuse from
players and fans can become burdensome. He spends his winters and early
springs in Sarasota, golfing, boating, and checking in on his former colleagues
when spring training camps open. Come April, when weather in the Northeast becomes suitable for outdoor activities, he and Denise head up to their
country home in North Lima, Ohio. He is a man of many interests and is
always keeping himself busy, leaving no time for wallowing in self-pity.

As Hirschbeck told the *New Haven Register* (essentially his hometown
newspaper as he grew up in nearby Stratford) in 2017, "I've been very, very
blessed. I really have," Hirschbeck insisted. "Things happen to people. You
don't say, 'Why me?' You say, 'Why not me? What makes us any different?'
You handle it, you deal with it, and you move on."[14]

Naturally, of course, the same holds true regarding his long-ago confrontation with Alomar.

"Baseball gave me everything I have in my life," says John. "From meeting
my wife to living where I live, my children, everything. It [incident with Alo-
mar] is just a little thing in the big scheme of a thirty-four-year career. To me,
it's a very little thing, because he and I have moved on from it."[15]

15

Hell on Earth

At 6:15 a.m. on September 20, 2017, Hurricane Maria made landfall on the southeastern coast of Puerto Rico. Several hours later, the first Category 4 storm to batter the US territory since 1932 was wreaking havoc on the entire 100-mile-long island. Torrential rainfall (up to seven inches per hour) sparked flooding that decimated coastal regions before raging inland and deluging villages with stormwater. Sustained winds up to 155 mph tore off roofs from commercial buildings, snapped palm trees, pulverized homes, and spewed debris across beaches and streets. The gale was so unprecedented in its ferocity that it paralyzed radar, weather stations, and cell towers (essentially the island's entire electrical grid), resulting in an information vacuum in which government officials could only make conjectures about property destruction and the aggregate number of injuries and fatalities.

(With such limited means of communication, it was virtually impossible to fathom the scale of destruction—particularly regarding the loss of human life. Initially, it was reported by Puerto Rico's public safety director, Héctor M. Pesquera, that at least six people had died. Less than a year later, as the hurricane's one-year anniversary approached, the Puerto Rican government announced the official death toll stood at 2,975, making the storm the deadliest US-based natural disaster in a century.)

But even in the immediate aftermath, CNN, naturally, was able to broadcast harrowing stories of the doomsday destruction into Americans' living rooms. Consider, for example, that of the three hospitals CNN visited, none had running water. This was but a miniscule sample. It was estimated that in the days following Maria's landfall, over three million residents were running out of food and drinkable water. In fact, several months later, rampant broken water mains and powerless pumps led to an outbreak of leptospirosis, a deadly bacterial disease caused by drinking water tainted with animal feces. With hospitals not being spared from the seemingly interminable power outages, an untold number of patients relying on breathing machines or dialysis died prematurely without the presence of loved ones.

And yet, even as Puerto Rico remained in the throes of widespread chaos and destruction, the US commonwealth, one already hammered by a prolonged debt and bankruptcy crisis, was clearly not receiving sufficient resources. While the island had been afflicted by Hurricane Irma–level winds and besieged by Hurricane Harvey–level floodwater, the US government was, quite frankly, acting at a glacial pace. Despite Puerto Rican governor Ricardo Rossello declaring that his island was facing a humanitarian crisis and imploring Congress to approve a commensurate aid package, it soon became evident that no comprehensive relief package—or the designation of Department of Defense resources for search-and-rescue operations, law enforcement, and transportation needs—was immediately forthcoming.

In light of the federal government's lack of urgency in responding to the catastrophe, many Puerto Ricans continued to feel like second-class US citizens. They already couldn't vote in presidential elections and lacked representation in Congress and now had to wait longer for life-saving resources than did US citizens in Florida and Texas following their respective hurricanes. It was a grave injustice, considering that for the past century Puerto Ricans, while subject to US federal laws, had perished in American wars, performed on Broadway, and, perhaps most notably, played in every MLB ballpark from Fenway Park to Dodger Stadium.

Now a middle-aged adult, Roberto Alomar had actually spent more of his life in the United States and Canada than in Puerto Rico. But his transient lifestyle hadn't dimmed his passion for all things Puerto Rico, where of course he still had hundreds of relatives and friends residing. (Immediately after the catastrophe had struck the island, the former MLB star couldn't reach his parents or sister in their hometown of Salinas; eventually, he learned that they were safe and sound.) Within a week of the hurricane making landfall, Robbie made arrangements to return to his native land. He couldn't stay stateside (or north of the border) while knowing that tens of thousands of young children were without food and shelter in his native land. Providing significant monetary assistance wouldn't suffice—he needed to be immersed in the recovery efforts while exuding genuine empathy toward those afflicted by the seemingly apocalyptic conditions in the wake of the recent tempest.

By the time Alomar had arrived, the devastation was overwhelming. Hardly any Puerto Ricans had electric power and nearly half lacked running water. Meanwhile, those who had taps functioning only had access for restricted hours. Many roads were left impassable because there were so many downed trees and utility poles. Cell phone service was spotty at best, in many places nonexistent. With gasoline in such scarce supply, motorists fueling their vehicles sometimes had to wait over four hours in the tropical heat without the air conditioning running . . . only to learn that there was a $20 limit per customer. Grocery shoppers searching for essential items like packs of water bottles, milk, bread, and batteries often found themselves staring up at barren shelves.

Ordinarily, a Robbie Alomar public appearance in Puerto Rico would prompt his starry-eyed countrymen to jostle for autographs and photos. In addition to being a Hall of Famer, Robbie grew up in a royal baseball family in a land where the sport is a way of life. Aside from global entertainment icons such as Ricky Martin and Benicio Del Toro, there are precious few Puerto Rican celebrities whose sightings on the island spark more excitement than Alomar's. But needless to say, September 2017 was no ordinary time. During this moment of great turmoil, survivors on the storm-ravaged island simply craved bottles of Poland Spring water and thus cared little whether it was a contracted humanitarian aid worker or visiting Hall of Fame ballplayer providing them with the vital nutrients.

While his nuclear family was unharmed and, unlike most Puerto Ricans, had access to a generator, there were others in Roberto's circle who were far less fortunate. Alomar's uncle, Demetrio, with whom he was very close, lost his house. As did many friends whose homes also could not withstand the hellacious winds buffeting their wooden frames. When Roberto arrived in his old neighborhood of Salinas sporting a backwards cap, jeans, and sunglasses, it seemed like the lines of malnourished children waiting for water and canned foods were endless. Puerto Rico had never been in such a dilapidated state in his lifetime—or anyone's for that matter. This was, quite simply, a once-in-a-century natural disaster that necessitated drastic measures.

Alomar was especially concerned that only seven thousand US troops had been deployed to the island (this figure would eventually swell to approximately seventeen thousand); his subsequent message calling for a heightened US military presence reflected the urgency of the situation.

"The quicker we can get more military personnel to help, the quicker we can recover because in this type of devastation, they know what to do," Alomar said. "They can help us to clean Puerto Rico faster.

"I think if we can get more troops out there to do the right thing, to help us with the electricity, fix the poles, fix this, fix that, I think that is a big help."[1]

There was one person in particular whom Alomar was trying to reach: US president Donald Trump. This wasn't so easy. Even with hundreds dying, children starving, women going into labor in collapsing buildings, Trump often came across as insensitive to the plight of the Puerto Rican community. At one point during his stop in Puerto Rico (nearly two weeks after the hurricane had pummeled the territory home to 3.4 million American citizens) he felt inclined to crack a "joke" at the expense of Puerto Ricans when he quipped, "You've thrown our budget a little out of whack." Mind you, this came on the heels of the commander in chief—one who didn't conduct a Situation Room meeting on the catastrophe until six days after landfall—accusing residents of Puerto Rico of being unwilling to help themselves.

Alomar could have engaged in a tweetstorm with Trump to express the resentment and bitterness many of his fellow Puerto Ricans were surely feeling. He could have joined the chorus of criticism of the president's lackluster response to the calamity or his condescending remarks. Instead, Alomar responded diplomatically to Trump's comments that Puerto Ricans needed to be more self-sufficient. Eschewing politics and personal grievances, Alomar was straightforward in his aforementioned public message that more manpower and equipment were needed to clear flood-ravaged roads that remained closed to local traffic.

Later on, in an interview with Jorge L. Ortiz of *USA Today*, Roberto rationalized his diplomatic (but not political) response by matter-of-factly explaining, "Things are slowly getting better, but the improvement has been really slow. That's why I sent a message to our president. I don't want to make this a political issue. This is all positive. I know the president has a lot on his plate right now. I just want to send him a message so he understands we need that help."[2]

Understandably, not every Puerto Rican ballplayer was able to overlook Trump's antics. Perhaps the most notable example was Boston Red Sox manager Alex Cora's outspokenness toward the president followed by his 2019 decision not to visit the White House when his club was honored for winning the prior year's World Series.

In addition to spending several days in his homeland delivering thousands of water bottles, canned goods, and shirts to survivors, Alomar donated an undisclosed sum toward relief efforts and used his own charitable organization, Foundation 12, one that ordinarily provided financial support to young underprivileged Canadian baseball players, to raise additional funds for hurricane recovery efforts.

With Puerto Rico having such a prominent MLB presence, Robbie was far from the only Puerto Rican big-league star (past or present) making significant financial contributions. Outfielder Carlos Beltran, then a member of the Houston Astros, was particularly generous, donating $1 million while raising an additional $343,000. Another active player, longtime St. Louis Cardinals backstop Yadier Molina, raised $134,000 through a GoFundMe page. Former New York Yankees catcher Jorge Posada and his wife, Jessica, not only visited the island several times in the immediate aftermath but also fund-raised over $250,000, while newly minted Hall of Famer Ivan Rodriguez contributed by collecting and sending supplies.

Generally speaking, Alomar has tried to perform charitable work without flashbulbs and digital recorders present. Like many prominent athletes (Ted Williams comes to mind), he doesn't want to draw attention to himself when helping others. But this time was different. This time he was trying to raise awareness of the plight of his countrymen and the most compelling way to do so was to publicly share his firsthand experiences of observing their distress.

As Alomar also told USA Today, "It's one thing to donate, but it's another to be there and feel what they're feeling. What I saw was a lot of sorrow. When I would give people water they would say, 'Oh my God, this water tastes so good.' They had barely had any water in a week. There's a sense of desperation, but I also saw happiness over getting some help."[3]

Once October dawned, upcoming postseason baseball promised to be bittersweet for many Puerto Ricans. On one hand, the playoffs were showcasing three young Puerto Rican stars (Francisco Lindor of the Indians, Carlos Correa of the eventual world champion Astros, and Javier Baez of the Cubs) whose feats could provide a much-needed diversion from Hurricane Maria. But, on the other hand, even several weeks after Maria had made landfall, there were still tens of thousands of Puerto Ricans living in fairly remote areas who lacked electricity . . . and thus the ability to watch the current crop of stud ballplayers representing their island. Compared to basic necessities like drinkable water, baby formula, and fuel for generators, the ability to watch MLB playoff games was not a high priority. But that didn't make it any less frustrating.

In early October, just after returning to the mainland, Alomar visited the MLB.com studios in Manhattan for an in-person interview about his recent trip. He made some insightful comments, including the following:

"In the south of Puerto Rico, you don't get internet, cell phones aren't working. . . . With no electricity, you cannot watch the games. That's what people don't understand. You can't watch the game. We might be able to watch it in San Juan, but not everybody lives in San Juan. I know where I'm from, they cannot watch the games."[4]

It just served as one more reminder of how the fabric of Puerto Rican society had been torn asunder by Hurricane Maria.

In April 2018, seven months after Maria had touched down, Puerto Rico was set to host a two-game series between the Cleveland Indians and Minnesota Twins at San Juan's venerable Hiram Bithorn Stadium. While MLB's return to Puerto Rico sparked great excitement from Mayaguez to Carolina, a stark reminder of the hurricane's long-lasting impact was glaringly present right outside the ballpark as passersby noticed that all that remained of the (now former) landmark bronze statue commemorating Hiram Bithorn, the first Puerto Rican to play in the majors, was its massive base. The statue had toppled over in the storm, landing face-first on the unforgiving concrete, and was nowhere to be found.

It was an awkward sight, but a fittingly painful reminder of Puerto Rico's drawn-out recovery, one that was strikingly conspicuous practically anywhere you looked. In neighborhoods surrounding Hiram Bithorn Stadium, blue tarps still covered demolished roofs; dozens of electronic signs along highways and traffic lights weren't functioning; palm trees, normally standing erect, now arched over buildings and homes.

And, of course, San Juan was faring significantly better than many of the rural (particularly mountainous) areas where thousands upon thousands of dehydrated and undernourished American citizens languished in dark and roofless homes. Although the announced death count stood at sixty-five, everyone was bracing for the actual chilling numbers to be released upon the conclusion of the official government review. Meanwhile, Maria, ultimately causing over $100 billion in collateral damage, was now the third-costliest hurricane in US history. Surely, the territory's already precarious economy would feel the financial shockwaves for years, maybe even decades, to come. And a couple of years later the COVID-19 pandemic would only exacerbate Puerto Rico's post-Maria economic situation. Some statistics, such as those documenting the number of children suffering from PTSD or families fleeing to the mainland, will never be ascertained.

16

A Global Reach

Roberto's volunteer efforts during Hurricane Maria marked a continuation of his North American–wide presence throughout the 2010s. In addition to calling Tampa and Toronto home, the newly minted Hall of Famer and special assistant to the Blue Jays organization would often return to Puerto Rico to visit his parents and extended family and hold clinics for the legions of young ballplayers who fantasized about being the next Roberto Alomar. With his brother a fixture on the Cleveland Indians' coaching staff, it was not uncommon to see Roberto hanging out in the home dugout of Progressive Field (known as Jacobs Field when he was with the franchise) during the team's pregame workouts.

And effective 12/12/12, he was doing all these things as a once-again married man. On the twelfth day of the twelfth month of 2012 ("12" was of course his uniform number), in front of dozens of former teammates, friends, and Blue Jays employees at the Art Gallery of Ontario in downtown Toronto, Roberto, wearing a suit designed by Pat Monardo, a renowned tailor for the likes of Tony Bennett and Harrison Ford, married Montreal native Kim Perks. Given Roberto's background, the attendee list was unsurprisingly diverse, with some of the more notable names including former ballplayers Jose Cruz Jr.; Kelly Gruber; Eduardo Perez; Devon White; Baseball Hall of Fame president Jeff Idelson; his favorite manager, Cito Gaston; one-time Jays executive

Pat Gillick; close friends Spencer Miller and Rob Jack; his financial advisor, Scott Merrill; and of course, his brother and best man, Sandy.[1]

Roberto had first met Kim in 1991 when she was a sky box hostess at the SkyDome for Blue Jays games and later became reacquainted with her during a 2010 chance encounter at the dental office of Dr. Sol Weiss in the high-end Toronto neighborhood of Yorkville. Just like Roberto, Kim had been previously married. She also had a daughter, a sixteen-year-old budding actress named Robyn who would soon assume the Alomar surname and a decade later make her mark on the Hulu series *Utopia Falls*. And in April 2014, just over a year after Kim and Roberto's lavish wedding and Atlantis honeymoon, Robyn became a big sister when the couple welcomed their daughter Lourdes into the world.

It was also in 2014 when Alomar, ensconced with his wife and daughters in his Tampa mansion, learned about Ben Sheppard, a far less fortunate eight-year-old boy from Whitby, Ontario, who was battling spastic hemiplegic cerebral palsy. Sheppard was (and still is) a die-hard Jays fan who lived for baseball, but his condition, one that causes significant tightness and spasticity in the muscles, rendered him mostly wheelchair bound, as walking, never mind running, became too cumbersome of a task. It was quite depressing—as Ben grew older, his mobility actually deteriorated because the tightness in his muscles hindered his bones from growing properly—to see his healthily maturing classmates rushing off to Little League games and sharing stories of their experiences at "Kids Run the Bases Days" at the Rogers Centre.

But by 2014 there was hope. A cutting-edge surgery, Selective Dorsal Rhizotomy (SDR), which could potentially release some of the muscle tension to the point that Ben could move around more freely, was now a viable option. However, the procedure was exorbitantly expensive (as in over $100,000), and there would be other considerable costs such as those associated with transportation and accommodations. Ben's family was of limited financial means (they were constantly saddled with large medical bills with another child also suffering from cerebral palsy), and their health insurance didn't cover a specialized treatment like SDR.

When Roberto found out about the family's dire situation (and that Ben just really wanted to be able to play baseball with other kids), he took it upon himself to make sure the surgery happened. What did that entail? For starters, recruiting other former Blue Jays (Duane Ward, Carlos Delgado, and Jesse

Barfield were some of the splashier names) to put on a one-time skills clinic for kids at Whitby's Iroquois Park with all proceeds from registration fees going toward Sheppard's medical bills. With the backing of such prominent Jays alumni, the Blue Jays Baseball Academy, in conjunction with the Whitby Minor Baseball Association (WMBA), were able to organize a first-rate event attended by over four hundred youth ballplayers. The turnout was solid and accounted for $34,000, a sum that was soon matched by the event's chief sponsor, Honda Canada. Simple math, however, would indicate that the goal of raising over $100,000 was not met. Although there had also been funds contributed through a small golf tournament and private donations, it simply wasn't enough: the Sheppard family was going to need more help to get their son the requisite medical care in a timely fashion.

They didn't have to wait long. Soon after the final proceeds were tallied, Roberto made his personal donation to ensure all medical expenses were covered.

The following month, Ben, along with his parents, Robyn and Norman, were headed to St. Louis Children's Hospital for the procedure.

Flash forward to April 13, 2015. A then nine-year-old Ben Sheppard, no longer dependent on his wheelchair to get around and on his parents to get dressed and go down the stairs, walked onto the Rogers Centre infield alongside Roberto and new MLB commissioner Rob Manfred and threw out the first pitch before Toronto's home opener.[2]

Two years later, during a visit to his home island, Alomar came across an opportunity to honor someone who was not among the living, that being Roberto Clemente. Upon learning from a mutual friend that Justino Clemente, Roberto's older brother and lone surviving sibling, always wanted to meet him, Alomar made plans to stop by the ninety-year-old man's home in Puerto Rico. A visit that Roberto had anticipated lasting no more than ten minutes eventually turned into a two-hour-long conversation in which Justino revealed his lifelong desire to visit the National Baseball Hall of Fame and Museum. Soon thereafter, Alomar arranged for Justino, along with his wife Carmen and daughters Janet and Judy, to visit Cooperstown and see Uncle Roberto's HOF plaque for the very first time. On September 29, 2018, a day before the forty-sixth anniversary of Roberto Clemente's three-thousandth career MLB hit and in the middle of National Hispanic Heritage Month (Sept. 15–Oct. 15), Justino and Roberto not only went to the sacred plaque and toured the Hall (quite a few artifacts from Clemente's career including the cap he wore when he collected his career-record hit are on display), but they also participated in a "Voices of the Game" program during which they told the audience of their blossoming friendship that led to them sharing a stage in Cooperstown's recently renovated Grandstand Theater.

Via a translator, Justino shared stories of growing up with Roberto and his younger brother's eventual journey to the mainland where he embarked on a Hall of Fame career. He was rather candid in describing his brother's struggles, at one point sharing with the audience, "His experience in the United States dealing with the racism really affected him quite a bit and it changed his personality. He became more guarded. When the press would come into the locker room he would try to hide. What Roberto would be wary of was would they be translating exactly what he was saying to the public or would they twist his words."[3]

There was a sizable crowd on hand, but two people who weren't present were Clemente's sons, Luis Clemente and Roberto Clemente Jr. In fact, they didn't even know about the arranged tour and program until afterward. The reason being that, according to Roberto Clemente Jr., Justino had actually been more or less estranged from his late brother's family ever since the tragic accident.

"That is a very touchy subject for me about my uncle because from the day that my father passed away, he never set foot in my house to visit," explains Roberto Jr. "People want to ask me [about the Hall of Fame visit]. I say, 'Please don't ask me because I don't know that guy.' I don't know who he is. He can talk of his knowledge about my father, but for me, he is a stranger. It's unfortunate, but it's a fact."[4]

Roberto's work in arranging Justino's visit exemplified how he used to leverage his influence in Cooperstown (he was formerly a member of the National Baseball Hall of Fame and Museum's Board of Directors) toward opening the Hall's doors for others—both figuratively and literally. Before resigning from the board amid the sexual misconduct allegations in April 2021, Roberto served on the Today's Game Committee, one of four such committees that used to meet every several years to vote on players and baseball personnel from a specific era for induction. While Roberto's committee focused on former players from 1988 to the present, his participation did provide exposure to members of the Modern Baseball Committee who considered the qualifications of ballplayers from 1970 to 1987, one of whom was old friend Luis Tiant. (Effective 2022, the Hall of Fame election eras were consolidated into two time frames—the Contemporary Baseball Era, spanning the period from 1980 to present day, and the Classic Baseball Era, spanning the period before 1980 and including Negro Leagues and pre–Negro Leagues stars.)

"He [Roberto] tried to talk to the guys to put me in the Hall of Fame," says Tiant. "He was mad because he said I'm supposed to be in the Hall of Fame. He doesn't know why they don't put me in. I really appreciate what he's trying to do for me. He didn't have to do any of that. Every time he sees me, he hugs me, we sit down, and we talk."[5]

For Tiant, who's in his eighties and not getting any younger, it's comforting to know that a formerly influential Hall member once lobbied for his inclusion.

"I don't know why but they wait until people die—like they did to Ron Santo and a few other guys—to put them in," adds Tiant, who is still awaiting baseball's greatest honor.[6]

In March 2017, Commissioner Manfred named Alomar MLB's Special Consultant in Puerto Rico, a role that entailed advising the Commissioner's Office on matters pertaining to youth baseball in Puerto Rico and serving as an ambassador at events and development initiatives throughout the territory, including youth camps and tournaments. (Alomar would later serve on Manfred's competition committee, but Puerto Rican affairs would remain his primary focus.) At the time, there were few people more qualified to be in charge of developing Puerto Rican players, coaches, and even front-office personnel.

A few years later, during the first winter of the pandemic when scores of young Puerto Rican ballplayers' careers were in flux, Roberto launched an expansion franchise, RA12, in the Liga de Béisbol Profesional Roberto Clemente (Winter League), with the primary goal of providing up-and-coming ballplayers an opportunity to compete at the professional level. Interestingly, when Roberto himself played in the winter league, the rosters were stacked with young guys. But over the years, young prospects were nudged out as the league started gravitating more toward MLB journeymen. In seeking to reverse that trend—while admittedly not being concerned with wins and losses—Roberto built a roster in which the oldest player was twenty-six. While the team finished 2–16 during a COVID-truncated schedule, a couple dozen Puerto Rican ballplayers fulfilled their collective dream of playing pro ball in their native land. As of winter 2022, Roberto remained the owner of the RA12 franchise, while his father served as co–general manager.

"Sometimes you have to do things differently so that you get different results," says Luis Clemente. "Many times, people are just too comfortable with the way things have been for many, many, many years. People like Robbie are the ones who really make a difference."[7]

Naturally, the current crop of Puerto Rican big leaguers is one that grew up idolizing Robbie. In particular, he was a childhood favorite of Mets shortstop Francisco Lindor, the flossy switch-hitter, who, like Alomar, struggled mightily during his first season in Queens. When Lindor, who wears number 12 in honor of Alomar, broke into the big leagues with Cleveland, Sandy Alomar Jr. was the first base coach; as Roberto would often visit his brother, Lindor was able to become acquainted with his childhood hero. In the following years, whenever Cleveland visited Toronto, where Robbie was working as a special assistant to CEO Mark Shapiro, Alomar and Lindor would reconnect.

That Alomar was employed by his former boss Shapiro for a number of years in Toronto was rather ironic. Remember, after the red-headed executive had dealt him to the Mets in December 2001, the star publicly accused the Cleveland front office of being deceitful. But whatever frosty relationship existed between the two men earlier in the century eventually thawed to the point that they could coexist peacefully as colleagues. Alomar, who started serving Toronto as a "special assistant" (many former MLB players hold this ambiguous part-time role) in 2011, began reporting to Shapiro in 2015 when the latter was hired as the club's CEO. They enjoyed a healthy working relationship, with Roberto supporting efforts in baseball operations—he was often mentoring guys during spring training—and outreach projects in different communities throughout eastern Canada.

By early 2020, tired of shuttling back and forth from Tampa to Toronto (not to mention making pit stops in Puerto Rico), he sold his 18,703-square-foot home north of Tampa and moved with his wife to Toronto, where they became full-time residents. A child of the Caribbean settling down in the Great White North? It actually made a lot of sense considering that his sports marketing agency, Alomar Sports, as well as his charitable organization, Foundation 12, one that was continuing to serve special needs children throughout Ontario, were both headquartered in Toronto. He was already a regular at the Jays' annual Winter Fest, glad-handing starry-eyed fans and reminiscing about the glory days of the early 1990s. An avid hoops fan (and a damn good player by the way), Robbie was often spotted courtside cheering on the Raptors—although not nearly as visibly as musician Drake. The sports talk show *Tim & Sid* that used to air on Sportsnet frequently had the Jays legend on as a guest before it disbanded. Perhaps most importantly, by living permanently in Toronto, Alomar was not only constantly immersed in the fabric of a city that still lionized him but was also within driving distance of older brother Sandy and his children, including Marcus, a physical therapist, and Brianna, a gifted singer who recited the National Anthem before the All-Star Futures Game at Cleveland's Progressive Field in July 2019.

July 2019. How much life would change for everyone, and in particular Roberto Alomar, over the next few years.

17

Spring 2021

In the end, Major League Baseball is no different from politics, entertainment, business, medicine, law, culinary arts, and broadcasting.

Just as allegations tied to the #MeToo movement rocked the aforementioned industries beginning in October 2017 when the *New York Times* published its explosive report chronicling repeated acts of sexual harassment committed by Hollywood mogul Harvey Weinstein, similarly disturbing accusations were eventually made against towering figures in the world of sports, in particular that of professional baseball. Ultimately, neither former players (Kenny Lofton, Mickey Callaway) nor active ones (Yasiel Puig, Trevor Bauer) would prove to be immune from such deeply personal charges, while one franchise, the New York Mets, was ultimately exposed as having a particularly toxic workplace culture rife with systemic unaccountability.

In January 2021, ESPN's intrepid journalists Mina Kimes and Jeff Passan reported that New York's recently-hired GM, Jared Porter, had sent dozens of sexually explicit, unsolicited texts and pictures to a female reporter who had relocated to the United States to cover Major League Baseball.[1] Less than 12 hours after ESPN's report was published, the New York Mets announced that they were firing Porter.

Steve Cohen, the franchise's new principal owner, tweeted, "In my initial press conference I spoke about the importance of integrity and I meant it. There should be zero tolerance for this type of behavior."[2]

It would soon become evident that Porter's "type of behavior" was not an isolated incident in the Mets organization. On January 22, 2021, three days after Porter was relieved of his duties, the Mets terminated hitting performance coordinator Ryan Ellis for his alleged acts of sexual misconduct that had occurred in 2017–2018.[3]

Meanwhile, on February 1, 2021, *The Athletic* also reported that Mickey Callaway, who had managed the Mets from 2018 to 2019 and at the time was the pitching coach of the Los Angeles Angels, was accused of making unsolicited sexual advances to five female reporters over at least five years, a time span that overlapped with his managerial stint in New York. The five accusers, all of whom spoke to *The Athletic* on the condition of anonymity, detailed Callaway constantly sending unwanted emails and text messages, including images of himself shirtless. Per the report, one lady claimed that Callaway asked her to send nude photos while another recalled Callaway thrusting his crotch toward her face in the midst of an interview. The Angels immediately suspended Callaway before ultimately firing him. The Mets, in an initial response to a request for a statement, told *The Athletic* that the organization "learned" in August 2018 of an incident that had occurred before it hired Callaway (he had previously been the pitching coach of the Cleveland Indians) and that it had investigated the incident. The Mets, however, did not disclose further details or the outcome of said investigation. After learning of Callaway's past history, the Mets allowed Callaway to continue managing the ballclub for another fourteen months before dismissing him in October 2019 following their disappointing third-place finish in the National League East race.[4] A month following the February 1, 2021, article, *The Athletic* published another report that revealed that some within the Cleveland Indians organization, including manager Terry Francona, were aware of Callaway's inappropriate behavior when he was the team's pitching coach before joining the Mets.[5]

Spring forward three months—as the coronavirus vaccines were being rolled out to the masses and stadiums were no longer vacant buildings, baseball was once again impacted by the #MeToo movement, as Roberto Alomar, yet another person associated with the New York Mets franchise, albeit formerly in his case, was accused of sexual predatory behavior. On April 30, 2021, it was revealed that earlier in the year a "baseball industry employee" had come forward with a 2014 sexual misconduct claim against Alomar, who was continuing to serve a dual role in baseball as a consultant to MLB Commissioner Rob Manfred and Blue Jays special advisor. Several hours after the allegation was made public, Manfred released the following statement explaining how his office decided to proceed following the reported workplace complaint against Alomar:

> At my office's request, an independent investigation was conducted by an external legal firm to review an allegation of sexual misconduct reported by a baseball industry employee earlier this year involving Mr. Alomar in 2014. Having reviewed all of the available evidence from the now completed investigation, I have concluded that Mr. Alomar violated MLB's policies, and that termination of his consultant contract and placement on the MLB's Ineligible List are warranted.[6]

Following Manfred's declaration, the Blue Jays announced that they were immediately severing all ties with Alomar. He wasn't just getting relieved of his special advisor duties which included serving as an ambassador for the club's global initiatives. The Blue Jays were effectively scrubbing Alomar's name from their records by delivering the following statement: "The Blue Jays are committed to advancing respect and equity in baseball and are taking further action by removing Alomar from the Level of Excellence and taking down his banner at Rogers Centre."[7] (In summer 2022, when the franchise celebrated the 30th anniversary of its first-ever World Series title, Alomar, arguably the most valuable member of the 1992 Jays, was not present.)

The saving grace, at least for Alomar, was that the National Baseball Hall of Fame opted not to revoke his esteemed membership. The official statement from Hall of Fame board chairman Jane Forbes Clark read as follows:

> The National Baseball Hall of Fame was shocked and saddened to learn of the news being shared today about Roberto Alomar. When he was elected to the Hall of Fame by the Baseball Writers' Association of America in the Class of 2011, Alomar was an eligible candidate in good standing. His plaque will remain on display in the Hall of Fame in recognition of his accomplishments in the game, and his enshrinement reflects his eligibility and the perspective of the BBWAA voters at that time.[8]

It should be noted that a couple of days after this story broke, Alomar did resign from his position on the Hall of Fame's board of directors.

While the Canadian Baseball Hall of Fame in St. Marys, Ontario, came to a similar conclusion by saying that Alomar's 2010 induction would not be rescinded, officials said in no uncertain terms that Alomar would not be welcome at future events.

A month later, another courageous woman came forth. This time, the accuser, Melissa Verge, chose to reveal her identity as well as provide a vivid account of what (allegedly) transpired. According to Verge's self-written report in the *Toronto Star*, one that she felt empowered to write after the aforementioned allegations had been made public, there was a 2014 incident when she was an eighteen-year-old volunteer at a youth baseball camp run by the Blue Jays. Reportedly, a forty-six-year-old Roberto Alomar, employed by the team at the time, cornered her in the team's weight room while giving her a tour of the clubhouse before propositioning her for sex by pressing his body into hers without consent . . . and then confronting her again the following day at the ballpark.

As published in the May 28, 2021, edition of the *Toronto Star*, Verge's story ("All I Wanted Was Baseball Advice. Instead, Roberto Alomar Pushed His Unwelcome Body up against Mine") included the following:

> We're alone inside the Blue Jays' clubhouse.
>
> A few minutes ago, this was the only place I wanted to be. My favourite place on earth. I would have happily made my home a tent in centrefield and lived out my days munching over-priced hotdogs and watching baseball.
>
> But now, my happy place has been taken away. I can't get out of here fast enough.
>
> . . . I was an 18-year-old Blue Jays fan, and Roberto Alomar was a 46-year-old Hall of Famer and we were alone in the clubhouse. He pushed his unwelcome body up against me from behind. He assumed I wanted it without even asking my permission.
>
> If he had asked, and I had the courage, I would have told him I didn't want him grabbing my arm and rubbing up against me. I wanted him to step away from me. I wanted to step away from him. I stood there, frozen. . . .
>
> I remember we left the clubhouse and as we were walking back towards the field, he had his arm tight around me—too tight. He asked me what my favourite alcoholic drink was and gave me his phone number.

He asked me not to tell anyone. I idolized him. I had been there at the Rogers Centre, one of more than 40,000 fans on the day his number was retired. I remember the song that played, "Beautiful Day," ringing throughout the stadium, and the chills that ran through my body. And now, here I was, and here he was.

I was scared. It was such a big power imbalance, I physically felt incapable of telling him no.

That was day one of the Blue Jays camp. I don't remember anything else about it. But on day two, I remember clearly, he asked me to go up to his private suite with him at the Rogers Centre.

"We can close the door and have some kissing and some loving," he said. "Just don't tell your boyfriend."

I didn't say no to his face. I felt nothing but dread, as I sat there waiting for him to approach me again to see if I was ready to go with him. I'd never been in a suite before, and I remember picturing a hotel room with a giant bed and nobody else around, which scared me even more. I didn't want to go. But I also didn't know how to say no to this powerful man who I had looked up to for years.

I sat down on the bench inside the dugout beside a group of young guys who were also helping out at the camp. I told a couple of them what had happened and they seemed shocked. It was hard for them to believe, probably because they idolized him, too.

Before he had a chance to confront me again, I did one of the hardest things I've ever done, and told a Jays official in charge of the camp. We sat inside the Away dugout at the stadium. I was crying. He looked shocked and worried.

He went to talk to Alomar about it, and later, they both came out and Alomar apologized to me, saying he saw me like a sister and would protect me. It seemed very insincere to me even then. It was nowhere close to a brother sister dynamic.

I thought about writing about my experience then, because it seemed wrong to me that he could continue working in amateur baseball when he was clearly abusing his position of power. After speaking with one of my professors at Ryerson, I decided against it. At the time, I didn't want to jeopardize my chances of working with the organization in the future.

But, when I opened up my phone and saw the article about him last month, that day at the camp seven years ago came back. I knew the time had come for me to share what happened.[9]

Once Verge went public with her story, the Blue Jays immediately released a statement, saying they were, "troubled to learn about Ms. Verge's experience in 2014 involving Roberto Alomar and another former employee. Since we were made aware of the incident by the *Toronto Star*, we have commenced an internal investigation using an outside firm."[10]

It was soon revealed that the other former team employee cited was one Rob Jack, the Jays' erstwhile manager of social marketing and a close friend and former groomsman of Alomar's, who, upon talking to Verge, apparently did not notify any members of the team or the HR department. (A year later, Jack was fired by the team, presumably for unrelated reasons, and went to work for Roberto as president of Alomar Sports.) More than a week before the *Toronto Star* published Verge's first-person narrative, Alomar and Jack were sent detailed questions, but neither responded.

Accompanying Verge's piece, the *Star*'s social justice reporter, Brendan Kennedy, wrote an article titled "Blue Jays Investigating New Allegations against Roberto Alomar," which shed light on some tangentially related developments. While MLB hadn't disclosed any details about its investigation regarding the initial allegations or what led Commissioner Manfred to punish Alomar so harshly, Kennedy wrote that "according to multiple sources with knowledge of the investigation, the allegations in that case are far more serious than what is now being alleged by Verge."[11] The investigation, which took three months to complete, involved the interrogation of fourteen people, including Alomar and Jack, and resulted in an eleven-page report, the contents of which prompted Manfred to place Alomar on MLB's Ineligible List without hesitation.

In the next paragraph in Kennedy's report, it was noted that the Blue Jays had also hired yet another external firm to conduct a different probe into unrelated accusations of "inappropriate behaviour" against Alomar involving a *third* woman.[12] The Jays confirmed to the *Star* that the investigation was recently finished, but refused to disclose any details. Naturally, there weren't many people willing to go on the record here, but Kennedy was able to get ahold of one former Jays employee who, speaking on the condition of anonymity, acknowledged that while he couldn't recall hearing of any specific complaints against Alomar, the recent allegations shouldn't come as a surprise to anyone in the organization. "I think the organization was well aware of [his] nature, let's put it that way."[13]

Epilogue

The trail of controversies has tarnished Roberto Alomar's legacy, but his greatness on the ballfield remains undeniable—especially when one considers the profound impact that he had on the history of late twentieth-century baseball. Without Alomar, Toronto doesn't win back-to-back World Series titles, Baltimore doesn't make it to two consecutive ALCS, and the 1999 Cleveland Indians don't win ninety-seven games en route to becoming one of the five fastest clubs to clinch a division title. Without Alomar, these teams may have been good, but not great.

In terms of his individual performance, the offensive numbers alone are most likely worthy of Cooperstown, especially considering the increasingly liberal standards by which today's candidates are judged. Terms such as "launch angle" and "exit velocity" weren't commonplace in Roberto's heyday, but even if they had been part of baseball jargon in the 1990s, such terminology would not have been necessary to confirm he was one of the best switch-hitters in MLB history. In seventeen seasons, number 12 recorded ("compiled" doesn't seem like the appropriate verb) 2,724 hits, 1,134 RBIs, and 474 stolen bases. A lifetime .300 hitter (in the most literal sense), Alomar also snuck in 210 home runs, a respectable number that doesn't even account for his shot during the 1992 ALCS (off Dennis Eckersley, no less) that would forever alter the trajectory of the Blue Jays franchise. He was perennially atop the league leaders in on-base percentage, never whiffed more than ninety-six times in a season, and established himself as one of the most capable bunters of his generation—a skill criminally overlooked by casual fans but not lost on the purists such as, say, Alex Rodriguez, who, while previously serving as a commentator for ESPN, cited Robbie's ability to lay down bunts straight out of a Tom Emanski instructional video.

Jose Cruz Jr. recalls that,

> He was my favorite player growing up. A lot of how I ended up playing and switch-hitting and everything, he was a part of that. He was just really fun to watch in person. [One time] I was watching Robbie Alomar hit as I was playing left field in the middle of our game. I was like, "C'mon snap out of it, man. Focus on the game." He was someone that you wanted to be like on the field.[1]

Even with the remarkable numbers on the back of his baseball card, defense was, without question, Roberto's forte—a true testament to his unparalleled wizardry in the middle of the diamond.

"From my personal view, and I've covered baseball every year since 1976, Robbie is by far the best second baseman I've ever seen," says veteran BBWAA member Barry Bloom. "And there is nobody even close."[2]

Not even Cincinnati Reds great Joe Morgan, whose name, along with Alomar's, invariably comes up in the debate over who was the greatest defensive second baseman in modern baseball?

"I mean Joe Morgan was a prototype second baseman," responds Bloom. "Joe Morgan was great as the type of second baseman he was. Robbie totally rewrote the position. His range and his ability to get to balls was far greater than that of any second baseman I've ever seen. The guy played second base like a shortstop."[3]

Coincidentally, the other all-time great defensive second basemen (with the exceptions of maybe Ryne Sandberg and Lou Whitaker) played before World War II. Drawing comparisons between Alomar and the likes of Eddie Collins, Charlie Gehringer, and Rogers Hornsby is a slippery slope given the vastly different eras in which Alomar and his predecessors played. Consider that the Gold Glove Award was not even created until 1957, long after the triumvirate of Collins, Gehringer, and Hornsby had retired. It's certainly possible that each may have surpassed Alomar's total of ten Gold Gloves, but no one will ever know. For what it's worth, what we do know is that Morgan,

Sandberg, and Whitaker, who won five, nine, and three, respectively, did not reach double digits. (A cursory glance at baseball-reference.com indicates that Collins, Gehringer, and Hornsby had superior offensive numbers to Alomar's; meanwhile, Morgan, Sandberg, and Whitaker were, generally speaking, less productive offensively.)

In the twenty-first century, the second baseman most frequently compared to Alomar is Houston Astros great Jose Altuve. As of this book's publication date, Altuve is on pace to finish with more hits and homers than Alomar's respective totals (2,724 base knocks, 210 long balls). Also, unlike Alomar, Altuve has won an AL MVP (2017) and three batting titles (2014, 2016, 2017). But, defensively speaking, there's no comparison, at least as far as end-of-season hardware goes. Alomar finished with 10 Gold Glove Awards while, as of February 2023, Altuve only had one to his name. Coincidentally, each ballplayer, while being an integral member of multiple World Series–winning teams, had his own legacy-defining scandal that, in the eyes of some, is grounds for being barred from Cooperstown, at least initially. For Alomar, the spitting incident derailed his pursuit of being a first-ballot Hall of Famer; for Altuve, his role in the Astros' nefarious sign-stealing operation may very well preclude him from being elected when he is first eligible.

Alomar's on-field accomplishments—and how they compare historically to those of other Hall of Fame–caliber second basemen—can be analyzed ad nauseam by stat geeks worldwide. (And they surely have been.) Meanwhile, no advanced metric can quantify his other defining trait, that being the intangible known as having an exceptional baseball IQ.

"I don't think there was anybody better than Robbie at being able to sit on the bench and know exactly what a pitcher was going to do," adds Bloom.[4]

Former players concur. Alomar was, in the words of fellow Hall of Famer Randy Johnson, "not only smart between the lines, but a very smart player in the dugout watching opposing pitchers."[5]

While Alomar hadn't exactly been on his mind of late, The Big Unit was able to elaborate during a November 2020 interview:

> As an opposing pitcher, I think there was a time or two when he probably knew what pitch I was getting ready to throw. As an opposing player, I just heard that he was a very smart ballplayer. There are just certain things that you can't teach a player. It goes without saying it's probably one reason why he's in the

Hall of Fame is because he made himself smart. He already had natural ability, and I think that there are lots of things that you have to do sometimes that are beyond the numbers or what will show up in the box score. [Alomar] always seemed to get the things done that needed to be done. [In the 1997 ALDS against Johnson's Mariners, Alomar managed to hit .300 while dealing with excruciating pain in his left shoulder.] Obviously, it goes without saying what kind of defensive player he was. He was unbelievable. I don't know how many Gold Gloves he had. He was kind of like Pudge Rodriguez, every year he got one. But there's more than just wanting to be known for your defense. He was a great offensive threat and was a very bright player. And that's probably one of his greatest attributes.[6]

Alomar was, in fact, exceptionally bright, and his uncanny ability to pick up the most subtle details was a considerable asset to whichever team he was playing for at the time. Former Baltimore Oriole southpaw Rick Krivda recalls one game he was pitching when Alomar essentially took over as *pitching coach* for an inning. This was in the 1990s, when it was customary for pitchers to keep their index fingers out of their gloves when delivering pitches. However, during this particular outing, Alomar noticed that this habit posed a disadvantage to his young teammate. So, one inning, in between batters, Roberto requested time and jogged over to the mound, instructing Krivda to tuck in his pointer finger. No explanation, just do it. After the side was retired, Alomar explained something to Krivda that he had never heard from any pitching coach in his past: by not concealing his pointer finger, he was tipping pitches. Apparently, Alomar noticed that Krivda had a tendency to press down with his index finger when he was about to fire a fastball but leave it in the air when delivering an off-speed pitch.

"Nobody had ever told me that," says Krivda. "No wonder he's an all-star. He just saw things."[7]

Krivda is not the only former teammate of Alomar's who can recall the man having a sixth sense on the diamond. As Jeff Reboulet shares:

Oftentimes I was playing shortstop with him. You always had to be ready for a throw behind. He would catch a ball from the outfield and he would just turn and fire it behind the guy at first, when nobody's even thinking about the guy at first.

Or he would catch a ball and they're going to hold the runner at third base from scoring. You know they're not going to score because it's not going to be that close—the coach is going to stop the runner. As soon as he would catch it, he would throw before the guy even got to third because he knew he was going to round it. If he rounded it too far, the ball would be there by the time he was able to put the brakes on and get back.

Nobody does those kinds of things, or rarely do they do those things. You have to have a complete understanding of what's going to happen—what that coach is going to do, what the player is going to do—and then you have to have the balls to throw it behind [in case you throw it away]. That was kind of the epitome of Robbie Alomar and how he would play the game.[8]

Prior to the bombshell allegations in spring 2021, Alomar had expressed mild interest in becoming an MLB manager one day. For many Hall of Famers—Ted Williams, Ryne Sandberg, Mel Ott, and even the trailblazing Frank Robinson, just to name several—this has not been a wise career move. Their stellar playing careers didn't translate to success in overseeing winning clubs. But because of his brilliant baseball mind and keen attention to the most minute details (not to mention vastly improved English communication skills), it seems quite possible that Roberto would have been able to buck that trend.

Interviews with dozens of former teammates and opponents indicate that no one knew more about the game—or had as much fun playing it. The latter was particularly true during the halcyon days of his blossoming career with the two-time world champion Toronto Blue Jays.

"When I think of Robbie, I think when you do something you love, it's not a job. It's not work," says former Toronto teammate Dave Winfield. "He just came out there and put his abilities and his heart and his desire on stage. He had a ball. I think he would be happy with his career and life in baseball. And he should be."[9] (Note: this interview was conducted in September 2020, months before Roberto's banishment from MLB.)

Undoubtedly, Robbie would have played for free. But it didn't hurt making over $76 million in career earnings either, at times being one of the game's highest-paid stars. Of course, had Robbie broken into the big leagues a quarter-century or so later, he could have made four times as much. If not more.

Not to be forgotten, one of the major reasons that Roberto became enamored with baseball was that he was able to share his passion for the sport with his father and brother. In this sense, he was no different from the millions of boys and girls who have ever stepped on a ballfield and enjoyed playing catch with their parents. Baseball lends itself to familial bonding—it's why so many young players gravitate toward the game in the first place—and Roberto just happened to be one of the incredibly rare ballplayers who rose to professional stardom in the footsteps of his proud father.

In terms of the impact the Alomar boys have had on Major League Baseball, consider that from 1964 through 2007, there were only nine seasons when an Alomar was not playing in the big leagues; meanwhile, Sandy Sr. spent some of those bridge years (1979–1987) as a coach. All told, the Alomars played in a grand total of 5,237 MLB games with Roberto accounting for 2,379. The family's collective résumé includes nineteen All-Star Game appearances and 5,128 career hits. In the 1990s, when Roberto and Sandy Jr. were in their prime, it seemed like nearly every postseason involved one of the brothers.

"When I think of families in the game, there are two prominent [ones] that stand out," says Shea Hillenbrand. "There's the Alomar family and the Molina family."[10]

There certainly have been quite a few prominent baseball families (the Griffeys, Bondses, Ripkens, Boones, Fielders, Alous, and Guerreros have to be atop any list) but it's only natural to associate the Alomars with the Molinas. Both families hail from Puerto Rico, have accounted for a whopping number of games played (for the Molinas, it is over four thousand), and within each of these royal baseball bloodlines, there is one member who stands out: Roberto is the only Alomar in the Hall of Fame while in the Molina family of catchers, youngest brother Yadier, likely bound for Cooperstown, had a far more productive career than those of his older siblings Bengie and Jose.

By any measure, the Alomars rank high on the list of baseball families, which, as it turns out, has further complicated Roberto's recent situation. While Roberto used to represent his honorable family well by virtue of his sparkling on-field performances and exemplary charity work, the recent allegations reflect poorly on the Alomars. Just like the alleged sexual misconduct behavior will remain an indelible part of Roberto's personal legacy, so too will it remain an everlasting part of the family's legacy, at least to some degree.

Legacy matters aside, it bears mentioning (or perhaps, reiterating) that back in the 1970s, if Maria, the matriarch of the family, had her way, the Alomar clan would never have become synonymous with baseball royalty. She knew that the game could be cruel and that it took a considerable toll on her husband. She didn't want a then-adolescent Roberto, as talented as he was, to waste his intellectual skills by obsessing over a career in baseball. Like many parents, Maria wanted her youngest child to pursue a more conventional career path by first getting a college degree.

However, all these years later, it's a pretty good thing that Roberto didn't heed his mother's advice to attend college. He probably would have been a fine student of higher education and found success in whatever profession he chose, but it seems safe to say that this baseball gig didn't work out too badly for him either.

Notes

INTRODUCTION

1. Albert Chen, "Roberto Alomar and John Hirschbeck," *Sports Illustrated*, July 8, 2013.

2. "Alomar's Post-Game Comments Infuriate Umpire," *Associated Press*, September 29, 1996.

3. Chen, "Roberto Alomar and John Hirschbeck."

4. Chen.

5. Rick Krivda, interview with author, August 4, 2020.

6. Dan Shaughnessy, "Alomar Hands Down Winner in Shame Game," *Boston Globe*, September 29, 1996.

CHAPTER 1

1. David Maraniss, *Clemente: The Passion and Grace of Baseball's Last Hero* (New York: Simon & Schuster, 2006), 19.

2. Bob Wolf, "Sandy Making Smooth Switch to Wigwam Keystone," *The Sporting News*, April 10, 1965.

3. Roberto Alomar, with Stephen Brunt, *Second to None: The Roberto Alomar Story* (New York: Penguin Books, 1993), 28.

4. John Wiebusch, "Alomar: Castoff Role a Nightmare," *Los Angeles Times*, June 19, 1970.

5. Alomar, with Brunt, 34.

6. Alomar, with Brunt, 34.

7. Maraniss, *Clemente*, 19.

8. Dick Heller, "The Way It Was: Clemente Gave Till the End," *Washington Times*, December 28, 2009.

CHAPTER 2

1. Roberto Alomar, with Stephen Brunt, *Second to None: The Roberto Alomar Story* (Toronto, ON: Penguin Books, 1993), 33.

2. Alomar, with Brunt, 51.

3. Alomar, with Brunt, 51.

4. Alomar, with Brunt, 41.

5. Alomar, with Brunt, 37.

6. Jose Cruz Jr., interview with author, September 20, 2022.

7. Marc Appleman, "Like Father Like Sons: Padres Bring More Than One Alomar to Camp," *Los Angeles Times*, March 5, 1985.

8. Alomar, with Brunt, *Second to None*, 54.

9. Milt Dunnell, "It Ain't Easy Being the Other Alomar," *Toronto Star*, April 25, 1992.

10. Bill Plaschke, "A Lot of Care, a Little Bit of Conniving Are Behind This Scouting Success Story," *Los Angeles Times*, January 26, 1989.

CHAPTER 3

1. Anonymous interview with author, February 2, 2021.

2. Anonymous.

3. Anonymous.

4. Anonymous.

5. Anonymous.

6. Roberto Clemente Jr., interview with author, February 5, 2021.

7. Clemente Jr.

8. Anonymous, interview with author, February 2, 2021.

9. Jim Wasem, interview with author, June 9, 2020.

10. Wasem.

11. Anonymous, interview with author.

12. Wasem, interview with author.

13. Jeff Yurtin, interview with author, June 8, 2020.

14. Wasem, interview with author.

15. Yurtin, interview with author.

16. Chris De Luca, "Alomar Is Upset after Demotion," *Escondido Times-Advocate*, March 26, 1988.

17. Bill Plaschke, "Alomar & Sons, Three from Same Family Keys to Organization's Future," *Los Angeles Times*, January 28, 1989.

18. Wire Report, "Padres Send Out the Call for Former Pilot Roberto Alomar," *Wichita Eagle-Beacon*, April 21, 1988.

CHAPTER 4

1. Jeff Sanders, "Padres History (April 22): Roberto Alomar's Debut, Tony Gwynn's 1000th Hit," *San Diego Union-Tribune*, April 22, 2020.

2. Doug Drabek, interview with author, March 12, 2021.

3. Mike Jackson, interview with author, June 10, 2020.

4. Barry Bloom, interview with author, December 7, 2020.

5. Anonymous, interview with author, February 2, 2021.

6. Phil Stephenson, interview with author, October 26, 2020.

7. Jeff Sanders, "Padres History (May 24): Jack Clark Takes On . . . Tony Gwynn?," *San Diego Union-Tribune*, May 24, 2020.

8. Bloom, interview with author.

9. Stephenson, interview with author.

10. Bloom, interview with author.

11. Bloom.

12. Tim Kurkjian, "Beginning Again," *Sports Illustrated*, March 11, 1991.

13. Kurkjian.

14. Barry Bloom, "Stars Are Out Tonight for Brothers Alomar," *Chicago Tribune*, July 10, 1990.

15. Alan Solomon, "Cubs/NL Report: The Week in Review," *Chicago Tribune*, July 22, 1990.

16. Roberto Alomar, with Stephen Brunt, *Second to None: The Roberto Alomar Story* (New York: Penguin Books, 1993), 102.

17. Stephenson, interview with author.

18. Gary Hyvonen, "Padres Hike Ticket Prices," *North County Blade-Citizen*, October 10, 1990.

19. Tom Lampkin, interview with author, April 16, 2021.

20. Scott Miller, "A Difference in the Climate: Ex-Padres Alomar and Carter Adjusting to Life in Toronto," *Los Angeles Times*, May 26, 1991.

21. Bloom, interview with author.

22. Stephenson, interview with author.

23. Lampkin, interview with author.

24. Lampkin.

25. John Lott, "Another Level: As Roberto Alomar Is Honored by the Blue Jays, the Star Hopes Fans Have Forgiven an Old Mistake," *National Post*, April 4, 2008.

26. Tim Kurkjian, "Our Best-Ever MLB Winter Meetings Trades, Rumors and Untold Tales from the Lobby," ESPN, December 8, 2020, https://www.espn.com/mlb/story/_/id/30465214/our-best-ever-mlb-winter-meetings-trades-rumors-untold-tales-lobby.

CHAPTER 5

1. Bruce Newman, "Home Suite Home," *Sports Illustrated*, June 8, 1992.

2. Rance Mulliniks, interview with author, July 7, 2020.

3. Mike Timlin, interview with author, September 21, 2020.

4. Mulliniks, interview with author.

5. Timlin, interview with author.

6. Matt Merullo, interview with author, May 12, 2021.

7. Jim Ingraham, interview with author, February 23, 2021.

8. Dave Winfield, interview with author, September 4, 2020.

9. Kevin Boland, "Alomar Makes Hard Landing on SkyDome's Artificial Field," *National Post*, May 22, 1991.

10. Tom Lampkin, interview with author, April 16, 2021.

11. "All-Star Game Notebook," United Press International, July 9, 1991.

12. Mike Terry, "Alomar Brothers Fulfill Dream of Playing Together," *USA Today*, July 9, 1991.

13. Jack Curry, "Don't Blame Alomar Jr. The Fans Did It!," *New York Times*, July 4, 1991.

14. Mulliniks, interview with author.

15. Newman, "Home Suite Home."

16. Newman.

17. Merullo, interview with author, May 12, 2021.

18. Jose Cruz Jr., interview with author, September 20, 2022.

19. Mulliniks, interview with author.

20. Winfield. interview with author.

21. Nick Cafardo and Bob Ryan, "Cone, Stewart Make Pitches," *Boston Globe*, October 12, 1992.

22. Danny Gallagher, *Baseball in the 20th Century* (Toronto, ON: Scoop Press, 2000).

23. Bob Ryan, "Gaining Respect with Their Heroic Performances," *Boston Globe*, October 12, 1992.

24. Winfield, interview with author.

25. Timlin, interview with author.

26. Ryan, "Gaining Respect."

27. Steve Rushin, "Border Conflict," *Sports Illustrated*, October 26, 1992.

28. Winfield, interview with author.

29. Neil Campbell, "Alomar Gives Press the Silent Treatment," *Toronto Globe and Mail*, June 3, 1993.

30. Campbell.

31. Dave Stewart, interview with author, February 3, 2021.

32. Stewart.

33. Jack Curry, "Alomar Truly Covers the Field Like a Hand in Glove," *New York Times*, October 18, 1993.

34. Timlin, interview with author.

35. Stewart, interview with author.

36. Timlin, interview with author.

37. Bill Lankhof, "Alomar Wants League to Help," *National Post*, July 4, 1995.

38. Timlin, interview with author.

39. Luis Tiant, interview with author, March 19, 2021.

40. Bob Elliott, "It's Time for Alomar to Leave," *National Post*, August 1, 1995.

41. Jim Byers, "Alomar Hints He'll Move," *Toronto Star*, July 31, 1995.

42. Timlin, interview with author.

CHAPTER 6

1. Tim Kurkjian, "Do Not Disturb Roberto Alomar," *Sports Illustrated*, January 29, 1996.

2. Kurkjian.

3. Kurkjian.

4. Peter Schmuck, "The Shining Star Likes His Space," *Baltimore Sun*, August 7, 1996.

5. John Eisenberg, interview with author, October 27, 2020.

6. Mark Maske, "Orioles' Multitalented Alomar Is Second to None," *Washington Post*, March 31, 1996.

7. B. J. Surhoff, interview with author, February 25, 2022.

8. Buster Olney, "Alomar Hitting His Prime at Plate," *Baltimore Sun*, May 28, 1996.

9. Eisenberg, interview with author.

10. Rick Krivda, interview with author, August 4, 2020.

11. Krivda.

12. Krivda.

13. Krivda.

14. Schmuck, "The Shining Star Likes His Space."

15. Olney, "Alomar Hitting His Prime at Plate."

CHAPTER 7

1. B. J. Surhoff, interview with author, February 25, 2022.

2. John Eisenberg, interview with author, October 27, 2020.

3. Roch Kubatko, "Cheered Alomar Pivots Away from Spat," *Baltimore Sun*, October 2, 1996.

4. Tim Kurkjian, "Public Enemy No.1," *Sports Illustrated*, October 14, 1996.

5. Albert Chen, "Roberto Alomar and John Hirschbeck," *Sports Illustrated*, July 8, 2013.

6. Claire Smith, "An Error That the Official Scorer Cannot Take Away," *New York Times*, October 8, 1996.

7. Smith.

8. Kurkjian, "Public Enemy No.1."

9. Phil Stephenson, interview with author, October 26, 2020.

10. Barry Bloom, interview with author, December 7, 2020.

11. Surhoff, interview with author.

12. "Alomar's Post-game Comments Infuriate Umpire," *Associated Press*, September 29, 1996.

13. Eisenberg, interview with author, October 27, 2020.

14. Eisenberg.

15. Frank Ahrens, "Roberto Alomar, Keeping His Eye on the Ball," *The Washington Post*, October 7, 1996.

16. Lisa Pollak, "The Umpire's Sons," *Baltimore Sun*, December 29, 1996.

17. Dan Shaughnessy, "Bronx Cheer to Alomar," *Boston Globe*, October 9, 1996.

18. Shaughnessy.

19. Jim Leyritz, interview with author, August 12, 2020.

20. Steve Wulf, "The Spit Hit the Fan," *Time*, October 14, 1996.

21. Leyritz, interview with author.

22. Smith, "An Error."

23. Mark Maske, "Umpire Enraged by Alomar's Comments," *Washington Post*, September 29, 1996.

24. Davey Johnson, with Erik Sherman, *Davey Johnson: My Wild Ride in Baseball and Beyond* (Chicago: Triumph Books, 2018), 314.

CHAPTER 8

1. Wire Report, "Kansas City Fans Sound Off about Alomar's Return," *USA Today*, April 8, 1997.

2. Scott Kamieniecki, interview with author, March 9, 2021.

3. Mark Maske, "Alomar, Hirschbeck Shake Hands," *Washington Post*, April 23, 1997.

4. Albert Chen, "Roberto Alomar and John Hirschbeck," *Sports Illustrated*, July 8, 2013.

5. Bill Koenig, "Sibling Revelry," *USA Today Baseball Weekly*, July 16, 1997.

6. Jack O'Connell, "The Healing Has Begun for Both Alomar Brothers," *Hartford Courant*, July 8, 1997.

7. Kamieniecki, interview with author.

8. Jeff Reboulet, interview with author, August 10, 2020.

9. B. J. Surhoff, interview with author, February 25, 2022.

10. Reboulet, interview with author.

11. Reboulet.

12. Kamieniecki, interview with author.

13. Doug Drabek, interview with author, March 12, 2021.

14. Surhoff, interview with author.

15. Reboulet, interview with author.

16. Rick Krivda, interview with author, August 4, 2020.

17. Tom Verducci, "Tribal Warfare," *Sports Illustrated*, October 20, 1997.

18. Verducci.

19. Kamieniecki, interview with author.

20. Krivda, interview with author.

21. Ken Rosenthal, "O's Have Nothing to Lose by Making Deal," *Baltimore Sun*, May 24, 1998.

22. Ken Rosenthal, "Only Alomar Can Turn Jeers into Cheers," *Baltimore Sun*, May 11, 1998.

23. Drabek, interview with author.

24. John Eisenberg, interview with author, October 27, 2020.

25. Joe Strauss, "Alomar Cleans Locker, Perhaps for Last Time," *Baltimore Sun*, September 27, 1998.

26. Reboulet, interview with author.

27. Reboulet.

28. Kamieniecki, interview with author.

29. Strauss, "Alomar Cleans Locker."

30. Surhoff, interview with author.

CHAPTER 9

1. Tom Verducci, "Scoring Machine," *Sports Illustrated*, May 24, 1999.

2. Verducci.

3. Phil Rogers, "Indians' Regular-Season Challenge Comes from Within," *Chicago Tribune*, April 5, 1999.

4. Jim Ingraham, *Mike Hargrove and the Cleveland Indians: A Baseball Life* (Cleveland: Gray & Company, Publishers, 2019), 268.

5. Jim Mecir, interview with author, December 14, 2020.

6. Mike Jackson, interview with author, June 10, 2020.

7. Jackson.

8. Jim Ingraham, interview with author, February 23, 2021.

9. Dave Burba, interview with author, January 5, 2021.

10. Verducci, "Scoring Machine."

11. Paul Hoynes, interview with author, July 3, 2020.

12. Ingraham, interview with author.

13. Wire Report, "One Team, Two Alomars," *Oneonta Star*, November 24, 1998.

14. Jackson, interview with author.

15. Nomar Garciaparra, interview with author, August 10, 2020.

16. Garciaparra.

17. Hoynes, interview with author.

18. Ingraham, interview with author.

19. Ingraham, *Mike Hargrove*, 269.

20. Burba, interview with author.

21. Omar Vizquel, with Bob Dyer, *Omar! My Life on and off the Field* (Cleveland: Gray & Company, Publishers, 2002), 198.

22. Vizquel, with Dyer, 148.

23. Anonymous, interview with author, June 28, 2020.

24. Chris Assenheimer, "Robbie Is Great on Diamond, Below-Average in Clubhouse," *Chronicle-Telegram* (Elyria, OH), June 9, 2002.

25. Garciaparra, interview with author.

26. Pedro Martinez, with Michael Silverman, *Pedro* (New York: Houghton Mifflin, 2015), 160.

27. Paul Hoynes, "Failure to Retaliate Leaves Robbie Alomar Fuming," *Plain Dealer*, June 19, 2000.

28. Hoynes.

29. Hoynes, interview with author.

30. Assenheimer, "Robbie Is Great on Diamond."

31. Burba, interview with author.

32. Hoynes, interview with author.

33. Anonymous, interview with author, June 28, 2020.

34. Jackson, interview with author.

35. Ingraham, interview with author.

36. Hoynes, interview with author.

37. Burba, interview with author.

38. Hoynes, interview with author.

39. Adam Rubin, "Alomar: Tribe Lied to Me," *New York Daily News*, March 7, 2002.

CHAPTER 10

1. Bobby Valentine, interview with author, August 11, 2020.

2. Valentine.

3. Valentine.

4. Valentine.

5. Valentine.

6. Bob Klapisch, "Mets Desperate for Alomar to Bust Out in '03," https://www.espn.com/mlb/columns/story?columnist=klapisch_bob&id=1492338, January 14, 2003.

7. David Waldstein, "Mets: It's Feat First for Sanchez, Alomar," *Star-Ledger*, March 4, 2003.

8. Jeff Duncan, interview with author, July 23, 2020.

9. Valentine, interview with author.

10. Duncan, interview with author.

11. Duncan.

12. Jack Curry, "A Mistake Is Erased, but a Mystery Remains," *New York Times*, July 2, 2003.

13. Editorial Staff, *Chicago Tribune*, "Mets Won't Miss Alomar," *Chicago Tribune*, July 2, 2003.

14. Paul Schwartz, "Roberto out the Door: Mets Get 3 Players from Sox in Return for Dud," *New York Post*, July 2, 2003.

15. Duncan, interview with author.

CHAPTER 11

1. Rick Morrissey, "Williams Shows He Understands What's at Stake," *Chicago Tribune*, July 2, 2003.

2. Mike Porzio, interview with author, September 15, 2021.

3. Teddy Greenstein, "Alomar No Iron Man, Gets Day Off," *Chicago Tribune*, July 12, 2003.

4. Teddy Greenstein, "A New Flag Is Flying," *Chicago Tribune*, July 2, 2003.

5. Porzio, interview with author.

6. Porzio.

7. Porzio.

8. Teddy Greenstein, "He Accepts Less—Happily," *Chicago Tribune*, January 8, 2004.

9. Greenstein, "He Accepts Less."

10. Shea Hillenbrand, interview with author, September 28, 2020.

11. Hillenbrand.

12. Hillenbrand.

13. Hillenbrand.

14. Phil Rogers, "Bad Break for Alomar, Good for Sox," *Chicago Tribune*, April 25, 2004.

15. Hillenbrand, interview with author.

16. Randy Johnson, interview with author, November 23, 2020.

17. Johnson.

18. Tom Jones, "Phenom Turns Teacher," *St. Petersburg Times*, February 24, 2005.

19. Wire Report, "Devil Rays 2B Roberto Alomar Retires," March 20, 2005.

CHAPTER 12

1. Jack Curry and Joshua Robinson, "Legal Dispute Hinges on Whether Alomar Has H.I.V.," *New York Times*, February 11, 2009.

2. Curry and Robinson.

3. Erica Pearson, "It's All a Vile Lie!," *New York Daily News*, February 12, 2009.

4. Kristen Hamill, "Ex-girlfriend Files Suit, Says Alomar Exposed Her to AIDS," CNN, http://www.cnn.com/2009/CRIME/02/11/alomar.aids.lawsuit/, February 11, 2009.

5. Sarah Netter, "Lawsuit Claims Baseball Star Alomar Has AIDS, Lied about Status," ABC News, https://abcnews.go.com/Sports/OnCall/story?id=6857096&pag =1, February 11, 2009.

6. Netter.

7. Mike Fish, "Alomar Scores Legal Victory," ESPN, https://www.espn.com/mlb /news/story?id=4142266, May 5, 2009.

8. Mike Fish, "Drama Follows Retired Baseball All-Star," ESPN, https://www.espn .com/espn/otl/news/story?id=5765281, November 4, 2010.

9. Fish.

10. Fish.

11. Fish.

12. "Wife Accuses Alomar of H.I.V. Exposure," *Toronto Sun*, October 7, 2010.

13. Fish, "Drama Follows Retired Baseball All-Star."

14. Josh Poltilove, "Ex-baseball Star Alomar Ordered to Avoid Wife," *Tampa Tribune*, August 4, 2010.

15. Fish, "Drama Follows Retired Baseball All-Star."

16. Fish.

17. Fish.

18. Fish.

19. Fish.

CHAPTER 13

1. Peter Schmuck, "Hirschbeck Backs Alomar for Hall of Fame," *Baltimore Sun*, January 5, 2010.

2. John Hirschbeck, interview with author, November 2, 2020.

3. Ken Davidoff, "Stunned Alomar Still Waiting," *Newsday*, January 7, 2010.

4. Roberto Clemente Jr., interview with author, February 5, 2021.

5. Barry Bloom, interview with author, December 7, 2020.

6. Todd Blyleven, interview with author, December 30, 2020.

7. Blyleven.

8. Roberto Alomar 2011 Hall of Fame Speech, National Baseball Hall of Fame and Museum Archives.

9. "Roberto Alomar Enters Hall of Fame," Associated Press, July 24, 2011.

10. Blyleven, interview with author, December 30, 2020.

11. Arden Zwelling, "Alomar 'Blessed to Play for a Great City,'" Major League Baseball, mlb.com, July 31, 2011.

12. Zwelling.

13. Zwelling.

14. Zwelling.

15. Zwelling.

CHAPTER 14

1. Albert Chen, "Roberto Alomar and John Hirschbeck," *Sports Illustrated*, July 8, 2013.

2. John Hirschbeck, interview with author, November 2, 2020.

3. Hirschbeck.

4. Hirschbeck.

5. Hirschbeck.

6. Wire Report, "Alomar, Hirschbeck Form Bond with Cause," *USA Today*, May 16, 2000.

7. Erin Hirschbeck, interview with author, October 30, 2020.

8. Erin Hirschbeck.

9. Albert Chen, "Roberto Alomar and John Hirschbeck," *Sports Illustrated*, July 8, 2013.

10. John Hirschbeck, interview with author.

11. Erin Hirschbeck, interview with author.

12. John Lott, "Another Level," *National Post*, April 4, 2008.

13. Erin Hirschbeck, interview with author.

14. "Former MLB Umpire and State Native John Hirschbeck Already Enjoying Retirement," *New Haven Register*, March 29, 2017.

15. John Hirschbeck, interview with author.

CHAPTER 15

1. Andrew Marchand, "'We Are Going to Survive,'" ESPN, https://www.espn.com /mlb/story/_/id/20905279/we-going-survive-roberto-alomar-wants-give-voice -puerto-rico, October 3, 2017.

2. Jorge Ortiz, "Roberto Alomar Has Message from Puerto Rico to Trump: 'We Need That Help,'" *USA Today*, October 3, 2017.

3. Ortiz, "Roberto Alomar Has Message."

4. Mark Newman, "Alomar Rallies Continued Aid for Puerto Rico," MLB.com, https://www.mlb.com/news/roberto-alomar-asks-for-aid-for-puerto-rico-c25738 1422, October 4, 2017.

CHAPTER 16

1. Bob Elliott, "Hall of Famer Roberto Alomar Marries in Toronto on 12-12-12," *Toronto Sun*, December 12, 2012, https://torontosun.com/2012/12/12/hall-of-famer -roberto-alomar-marries-in-toronto-on-12-12-12.

2. Brian McNair, "Whitby's Ben Sheppard Throws Out First Pitch at Toronto Blue Jays' Home Opener," DurhamRegion.com, April 14, 2015, https://www.durham region.com/community-story/5557360-whitby-s-ben-sheppard-throws-out-first -pitch-at-toronto-blue-jays-home-opener/.

3. Bill Francis, "Justino Clemente, Brother of Roberto, Visits Hall of Fame," National Baseball Hall of Fame, https://baseballhall.org/discover/justino-clemente -visits-hall-of-fame, October 2, 2018.

4. Roberto Clemente Jr., interview with author, February 5, 2021.

5. Luis Tiant, interview with author, March 19, 2021.

6. Tiant.

7. Luis Clemente, interview with author, February 5, 2021.

CHAPTER 17

1. Mina Kimes and Jeff Passan, "New York Mets GM Jared Porter Acknowledges Sending Explicit Images to Female Reporter When He Worked for Chicago Cubs," ESPN, January 18, 2021, https://www.espn.com/mlb/story/_/id/30737248/ny-mets-gm-jared-porter-acknowledges-sending-explicit-images-female-reporter-worked-chicago-cubs.

2. Mina Kimes and Jeff Passan, "New York Mets GM Jared Porter Fired for Sending Explicit Texts, Images to Reporter," ESPN, January 19, 2021, https://www.espn.com/mlb.

3. David Waldstein, "The Mets Quietly Fired a Second Employee for Sexual Harassment," *New York Times*, February 17, 2021.

4. Kevin Draper, "Former Mets Manager Accused of Making Unwanted Sexual Advances," *New York Times*, February 1, 2021.

5. Rob Piersall, "Disgraced Ex-New York Mets Manager Mickey Callaway Fired by Mexican League Team," *Sports Illustrated*, June 1, 2022, https://www.si.com/mlb/mets/news/new-york-ex-manager-mickey-callaway-fired-mexican-league-mets.

6. Mollie Walker, "Roberto Alomar Banished by MLB after Sexual Misconduct Claim," *New York Post*, April 30, 2021.

7. Walker.

8. Bill Shaikin, "MLB Puts Roberto Alomar on Ineligible List; Hall of Fame Says He'll Stay Put," *Los Angeles Times*, April 30, 2021.

9. Melissa Verge, "All I Wanted Was Baseball Advice. Instead, Roberto Alomar Pushed His Unwelcome Body Up against Mine," *Toronto Star*, May 28, 2021.

10. Brendan Kennedy, "Blue Jays Investigating New Allegations against Roberto Alomar," *Toronto Star*, May 28, 2021.

11. Kennedy.

12. Kennedy.

13. Kennedy.

EPILOGUE

1. Jose Cruz Jr., interview with author, September 20, 2022.

2. Barry Bloom, interview with author, December 7, 2020.

3. Bloom.

4. Bloom.

5. Randy Johnson, interview with author, November 23, 2020.

6. Johnson.

7. Rick Krivda, interview with author, August 4, 2020.

8. Jeff Reboulet, interview with author, August 10, 2020.

9. Dave Winfield, interview with author, September 4, 2020.

10. Shea Hillenbrand, interview with author, September 28, 2020.

Bibliography

NEWSPAPER ARTICLES

Ahrens, Frank. "Roberto Alomar, Keeping His Eye on the Ball." *The Washington Post*, October 7, 1996.

Appleman, Marc. "Like Father Like Sons." *Los Angeles Times,* March 5, 1985.

Assenheimer, Chris. "Robbie Is Great on Diamond, Below-Average in Clubhouse." *The Chronicle-Telegram*, June 9, 2002.

Boland, Kevin. "Alomar Makes Hard Landing on SkyDome's Artificial Field." *National Post*, May 22, 1991.

Botte, Peter. "Dad: Mets to Blame, Not Robbie." *New York Daily News*, July 3, 2003.

Buckley, Taylor. "Blue Jays Drop In, Stay for a Few Days." *USA Today*, October 22, 1993.

Byers, Jim. "Alomar Hints He'll Move." *Toronto Star*, July 31, 1995.

Cafardo, Nick, and Bob Ryan. "Cone, Stewart Make Pitches." *Boston Globe*, October 12, 1992.

Campbell, Neil. "Alomar Gives Press the Silent Treatment." *The Globe and Mail*, June 3, 1993.

Chass, Murray. "Johnson, the A.L. Manager of the Year, Resigns from Orioles." *New York Times*, November 6, 1997.

Crowe, Jerry. "Padres Cautious in Bringing Up Young Alomar." *Los Angeles Times*, April 23, 1988.

Curry, Jack. "Alomar Truly Covers the Field Like a Hand in Glove." *New York Times*, October 18, 1993.

———. "Don't Blame Alomar Jr. The Fans Did It!" *New York Times*, July 4, 1991.

———. "A Mistake Is Erased, but a Mystery Remains." *New York Times*, July 2, 2003.

Curry, Jack, and Joshua Robinson. "Legal Dispute Hinges on Whether Alomar Has H.I.V." *New York Times*, February 11, 2009.

Davidoff, Ken. "Stunned Alomar Still Waiting." *Newsday*, January 7, 2010.

De Luca, Chris. "Alomar Is Upset after Demotion." *Escondido Times-Advocate*, March 26, 1988.

———. "Bowa Finally Gets His Second Baseman." *Escondido Times-Advocate*, April 20, 1988.

———. "Roberto Alomar's Future Is Bright." *Escondido Times-Advocate*, March 9, 1989.

Draper, Kevin. "Former Mets Manager Accused of Making Unwanted Sexual Advances." *New York Times*, February 1, 2021.

Dunnell, Milt. "It Ain't Easy Being the Other Alomar." *Toronto Star*, April 25, 1992.

Editorial Staff. "Mets Won't Miss Alomar." *Chicago Tribune*, July 2, 2003.

Editorial Staff. "'We Need Sports and Baseball More Than Ever,'—Roberto Alomar Makes Personal Plea for MLB Sanity." *Toronto Star*, June 16, 2020.

Elliott, Bob. "It's Time for Alomar to Leave." *National Post*, August 1, 1995.

"Former MLB Umpire and State Native John Hirschbeck Already Enjoying Retirement." *New Haven Register*, March 29, 2017.

Fraley, Gerry. "When Blue Jays Get Mad, They Get More Than Even." *Dallas Morning News*, October 12, 1992.

Ghiroli, Brittany, and Ken Rosenthal. "'This Is a Pattern': Three Women Told Mets about Sexual Harassment in 2018." *The Athletic*, February 17, 2021.

Goldiner, Dave, and Adam Rubin. "Mets Star: I'm Straight." *New York Daily News*, May 22, 2002.

Greenstein, Teddy. "Alomar No Iron Man, Gets Day Off." *Chicago Tribune,* July 12, 2003.

———. "He Accepts Less—Happily." *Chicago Tribune,* January 8, 2004.

———. "A New Flag Is Flying." *Chicago Tribune,* July 2, 2003.

Guest, Larry. "Spitting Image Still Haunts Orioles' Star." *Orlando Sentinel,* May 11, 1998.

Heller, Dick. "The Way It Was." *The Washington Times,* December 28, 2009.

Hoynes, Paul. "Failure to Retaliate Leaves Robbie Alomar Fuming." *The Plain Dealer,* June 19, 2000.

Hyvonen, Gary. "Padres Hike Ticket Prices." *The North County Blade-Citizen,* October 10, 1990.

Jenkins, Colleen. "Maripily and Roberto Alomar Divorce Has Puerto Rico Riveted." *St. Petersburg Times,* September 3, 2010.

Jones, Tom. "Phenom Turns Teacher." *St. Petersburg Times,* February 24, 2005.

Karstens-Smith, Gemma. "Woman Hopeful Sharing Story about Alleged Sexual Misconduct by Alomar Helps Others." *The Canadian Press,* June 2, 2021.

Keegan, Tom. "Alomar Brothers Gearing Up for a Family Feud." *New York Post,* October 8, 1997.

———. "Mussina's Town of Tears." *New York Post,* October 15, 1997.

Kennedy, Brendan. "Blue Jays Investigating New Allegations against Roberto Alomar." *Toronto Star,* May 28, 2021.

———. "Roberto Alomar Responds to Toronto Star Investigation, Says He Will 'Not Engage in a Trial by Media.'" *Toronto Star,* May 29, 2021.

Kepner, Tyler. "Roberto Alomar Is Removed from Baseball's Present, If Not Its Past." *New York Times,* April 30, 2021.

Koenig, Bill. "Sibling Revelry." *USA Today Baseball Weekly,* July 16, 1997.

Kubatko, Roch. "Cheered Alomar Pivots Away from Spat." *The Baltimore Sun,* October 2, 1996.

Lankhof, Bill. "Alomar Wants League to Help." *National Post,* July 4, 1995.

Lott, John. "Another Level." *National Post*, April 4, 2008.

Madden, Bill. "Once Locks, Mac & Robbie May Lose Hall Pass." *New York Daily News*, March 21, 2005.

Malnic, Eric. "Rain, Wind Will 'Dent' Dry Spell, Not End It." *Los Angeles Times*, April 20, 1988.

Maske, Mark. "Alomar, Hirschbeck Shake Hands." *The Washington Post*, April 23, 1997.

———. "Orioles' Multitalented Alomar Is Second to None." *The Washington Post*, March 31, 1996.

———. "Umpire Enraged by Alomar's Comments." *The Washington Post*, September 29, 1996.

McManaman, Bob. "Alomar Lost for 6-8 Weeks." *The Arizona Republic*, April 21, 2004.

Miller, Scott. "A Difference in the Climate: Ex-Padres Alomar and Carter Adjusting to Life in Toronto." *Los Angeles Times*, May 26, 1991.

Morrissey, Rick. "Williams Shows He Understands What's at Stake." *Chicago Tribune*, July 2, 2003.

O'Connell, Jack. "The Healing Has Begun for Both Alomar Brothers." *Hartford Courant*, July 8, 1997.

Olney, Buster. "Alomar Hitting His Prime at Plate." *The Baltimore Sun*, May 28, 1996.

Ortiz, Jorge. "Roberto Alomar Has Message from Puerto Rico to Trump: 'We Need That Help.'" *USA Today*, October 3, 2017.

Pearson, Erica. "It's All a Vile Lie!" *New York Daily News*, February 12, 2009.

Plaschke, Bill. "Alomar & Sons, Three from Same Family Keys to Organization's Future." *Los Angeles Times*, January 28, 1989.

———. "Chub Feeney Resigns as President of Padres." *Los Angeles Times*, September 26, 1988.

———. "A Lot of Care, a Little Bit of Conniving Are Behind This Scouting Success Story." *Los Angeles Times*, January 26, 1989.

Pollak, Lisa. "The Umpire's Sons." *The Baltimore Sun*, December 29, 1996.

Poltilove, Josh. "Ex-baseball Star Alomar Ordered to Avoid Wife." *The Tampa Tribune*, August 4, 2010.

Quinn, T. J. "Fonzie Will Move, but Only for Alomar." *New York Daily News*, December 12, 2001.

Reynolds, Tim. "'People Are Still Suffering.'" *Chicago Tribune*, April 15, 2018.

Rogers, Phil. "Alomar Joins Hall's Family." *Chicago Tribune*, July 24, 2011.

———. "Bad Break for Alomar; Good for Sox." *Chicago Tribune*, April 25, 2004.

———. "Indians' Regular-Season Challenge Comes from Within." *Chicago Tribune*, April 5, 1999.

Rosenthal, Ken. "Only Alomar Can Turn Jeers into Cheers." *The Baltimore Sun*, May 11, 1998.

———. "O's Have Nothing to Lose by Making Deal." *The Baltimore Sun*, May 24, 1998.

Rubin, Adam. "Alomar: Tribe Lied to Me." *New York Daily News*, March 7, 2002.

———. "Bobby V Has Juicy Theory." *New York Daily News*, June 26, 2002.

———. "Phillips: No Deal for Alomar." *New York Daily News*, February 18, 2003.

Ryan, Bob. "Gaining Respect with Their Heroic Performances." *Boston Globe*, October 12, 1992.

Sanders, Jeff. "Padres History (April 22): Roberto Alomar's Debut, Tony Gwynn's 1000th Hit." *The San Diego Union-Tribune*, April 22, 2020.

———. "Padres History (May 24): Jack Clark Takes on . . . Tony Gwynn?" *The San Diego Union-Tribune*, May 24, 2020.

Schmuck, Peter. "Hirschbeck Backs Alomar for Hall of Fame." *The Baltimore Sun*, January 5, 2010.

———. "The Shining Star Likes His Space." *The Baltimore Sun*, August 7, 1996.

Schwartz, Paul. "Roberto out the Door." *New York Post*, July 2, 2003.

Shaikin, Bill. "MLB Puts Roberto Alomar on Ineligible List: Hall of Fame Says He'll Stay Put." *Los Angeles Times*, April 30, 2021.

Shaughnessy, Dan. "Act Spits in Face of Justice." *Boston Globe,* October 3, 1996.

———. "Alomar Hands Down Winner in Shame Game." *Boston Globe*, September 29, 1996.

———. "Bronx Cheer to Alomar." *Boston Globe*, October 9, 1996.

Smith, Claire. "An Error That the Official Scorer Cannot Take Away." *New York Times*, October 8, 1996.

Solomon, Alan. "Cubs/NL Report: The Week in Review." *Chicago Tribune*, July 22, 1990.

Strauss, Joe. "Alomar Cleans Locker, Perhaps for Last Time." *The Baltimore Sun*, September 27, 1998.

———. "Alomar Set to Switch Off Troubles." *The Baltimore Sun*, February 15, 1998.

———. "Going from Resilient to Silent." *The Baltimore Sun*, May 24, 1998.

Terry, Mike. "Alomar Brothers Fulfill Dream of Playing Together." *USA Today*, July 9, 1991.

Topkin, Marc. "Alomar Expected to Call It a Career." *Tampa Bay Times*, March 19, 2005.

Verge, Melissa. "All I Wanted Was Baseball Advice. Instead, Roberto Alomar Pushed His Unwelcome Body up against Mine." *Toronto Star*, May 28, 2021.

Waldstein, David. "Mets: It's Feat First for Sanchez, Alomar." *The Star-Ledger*, March 4, 2003.

———. "The Mets Quietly Fired a Second Employee for Sexual Harassment." *New York Times*, February 17, 2021.

Walker, Mollie. "Roberto Alomar Banished by MLB after Sexual Misconduct Claim." *New York Post*, April 30, 2021.

Wire Report. "Alomar, Hirschbeck Form Bond with Cause." *USA Today*, May 16, 2000.

———. "Alomar's Defense Catching Phils' Attention." *Associated Press*, October 1993.

———. "Alomar's Post-game Comments Infuriate Umpire." *Associated Press*, September 29, 1996.

———. "Death Threat Made against Alomar." *Calgary Herald*, July 3, 1995.

———. "Devil Rays 2B Roberto Alomar Retires." March 20, 2005.

———. "Kansas City Fans Sound Off about Alomar's Return." *USA Today*, April 8, 1997.

———. "One Team, Two Alomars." *Oneonta Star*, November 24, 1998.

———. "Padres Send Out the Call for Former Pilot Roberto Alomar." *The Wichita Eagle-Beacon*, April 21, 1988.

———. "Roberto Alomar Enters Hall of Fame." *Associated Press*, July 24, 2011.

———. "Wife Accuses Alomar of H.I.V. Exposure." *Toronto Sun*, October 7, 2010. Wire Report. "All-Star Game Notebook." United Press International, July 9, 1991.

Zwolinski, Mark. "Blue Jays Alumni Gather to Help Boy with Cerebral Palsy." *Toronto Star*, June 4, 2014.

MAGAZINE ARTICLES

Chen, Albert. "Roberto Alomar & John Hirschbeck." *Sports Illustrated*, July 8, 2013.

Collins, Cory. "Roseanne Barr's National Anthem: An Oral History of the Barr-Bungled Banner." *Sporting News*, May 29, 2018.

Kurkjian, Tim. "Beginning Again." *Sports Illustrated*, March 11, 1991.

———. "Do Not Disturb Roberto Alomar." *Sports Illustrated*, January 29, 1996.

———. "Public Enemy No. 1." *Sports Illustrated*, October 14, 1996.

Newman, Bruce. "Home Suite Home." *Sports Illustrated*, June 8, 1992.

Rushin, Steve. "Border Conflict." *Sports Illustrated*, October 1992.

———. "Oh, Canada!" *Sports Illustrated*, November 1992.

Verducci, Tom. "Scoring Machine." *Sports Illustrated*, May 24, 1999.

———. "Tribal Warfare." *Sports Illustrated*, October 20, 1997.

Wulf, Steve. "Now or Never." *Sports Illustrated*, October 1992.

———. "The Spit Hit the Fan." *TIME*, October 14, 1996.

BOOKS

Alomar, Roberto, with Stephen Brunt. *Second to None: The Roberto Alomar Story.* New York: Penguin Books, 1993.

Gallagher, Danny. *Baseball in the 20th Century.* Toronto: Scoop Press, 2000.

Ingraham, Jim. *Mike Hargrove and the Cleveland Indians: A Baseball Life.* Cleveland: Gray & Company, Publishers, 2019.

Johnson, Davey, with Erik Sherman. *Davey Johnson: My Wild Ride in Baseball and Beyond.* Chicago: Triumph Books, 2018.

Martinez, Pedro, with Michael Silverman. *Pedro.* New York: Houghton Mifflin, 2015.

Rubin, Adam. *Pedro, Carlos, and Omar: The Story of a Season in the Big Apple and the Pursuit of Baseball's Top Latino Stars.* Guilford, CT: The Lyons Press, 2006.

Vizquel, Omar, with Bob Dyer. *Omar! My Life on and off the Field.* Cleveland: Gray & Company, Publishers, 2002.

Wendel, Tim. *Down to the Last Pitch: How the 1991 Minnesota Twins and Atlanta Braves Gave Us the Best World Series of All Time.* Boston: Da Capo Press, 2014.

WEBSITE ARTICLES

Castrovince, Anthony. "John Hirschbeck's Survival Guide." MLB, January 13, 2015. https://www.mlb.com/news/mlb-umpire-john-hirschbeck-survival-guide-ald.

Elliott, Bob. "Hall of Famer Roberto Alomar Marries in Toronto on 12-12-12." *Toronto Sun*, December 12, 2012. https://torontosun.com/2012/12/12/hall-of -famer-roberto-alomar-marries-in-toronto-on-12-12-12.

Fish, Mike. "Alomar Scores Legal Victory." ESPN, May 5, 2009. https://www.espn .com/mlb/news/story?id=4142266.

———. "Drama Follows Retired Baseball All-Star." ESPN, November 4, 2010. https://www.espn.com/espn/otl/news/story?id=5765281.

Francis, Bill. "Justino Clemente, Brother of Roberto, Visits Hall of Fame." National Baseball Hall of Fame, October 2, 2018. https://baseballhall.org/discover/justino -clemente-visits-hall-of-fame.

Hamill, Kristen. "Ex-girlfriend Files Suit, Says Alomar Exposed Her to AIDS." CNN, February 11, 2009. http://www.cnn.com/2009/CRIME/02/11/alomar.aids.lawsuit/.

Kimes, Mina, and Passan, Jeff. "New York Mets GM Jared Porter Acknowledges Sending Explicit Images to Female Reporter When He Worked for Chicago Cubs." ESPN, January 18, 2021. https://www.espn.com/mlb/story/_/id/30737248 /ny-mets-gm-jared-porter-acknowledges-sending-explicit-images-female-reporter -worked-chicago-cubs.

———. "New York Mets GM Jared Porter Fired for Sending Explicit Texts, Images to Reporters." ESPN, January 19, 2021. https://www.espn.com/mlb.

Klapisch, Bob. "Mets Desperate for Alomar to Bust Out in '03." ESPN, January 14, 2003. https://www.espn.com/mlb/columns/story?columnist=klapisch_bob&id =1492338.

Kurkjian, Tim. "Our Best-Ever MLB Winter Meetings Trades, Rumors and Untold Tales from the Lobby." MLB, December 8, 2020. https://www.espn.com/mlb /story/_/id/30465214/our-best-ever-mlb-winter-meetings-trades-rumors-untold -tales-lobby.

Marchand, Andrew. "'We Are Going to Survive.'" ESPN, October 3, 2017. https:// www.espn.com/mlb/story/_/id/20905279/we-going-survive-roberto-alomar -wants-give-voice-puerto-rico.

McNair, Brian. "Whitby's Ben Sheppard Throws Out First Pitch at Toronto Blue Jays' Home Opener." DurhamRegion.com, April 14, 2015. https://www.durham region.com/community-story/5557360-whitby-s-ben-sheppard-throws-out-first -pitch-at-toronto-blue-jays-home-opener/.

Netter, Sarah. "Lawsuit Claims Baseball Star Alomar Has AIDS, Lied about Status." ABC News, February 11, 2009. https://abcnews.go.com/Sports/OnCall/story?id =6857096&page=1.

Newman, Mark. "Alomar Rallies Continued Aid for Puerto Rico." MLB, October 4, 2017. https://www.mlb.com/news/roberto-alomar-asks-for-aid-for-puerto -rico-c257381422.

Piersall, Rob. "Disgraced Ex-New York Mets Manager Mickey Callaway Fired by Mexican League Team." *Sports Illustrated*, June 1, 2022. https://www.si.com/mlb /mets/news/new-york-ex-manager-mickey-callaway-fired-mexican-league-mets.

Zwelling, Arden. "Alomar 'Blessed to Play for a Great City.'" MLB, July 31, 2011. mlb.com.

Index

Pabon, Carmen, 6
Pabon, Nestor, 7
Pagliarulo, Mike, 42
Palmeiro, Rafael, 75, 96, 98, 104, 160
Palmieri, Demetrio Alomar, 1
Park, Chan Ho, 125
Passan, Jeff, 203
Pendleton, Terry, 63
Peppermill Resort Spa Casino, 25–26
Perez, Eduardo, 195
Perks, Kim, 174, 195–96
Perry, Gaylord, 171
Pesquera, Héctor M., 187
Pettitte, Andy, 86–87, 140
Philadelphia, 66, 75
Philadelphia Phillies, 66
Phillips, Steve, 135–36, 140–41, 143
Phoenix, 152
Piazza, Mike, 137, 141–42, 145
Pierce, Mary, 104, 120, 126
Piniella, Lou, *133*, 159
Pittoni, Luke, 162
Pittsburgh Pirates, 8, 37
Pizza Hut, 23, 28
Plain Dealer, 113
Plaschke, Bill, 32
PlayStation, 111
Poland, Ohio, xvi, 84, 180
Poland Spring, 26, 189
Polo Grounds, 63
Poltergeist, 153
Ponce, Puerto Rico, 1, 15
Pony League, 2
Porter, Jared, 203
Porzio, Mike, 147, 149
Posada, Jessica, 191
Posada, Jorge, 191

Prague Spring, 6
Progress Energy Park, 159
Progressive Field, 182, 195, 201
PTSD, 193
Puerto Rican Winter League, 13–14, 17, 38, 65
Puerto Rico, xvi, 1–2, 8–9, 14–15, 17–18, 24, 27, 39, 76, 103, 139–40, 142, 159, 161–63, 166–67, 170, 185, 187–93, 195, 197, 199–200, 214
Puig, Ed, *127*
Puig, Yasiel, 203

Quantrill, Paul, xiii
Queens, New York, 12, *133*, 136–37, 140–41, 144, 147–48, 152, 161, 170, 173, 200

RA12, 199–200
Ramirez, Manny, 101, 110, 124–25
Ramirez, Rafael, 36
Rawlings, 77
Ready, Randy, 30, 32
Reagan, Ronald, 37
Reboulet, Jeff, 92, 96–99, 106, 212
Reebok, xiv
Reilly, Mike, 102
Reno, Nevada, 25–28
Reno Padres, 25–26
Reyes, Jose, *132*, 142
Rhodes, Arthur, 96
Riddoch, Greg, 44–47
Riggan, Jerrod, 126
Riggleman, Jim, 123
Riley, Pat, 85
Ring, Royce, 144
Rio Piedras, Puerto Rico, 9, 140

About the Author

David Ostrowsky is a sportswriter for the *Atlanta Jewish Times* and the author of *Pro Sports in 1993: A Signature Season in Football, Basketball, Hockey and Baseball*. He lives with his wife, Lauren, and children, Colby and Camden, in the Greater Boston area.

Printed in the USA
CPSIA information can be obtained
at www.ICGtesting.com
CBHW031558160724
11525CB00001B/2